This Place Will Become Home

This Place Will Become Home

Refugee Repatriation to Ethiopia

Laura C. Hammond

CORNELL UNIVERSITY PRESS

ITHACA AND LONDON

First published 2004 by Cornell University Press
First printing, Cornell Paperbacks, 2004

Printed in the United States of America

Library of Congress Cataloging-in-Publication Data

Hammond, Laura, 1967–
   This place will become home : refugee repatriation to Ethiopia / Laura Hammond.
      p.   cm.
   Includes bibliographical references and index.
   ISBN 0-8014-4307-5 (cloth : alk. paper)—ISBN 0-8014-8939-3 (pbk. : alk. paper)
   1. Refugees–Ethiopia.   2. Refugee camps–Sudan.   3. Repatriation–Ethiopia.   4. Return migration–Ethiopia.   5. Land settlement–Government policy–Ethiopia.   I. Title.
   HV640.4.E77H36 2004
   323.6′4′0963—dc22

                                                    2004010284

Cornell University Press strives to use environmentally responsible suppliers and materials to the fullest extent possible in the publishing of its books. Such materials include vegetable-based, low-VOC inks and acid-free papers that are recycled, totally chlorine-free, or partly composed of nonwood fibers. For further information, visit our website at www.cornellpress.cornell.edu.

Cloth printing   10 9 8 7 6 5 4 3 2 1
Paperback printing   10 9 8 7 6 5 4 3 2 1

Contents

Ethiopian administrative boundaries under the Derg government (1974–1991)

Acknowledgments

Over the decade in which I researched, wrote, and rewrote this book, I benefited from the guidance, hospitality, friendship, criticism, and gentle (and not-so-gentle) nudges of innumerable people.

Barbara Harrell-Bond of the Refugee Studies Centre at the University of Oxford (now of American University in Cairo) gave me my first glimpse of refugee studies and has continued to encourage and challenge me to this day. Asfaha Hadera of In Exile introduced me to the Ethiopian community in New York City in 1988–89 when I was conducting my maiden fieldwork project as an undergraduate at Sarah Lawrence College. Lina Brock first ignited the spark that made me want to be an anthropologist, but unfortunately did not live to see the fruit of her efforts.

In Madison, Wisconsin, Solomon Woldesemayat and Markos Regassa provided intensive Amharic language lessons and fed me Ethiopian food, and Fereja Tahir gave me my first lessons in Tigrinya before I went to Ethiopia.

The research was funded by an Insitute for International Exchange Fulbright Award and by a fellowship from the John D. and Catherine T. MacArthur Foundation, in·conjunction with the Global Studies Program at the University of Wisconsin-Madison. I also received funds and logistical support from the United Nations High Commissioner for Refugees and the United Nations Development Programme–Emergencies Unit for Ethiopia (now known as UNOCHA–Ethiopia).

While in the field and writing, the Ethiopian studies community provided friendship, encouragement, and criticism. I wish to thank in particular Alan Hoben, Harold Marcus, Jim McCann, Alula Pankhurst, Bahru Zewde, and the staff of the Institute of Ethiopian Studies and Institute of Development Research at Addis Ababa University.

Numerous aid practitioners helped me to keep sight of the practical nature of my work: Jim Borton, my godfather throughout the fieldwork period, provided everything from advice and logistical support to meals at my favorite restaurant to a place to store my boxes. Past staff of the United Nations Emergencies Unit for Ethiopia has been extremely supportive, especially Ben Parker, Mark Bidder, and Matt Bryden. The staff of UNHCR–Ethiopia, particularly Denis Blair, was extremely helpful. The Administration of Refugee/Returnee Affairs and Mandefro Tegegne also provided assistance in developing the research plan.

For hosting me during my various stays in Addis Ababa I wish to thank Etagegnehu Mekonnen and family, Daniela Owen, Stevens Tucker, Vincent and Marie Chordi, Vanandura Chinadurai, Robert and Linda Shank, Bill and Ashton Douglass, Emma Ghevarian, Mitselal Gebre Selassie and family, Pascal Joannes, Frederic Vigneau, and Selamawit Abera. In Tigray, thanks to the staff at Genet Hotel Humera, the Kafta Humera *woreda* administration, the staff of the Humera Hospital and Outpatient Clinic, Wray and Karen Witten, Aregawi Araya, Berhane Gebre Egziabher, Teklewoini Assefa, and the Relief Society of Tigray for help in arranging the research and support throughout. Thanks also to Mehari Berhan, who checked my Tigrinya translations.

Throughout this process, the anthropology department at the University of Wisconsin–Madison has provided continuous support and patience in equal degrees. Particular thanks to my advisor, Sharon Hutchinson, who has been a fantastic colleague and friend. Also to Neil Whitehead, Thomas Spear, Maria Lepowsky, Alberto Palloni, and Herbert Lewis for their guidance and support. I learned as much from my classmates Joslyn Cassady and Mike Youngblood as from anyone.

At Cornell University Press, thanks to my editors Sheri Englund, Ange Romeo-Hall, John Raymond, and Catherine Rice.

Thanks also to my family—all of whom visited me in the field. Their visits and care packages helped me through the longest periods. Special thanks to Ben Ward, who edited several drafts, kept me writing, and has become gracefully resigned to my peripatetic character.

My research assistants, Abebe Bekele and Lettemeskel Gidey (who died before the study was finished), provided excellent translation and research skills, not to mention companionship; their work makes this very much a collective project.

Finally, to the people of Ada Bai whose patience, friendship, humor, and stories made this much more than a study, I offer my deepest gratitude. I have changed their names to protect their privacy, but I hope that they can recognize themselves and will forgive me for any errors I have made, for which, of course, I take full responsibility. This book is dedicated to them.

Ethiopian administrative regions and zones, 1993 to the present

Note on Transcriptions and Use of Tigrinya Terms

Tigrinya is a Semitic language, related to Amharic (the national language of Ethiopia), Hebrew, and Arabic. It is derived from the ancient liturgical language Ge'ez.[1] Its written form is made up of syllabic symbols (consonant-vowel combinations). The basic syllabary is made up of thirty-three different roots, and each root has at least seven variations. In addition, there are thirty-seven special characters.

I learned to read the Amharic and Tigrinya syllabary (the two languages use the same basic syllabary, which differs only in the way that a few symbols are pronounced) prior to beginning my research. However, most of my language learning was done through listening and speaking with Tigrayans. In the interests of accuracy and saving time, I relied on a research assistant to translate most formal interviews. However, as I became more proficient in the language, I also interviewed on my own in Tigrinya.

Throughout this book, I have included terms and some translated songs or proverbs in their English and Tigrinya written forms. In many cases, where I have been able to locate the Tigrinya spelling for a term, I have included it, since transliteration of Tigrinya terms is open to wide variation. This should help Tigrinya speakers who read this book to identify the exact term to which I refer. Unfortunately, it has not been possible to identify the Tigrinya written form for all terms. Most of my informants were illiterate, and even those who were not were not accustomed to reading and writing in Tigrinya, since that language only started to be used as an official medium of written communication and for educational purposes in Tigray Region when the Ethiopian People's Revolutionary Democratic Front came to power in 1991.

To my knowledge, there is no dictionary currently available for translation of Tigrinya to English. There are, however, several useful English to Tigrinya dictionaries. I have also benefited from Wolf Leslau's *Concise Amharic Dictionary* (University of California Press, 1976), Amsalu Aklilu and G. P. Mosback's *English-Amharic Dictionary* (Addis Ababa, 1973), and Yohannes Gebre Egziabher's *Mezgebe-K'alat Tigrinya–Amharinya* (Ethiopian Dictionary, Tigrinya–Amharic) (Asmara, 1958–59).

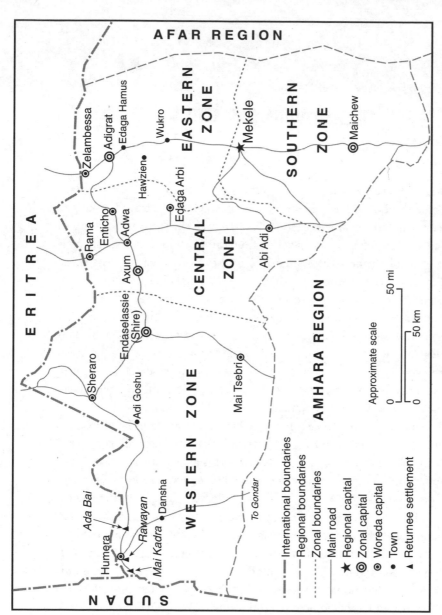

Tigray Region, showing locations of Ada Bai and other returnee settlements. Adapted from a map produced by the UN Emergencies Unit for Ethiopia (with permission). The designations used do not imply the expression of any opinion of the UN or the author regarding the legal status and delimitations of international, regional, or zonal boundaries.

This Place Will Become Home

Introduction

Early one afternoon in late June 1993, more than one hundred trucks—carrying more than seven thousand people together with all of their worldly possessions—rumbled along a muddy track across a plain in the far northwestern corner of Ethiopia. The going was slow, as the trucks had to maneuver through deep ruts left by tractors that had traveled the road while the black soil was still wet from the previous night's rain. Except for a low mountain ridge to the north, which ran along the Tekezze River that marked the border between Ethiopia and Eritrea, the landscape had few distinguishing features. The road cut through brown fields, flat and empty, with the occasional lone acacia tree providing shade for those who found themselves in the unlucky position of being out in the hot sun at midday. The people in the trucks, although already hot, covered their heads and shoulders with towels, blankets, and shawls to protect themselves from the scorching sun and the dust being kicked up by the convoy. They clung to each other and to the sides of the truck to keep from bouncing too hard. "Ayeeee!" many of them exclaimed wearily. "*Tsehai belina* [the sun is eating us]!"

The trucks came to a stop amid a scattering of twenty or so grass huts. Aside from these structures, the only permanent buildings were a small one-storey red brick warehouse and a smaller abandoned whitewashed brick house that, locals said, had originally belonged to a Catholic priest who had owned a fruit and vegetable farm there. Both priest and farm were long gone—these structures and a single collapsed well in the riverbed behind the house were all that remained to suggest that the farm had ever existed.

Amid a flurry of noise and confusion, the passengers got down from the trucks and attempted to locate their household's belongings, which in most cases consisted of not much more than a few battered suitcases carrying a few dingy, threadbare items of clothing and precious mementos; a bed frame made from wood and goat skin or (if the owner was a bit more wealthy) steel; a chair or table; some plastic jerry cans and a few cooking

Returnees arriving from Sudan. All photos by the author.

pots. Some of the more wealthy people had also brought a bicycle, a treadle-powered sewing machine, or a donkey cart, assets that could eventually be used to generate income. Several long shades, built from wood and grass but open on the sides, had been erected to provide relief from the sun. The government officials on hand to receive the new arrivals told them that they should sleep under the shades until they had been assigned a house plot; this might take several days. Within a few minutes of their arrival, the empty trucks restarted their engines and began to speed back toward town, their drivers anxious to find a beer, a meal, and a hotel bed before dark.

The newcomers, surrounded by their belongings, looked around them at the big empty field in which they found themselves. They had been told that this place was called Ada Bai, which appropriately enough comes from the Tigrinya words "Addi Abay" or "Big Land." None of them had ever been there before. Yet the place looked and felt (in that afternoon sun of 110°F) very much like the fields surrounding the refugee camps in Sudan where they had spent the last eight years. After all, despite the fact that they had officially repatriated to their country of origin, Ada Bai was still less than one hundred kilometers from the camps. It most definitely did not look like the Tigrayan highlands whose rugged mountains rose from the plain one hundred kilometers to the east, and which had been their home until war and famine forced them to leave in 1984–85. Yet this, they were told by the Ethiopian government, the United Nations, and their local leaders, was Ethiopia, and thus it was to be considered "home."

The experience of refugee repatriation and postreturn life that I describe in this book is an important piece of Ethiopia's postwar reconstruction story: it is the story of how return migrants, located at the edges of political and economic control and influence both geographically and practically, transformed an empty space into a meaningful place. Questioning the commonly held belief that refugees who return to their country of origin are necessarily people "going home," I follow the construction of social life in a postwar, postmigration context that involves careful manipulation by returnees of both local and global processes. Through an ethnographic lens, I examine the process by which Tigrayan returnees set about transforming an unknown and anonymous space first into a personalized place and finally into a "home."

This process involved two conceptually distinct but practically intertwined subprocesses. The first was one of emplacement, whereby people transformed an unfamiliar physical space into a personalized, socialized place. The second was that of community formation through creative action and structural transformation. While these dual processes were simultaneous and complementary, they were also distinct, each holding a different relationship to history, structure, antistructure, and the production of meaning.

"Returning" to a Strange Place

The new residents of Ada Bai were returning to a country headed by the Ethiopian People's Revolutionary Democratic Front (EPRDF), a coalition of movements led by the Tigrayan People's Liberation Front (TPLF), which had successfully fought a civil war between 1975 and 1991, finally ousting the socialist dictator, Colonel Mengistu Haile Mariam, and his regime, known as the Derg. One of the EPRDF's first moves was to institute a system of ethnic federalism, whereby the main ethnic groups were divided by regional boundaries and granted a considerable degree of autonomy to manage their internal affairs. Each region was able to use its own language in official communication and to teach it (in addition to Amharic, the national language) in schools. Regional boundaries were redrawn to reflect the ethnic composition of local populations. Under the new regional boundaries, Ada Bai and its surroundings were assigned to

Tigray Region; previously the area had been administered by the province of Gondar (Gondar itself was subsumed within the larger Amhara Region). In other words, although this land was new to the repatriating refugees, to the government and the international community the area was recognized as belonging to Tigray Region, and it was therefore said that the refugees were "returning" to their homeland.

This distinction was politically expedient, because the land that the returnees had left in the highlands had been reallocated to other land-poor farmers in their absence. The lowland area, being much less densely populated and potentially more productive, was considered by the Ethiopian government as a good site to resettle the returnees to avoid placing even greater pressure on the already degraded and overcrowded highlands. Thus, returnees were advised (although not required) to remain in the lowlands, where they would be allocated land, rather than return to the highlands, where they would likely be unable to support themselves.

Settling in the lowlands entailed a change not only in the physical surroundings of returnees but, far more significantly, in the very social organization and economic basis on which they would be able to support themselves. In the highlands, most rural dwellers lived in houses scattered across the mountain slopes rather than in villages; in the lowlands they would live in a town that was quite crowded. In the highlands there was no local market, and thus visits to the market were made as often as once a week or as rarely as once a month, depending on how far people had to travel from their homes to get to the marketplace. In the lowlands, a market operated in the village every day and sat at the center of the town. Prices in Ada Bai were high because of its physical remoteness, but people could also buy smaller amounts of what they needed on a daily basis without having to travel far. Wage labor played a more important role in the lowlands and could be undertaken on a more occasional basis because people did not have to leave their households for long periods to find work as they had done in the highlands. The heat was particularly oppressive and prevented people from working during the hottest hours of the day.

The lowlands were also considered more unhealthy than the highlands, with more communicable diseases and dangerous spirits that could kill a person. Because people lived in close proximity to strangers, and the town also attracted unknown people from distant places to its business district, the danger of attack by an evil spirit was considered greater. These factors made it more difficult for people to find potential partners for their sons and daughters to marry—a person's character became more important than his or her family's history in judging suitability for marriage, and the danger of not being able to find a suitable match was a source of anxiety for some parents.

Bursting the Bubble of the Imagined Homeland

For the first few days after the returnees' arrival, chaos reigned. Local leaders, cadres who had been chosen by the TPLF in the refugee camp, organized the population into groups.[1] These groups, which closely resembled the neighborhoods that had existed in the camp, were named after the provinces of Tigray from which people had originally come: Axum, Adwa, Tembien, Enticho, Agame, and so forth. The two hundred or so Muslims (who had come from all parts of Tigray) were given house plots close together. The Relief Society of Tigray (REST), a nongovernmental organization that had originally been the humanitarian wing of the TPLF, distributed to each household a plastic sheet for shelter, a 20-liter jerry can to haul and store water, a box of cups, plates, and other cooking utensils, and nine months' food ration. For the first few days people lived under the grass shelters or in the shade of the few acacia shrubs that dotted the area. The bright blue plastic sheets afforded little shelter from the nightly rains and strong winds that seemed to have arrived together with the refugees.

Mebrat,[2] a twenty-year-old single mother whose parents had left Ethiopia during the 1970s, was born in Eritrea and raised in the refugee camps in the Sudan. She came to Ada Bai with her four-year-old daughter and her father, mother, two brothers, and one sister. She recalled the first days after her family arrived in Ada Bai:

> We left [the Safawa refugee camp] and came to Ada Bai. When we were in Safawa, I knew nothing about Tigray. But I had heard that life was very hard. . . . that there was not a lot of work [i.e., employment opportunities] and that it is difficult to collect [save] money here. So I was unhappy when I thought of "coming home." But my parents said, "No, it is better to be in our country and to be poor than to be a refugee and to be rich." But even the Sudanese were telling us how difficult it is to live in Tigray. I had no memories of Tigray, so I was afraid.
>
> When we got here, we could not believe [what we saw]. This place was a field, and the place across the road [north, at the edge of the horizon along the banks of the Tekezze River that separates Ethiopia from Eritrea] was a forest. I remember that we waited two days to get our plastic shade [sheet]. Most everyone stayed under a [large grass] shade together, but we

Returnees spent their first nights under plastic sheeting.

went to the place that had been assigned to [the people from] Agame [a district in northeastern Tigray, from which her parents had migrated twenty years earlier]. We did that because we knew it would be hard to live with so many families together and we did not want to spend money transporting our things [by hiring donkey carts].

We were all alone for several days. I remember one day there was a strong wind and heavy rain. My father and Hagos [her brother] had to hold the plastic sheet [to keep it] from flying away. All our belongings, including our mattresses, were made dirty by the mud. After that first time the rain was not so bad.

At first we built a small shelter, like [a cooking hut that] people make for a *magogo* [traditional stove]. We stayed in that for fifteen days. All our belongings were outside and we were inside with our grain that we had brought from the Sudan.

Mebrat's mother, Azeb, was so discouraged by conditions at Ada Bai during those first few days that she felt physically ill and asked her daughter to take her to the clinic. The clinic had been set up by the government's regional Bureau of Health inside a series of white tents, located near the brick house at the eastern edge of the settlement. The tents were too hot to sit in for any length of time during the day and too low to the ground for people to stand in, so the government health workers assigned to the area examined most of their patients in the open air, using the tents to store medicine and equipment and the house as their own living quarters. Bags of intravenous solution were hung from the branches of trees, running into the arms of extremely ill, dehydrated patients who lay on the ground.

When Azeb got to the clinic, the health workers could find nothing wrong with her. She told me later that she realized she was really just depressed about the living conditions in Ada Bai and returned to the family's rudimentary shelter that passed for a house. Within a few weeks, her husband and eldest son had built a proper house, a single round room made from grass and wood poles, with mud walls inside and a thatched roof. She said that once she had moved her family into the new house and other people had come to the area assigned to those who were from Agame, she began to feel better.

Over the next weeks and months, people started to establish routines of daily life. They located the nearest water source (for most, this was the well behind the clinic, contaminated as a result of also being used to water animals and not having a cover to keep debris from dropping inside). They were assigned plots of land (16 by 20 meters each) on which to build, and found the areas in the surrounding fields and forests where grass and wooden poles could be cut for building their houses. Those who could not build their own houses—the elderly, single women, and the disabled— sought assistance from their neighbors or sold a few precious belongings to get enough cash to hire someone to help them. The community built one large church and two small mosques out of straw, wood, and mud. Once these basic needs had been attended to, those who had left their goats, sheep, or donkeys in Sudan returned there to bring them to Ada Bai. Others sold some of their food rations to buy animals. A few shops, bakeries, and grinding mills were opened, mostly by entrepreneurs from the nearby town of Humera, but some by people who had owned businesses in the refugee camps and had brought the corrugated iron from which the shops were built with them to Ada Bai. A tiny market was formed along the roadside where traders piled their limited wares on the ground in the dust for customers to pick over. Several teahouses and restaurants were opened, catering to the few health workers, truck drivers, government officials, and relief workers who came to Ada Bai to assess the situation or to bring supplies: most Ada Bai residents did not have the money to spend on tea or prepared food.

The local council began to allocate plots of land to (mostly male) heads of household. Much of this land needed to be cleared before it could be planted. In the highlands land was degraded and plots were as small as one acre (.4 hectare), making it difficult to produce enough barley, teff, or wheat for the household to survive. In Humera, by contrast, the land was fertile and had the potential to produce large quantities of sorghum and sesame. However, returnee farmers did not have experience growing these crops, and plowing was difficult and expensive to arrange (either through renting tractors or donkeys) because most people had no traction animals. The challenges of adjusting to the new agricultural system would bring smaller harvests for the first few years.

These small-scale entrepreneurial activities began the long process that would eventually transform Ada Bai from an empty "Big Land" into a returnee settlement and eventually into a village. This evolution marked the beginning of a process whereby people constructed a physical, social, and emotional "home" based on a redefined sense of community.

End of the War: A Time of Change for Everyone

The precipitating event that made return from exile possible for most Ethiopians living in Sudan was the end of the civil war that the TPLF had fought against the Ethiopian Derg government army. The war had devastated most of Tigray Region: bridges and roads had been bombed or mined, hospitals had been stripped bare of supplies, and schools had been destroyed or closed to be used as army barracks. Development had been brought to a standstill, and most of the region was without access to clean water, electricity, telephone service, and even the most basic social services. The vast majority of the region's population, estimated at three million, had known only war for most of their lives.

It is estimated that during 1984, two hundred thousand people fled from Tigray to Sudan.[3] Some people left their land and property in the hands of relatives when they fled to Sudan, and thus returned to Tigray the following year. They wanted to reclaim their property and to plant their fields, even though the war was still going on, for they did not want to remain dependent on food aid for another year. Those who remained in Sudan were poorer and had nothing to return to. They included those too weak, sick, or poor to leave the camps. Even after the end of the 1984–85 famine, they waited for an end to the war and the possibility of being assisted to return to Ethiopia to rebuild their asset base. The change of government made this return possible, though it was not as smooth or successful as most of the repatriating refugees had hoped.

The challenges of reconstruction following the end of the war were overwhelming. Tigrayan society and culture had changed dramatically: not only returning refugees but also local farmers and townspeople had to navigate their way toward a future that, while promising, was still largely uncertain. Their guerrilla movement had been victorious, but the implications of that victory were still unclear. Returnees would need to learn to grow new crops and to obtain all of their household requirements without external assistance for the first time in eight years.

Emplacement: A Dialectic of Practice and Representation

The process of emplacement in Ada Bai was enacted through the innumerable practices that made up everyday life, including house building, farming, cooking, tea drinking, trading, attending the church or mosque, and celebrating public holidays (Bodenhorn 1995; Hirsch and O'Hanlon 1995). Representations—conscious reflections on or about the place— were born from the relationship that individuals and groups forged between themselves and their environment through these practices, and were complementary to the immediate experiences of inhabiting the place through social practice. Emplacement involved the integration of the material and moral aspects of practice (Migdal 1988, 27). Practice and representation worked in a dialectic to mold "senses of place" (Feld and Basso 1996) that were at once utilitarian, reflective, and creative. Movement from exile to country of origin was the impetus that "offered [strategies] that lock[ed] horns with prevalent norms and modes of social control, proposing new forms of social life" (Migdal, 27).

Rather than develop a single sense of place whereby all who inhabited it considered their surroundings in the same way, spaces were emplaced differently by men and women, children, the elderly, tradespeople, and farmers. Different senses of place were based on the particular relationship forged through daily practice. Household space, wilderness, sacred spaces, and public spaces were all personalized and incorporated into mosaics of meaning that translated unknown, dangerous areas into known, safe places, experienced differently by different people.

Emplacement formed the basis for productive work, social organization, and different forms of community identity. As such, place was the locus of political and domestic negotiation over the processes of community construction. Local political leadership, regional, and even central government visions of the best use of the land often conflicted with local perceptions. Discussions about the best use of a place could turn into heated debate, for the implications often spelled the difference between subsistence and starvation or involved dramatically disparate visions of how the community imagined itself or how different individuals imagined their role in the collective. The multiplicity of views about how places should be used were made clear in public debate, neighborhood songs, and political propaganda.

Decentering the Notion of "Home"

The concept of "home" in anthropological discourse has been conceived of variously as the place where people live, to which they return, or where they dream of returning if they are obliged to leave. Home is where people who have similar lives and similar interests live. It is assumed to be a place to which people have a relationship that is unchanging. In recent years, perhaps as a result of highly publicized upheavals throughout the world, the challenges of homecoming have increasingly been the subject of focus. Some of the most useful texts in this respect have been written by returnees and immigrants themselves who have found themselves in the uncomfortable position of realizing that the home they had dreamt of returning to in fact does not exist anywhere but in the mind's eye (Kundera 2002).

In this book, I demonstrate how people may, as a result of changing circumstances associated with displacement and civil war, come to define "home" not in geographic terms but as the conceptual and affective space in which community, identity, and political and cultural membership inter- sect. In this sense, home is a variable term, one that can be transformed, newly invented, and developed in relation to the circumstances in which people find themselves or choose to place themselves. Returnees were settling in a physical place where they had never lived before, far from their birthplaces and extended families in the Tigrayan highlands and with different, sometimes unfamiliar, resources with which to support their households. They underwent the process of creating anew (rather than re-creating) meaning and associations with each other and with their new surroundings.

In this sense, they were similar to Russians who "returned" from the other republics of the former Soviet Union when the Communist regime ended. Many of these so-called returnees had family ties to Russia but had never actually lived there. They tended to have idealized images of what life there would be like and faced major tasks of reimagining their new surroundings in order to understand their new environment as home. Writing about this population of (so-called return) migrants, Hilary Pilkington and Moya Flynn say:

> Migrants must confront changes that have taken place in the space to which they are returning both in actual terms and in relation to their image of that space. Reidentification with the new homeland is thus a process of "becoming" which must take into account both the future and the past. . . . The experience of Russian returnees suggests that "home" is not a physical space which can be "returned to" but an imagined community which requires both physical and cultural reconstruction by migrants upon return. (Pilkington and Flynn 1999, 191–96)

The definitional transformation that notions of home underwent was, for the people of Ada Bai, the outcome of the emplacement process. My exploration of the means by which people made sense of their new environment follows the way that they constructed a home—a sense of belonging to a place such that it became the focal point of the person's social, economic, and political identity—from a space that, at the time of their arrival back in Ethiopia, they did not associate with any particularly significant meaning.

Community Formation

A key element in the process of emplacement was the subprocess of community formation, whereby a group of people, finding themselves thrown together by their circumstances but sharing no other common personal history, developed the bonds that tied them together and began to think of themselves as "Ada Bayans," people belonging to the village of Ada Bai. Community formation followed certain conventions that were both a reflection of the social structure familiar to the returnees and of the disruption that structure necessarily underwent as a result of the displacement.

Having been removed first from their original homes and then again from their adopted refugee camp home, the returnees found themselves in a kind of unstructured transitional state. The rules of proper or reasonable social behavior and interaction were thrown into question: some were still valid, some needed to be renegotiated and modified to accommodate the new context, and still others had lost their utility or meaning and were eventually discarded. Uncertainty about which social conventions and strategies to use in the new environment gave way to a general sense of confusion within the community. Such confusion could be uncomfortable, dangerous, and at times even life threatening. Returnees were like actors rehearsing a play, holding a script in their hands, but not sure whether they would be required to read from the script in its entirety or would be compelled to improvise here and there in order to enact a new story. To take the analogy even further, they were not even sure what the final act of the drama was about, so they had little sense of whether it would be better to follow the script or to ad-lib their lines.

Many explorations of cultural creativity (Turner 1974; Lavie, Narayan, and Rosaldo 1993) describe exhibitions of improvisation as celebrations of human ingenuity and resourcefulness, and for the most part as positive experiences. In contrast, in Ada Bai many expressions of cultural creativity were anxiety producing and difficult. Ada Bai residents did not, for the most part, enjoy the fact that the social mores and everyday practices that they had used for many years (in some cases for their entire lives) would have to be replaced. Rather than being a creative celebration, their approach to innovation might more aptly have been described as "making the best of a bad situation." Indeed, particularly during the first year after repatriation, many children died as a result of sickness and malnutrition; people attributed these deaths to the fact that they were not yet settled and thus were more vulnerable not only to infectious disease and poverty-related food shortages but also to attacks by spirits and unknown environmental factors.

In her work on the Gwembe Tonga in Zambia (then Northern Rhodesia), Elizabeth Colson outlines a scenario that she considers to be more or less generalizable to displaced and other crisis-affected populations:

> In the general insecurity, people will be unwilling to experiment with new
> technical possibilities except on a minimal basis that will not commit their
> resources to untried innovations. The first years will be marked by many
> small experiments as people test the potential of the new environment.
> They expand from this stage only when there is clear advantage to them
> in the next step. They will be equally unwilling to experiment with large-
> scale social innovation; and since the success of new forms of social
> organisation is less easily demonstrated than the success of crops or new
> productive techniques, such small-scale experimenting with social organi-
> sation as takes place is not likely to be followed by a massive reordering of
> social life. Instead they will consciously maintain the formal structure of
> their society, substituting actors without altering roles, providing symbolic
> actions when customary transactions cannot be carried out. Ultimately,

when the crisis is seen as over, the need to organize action with reference to the new physical and social environment may lead people to develop new formal structures as rationales and limiting definitions for expected behaviour. (1971, 1–2)

Especially at the outset, when Ada Bayans' very survival was seen to be dependent on their ability to reconcile structure and innovation, change could be frightening and anxiety producing. Innovation was often achieved reluctantly, as people tried to preserve known and trusted methods of managing their affairs only to find (sometimes after the loss of a child, a failed harvest, or some other personal catastrophe) that the old practices no longer worked. This was particularly true of the older people, who resisted change more than their children did. Over time, as innovation led to reformed structure and people "found their way," there was a palpable sense of relief in the community. People were able to reflect on the time in which "we were not settled" and contrast it with their subsequent feelings of being settled.

The Community's Relation to Larger Social Networks

Essential to the concepts of "home" and "community" are a group's connections to larger levels of social organization: in this case, to Tigray Region, to Ethiopia as a nation, and to the Horn of Africa. Global discourses on refugee protection and care, repatriation, development, and migration also become relevant to understanding social and symbolic meaning generated through the experience of return. Those who came to Ada Bai had developed their own understandings of these levels of organization and their own relationship to them. They saw themselves as having been persecuted civilians who had fled a war between the central government and a guerrilla army in which many (both men and women) had at some point served. They had been refugees in Sudan receiving food from international agencies and visits from high-ranking political officials. Later, upon their return, they became citizens of a country emerging from war, participating in local elections and in meetings on constitutional formation. These stages of their lives involved changing relationships to political authorities and to political power in general. Such power shifts affected them directly and served to define the personal freedoms, opportunities, and constraints of the community.

Despite the remoteness of their community, people in Ada Bai kept themselves informed about political affairs in the world. They never tired of telling me what they had heard on the Tigrinya-language radio evening news program; about goings-on in Mekele (the regional capital), Addis Ababa (the national capital), the United States, or in a country they had never heard of where a war was reported to be going on. One evening in 1995, I was quizzed by my neighbors about Rwanda and what I knew about the genocide going on there, particularly when they heard that Ethiopia had sent soldiers to join the UN peacekeeping force. One woman had heard from her son, who was a soldier, that he would be participating in the operation. In this way, international affairs often became personal issues as well.

During the late 1980s, the United States and other countries accepted thousands of Ethiopians and Eritreans from the refugee camps in Sudan to be resettled. Many people had relatives living abroad and came to me seeking assistance in making contact with them. In most cases the addresses they had were no longer valid; they had not kept in contact with each other. This may have been because there was no communications infrastructure (no telephone or postal service) in the camp or because people had moved many times after arriving in the United States. In addition, research that I have done with Ethiopian and other refugee and immigrant communities in the United States suggests that many people do not communicate with their relatives outside the United States because they are not able to send gifts or money (Hammond 1989). Those who come to the States expecting to be able to find a job that pays well right away are discouraged at the reality, which is that they often must hold two or more jobs just to cover their own household expenses. This may also account for why, unlike in other refugee situations, the role of remittances in the household economy was negligible (Horst 2002).

Temporality in Social Process

During the course of my stay in Ada Bai, I observed something being constructed from virtually nothing: village from field, place from space, home from settlement. This is not to say that people did not have their own shared history but that the relationship between their community and the physical place had not yet been developed. The process of emplacement was substantially under way by the time I finished the major period of fieldwork in July 1995, yet it will continue for as long as those who dwell there remain. On my return visits, I have observed ever-increasing and deepening connections between people and place; many of the bonds out of which a community is formed are now stronger than any that Ada Bai residents have ever known anywhere.

By contrast, however, in creating a narrative of community formation, beginnings and endings were harder, if not impossible, to delineate. Refugees repatriated to Ada Bai from Sudan not only with their physical belongings but with their cultural and historical baggage as well. They arrived with expectations, plans, fears, and dreams; few of these would ever be fully realized—most would be replaced by new visions of the future— but such images guided people in orienting their lives in their new location. Migration was for most people not a new experience. Although there is a sense in which they were "starting over" by establishing themselves in their new environment, they were doing so with a whole toolbox from which to develop strategies for living and thriving in this new place. They looked to Sudan for work opportunities, traveled to Eritrea to buy imported goods to sell in the local market, and searched for local seeds and raw materials for making tools from their immediate environment and in local markets. In this new space that was largely foreign (even though they were nominally in their home country) people were neither creating a new way of life from a clean slate nor going back to a previous state of being.

Although returnees negotiated and contested meanings of community and home in their practical, everyday lives, such debates and concepts were rarely articulated verbally in any objective fashion. Particularly during the first year after repatriation, constructing a community and a feeling of home were more matters of "getting on with life." Feeding one's family, building one's house, participating in local and national elections, finding a spouse for one's child or oneself, attending religious festivals, and healing one's sick infant were all ways of emplacing oneself and building a community. Most of these activities involved kin, neighbors, and spiritual and secular leaders. Community cohesion was generated through the daily exchanges of goods, favors, and knowledge; borrowing was considered the raw material that neighbors and kin used to weave their lives together. These were the building blocks of practice that fed changing ideas about socially appropriate behavior, neighborliness, and common sense. Discussions about community formation were about where to find the best farmland or sorghum seeds, how to bring down a baby's fever, or whose *sewa* (locally produced beer made from sorghum) was the best. It involved a reexamination of the criteria by which decisions were made, actions taken, and judgments formed. Mapping a social world onto a heretofore unknown physical space involved identifying resources, both human and economic, to make life in this place possible. Many of the resources of the highlands, from seeds to traditional medicines to long-standing and well-established political structures, were not available in the lowlands. These had to be procured from the natural environment or created anew. In the process, neighborhoods were developed that offered security, camaraderie, and support. The process was intensely personal for each individual and each household. It was also public, involving huge meetings attended by at least one adult from each household to discuss issues such as local elections, community work projects, environmental sanitation campaigns, or allocation of farmland.

The years from 1993 through 1995 were a period of intense change for the people of Ada Bai. The process of community construction changed over time in its character, quality, and focus. Whereas in 1993 people were concerned with obtaining access to farmland and making sure that they got their fair share of water from the well, by 1995 these things were no longer of as much concern to most people because they had obtained access to these things. More pressing were issues such as starting a business, improving one's house, or reestablishing links with relatives from whom people had been separated.

The Anthropologist as Witness, Neighbor, and Ambulance Driver

My analysis of postrepatriation community formation and emplacement is based on research carried out over the past decade in Ada Bai and Tigray. The primary focus of this book comes from research I carried out over twenty months (November 1993 to July 1995) in Ada Bai. During that time, I was a resident in the settlement, living in a one-room straw house that looked like every other house in the village. I also returned to Ada Bai for shorter visits in 1996, 1997, 2001, and 2002. (Ethiopia and Eritrea were at war from 1998 to 2000, and because of its proximity to the border, access to Ada Bai was prohibited by the Ethiopian government.) Prior to the twenty months I spent in Ada Bai, I spent four months (August–November 1993) in the highlands of Tigray, both in the regional capital, Mekele, and in the largest town in the northeastern part of the region, Adigrat. In Adigrat I worked as a volunteer assessing a soil and water conservation project run by the Ethiopian Catholic Church. This work helped to give me a sense of life for rural peasants who had endured the war from their homes in the highlands that I would later be able to contrast with the experiences of returnees in the lowlands. From 1995 through 1997 and throughout 1999 and 2000, I worked as a consultant field officer for the United Nations Emergencies Unit for Ethiopia (UN–EUE), a project of the United Nations Development Programme (UNDP) (now run by the UN Office for the Coordination of Humanitarian Affairs, or UNOCHA) and for other nongovernmental and bilateral donor organizations, including the United States Agency for International Development.[4] Through this work I was able to contextualize my experience in Ada Bai within wider national and regional spheres and to get a more complete sense of how life in the lowlands around Ada Bai contrasted with the highlands.

My discussion of emplacement and community construction is influenced as much by my personal experience in the returnee settlement as by my research observations. In their process of social mapping, the returnees left out nothing and nobody. That included me, the village anthropologist, who the community gave multiple identities as ambulance and taxi driver and as witness.

One month after I arrived in Ada Bai, the United Nations Emergencies Unit for Ethiopia loaned me an old Toyota Land Cruiser to use in the field in exchange for writing a series of reports on my research findings. This was the only privately owned vehicle in the village; the taxis and tractors that traveled back and forth to Humera were owned by businessmen in that town, and fares for rides were too expensive for many people. A few days after I had brought the vehicle from Addis Ababa, a man came to me to ask if I would drive his wife, who was having complications delivering her fourth child, to the hospital in Humera. I agreed to make the trip, and both mother and child survived the experience, although I was later to discover that another of their children was severely malnourished and would not live to see her fifth birthday.

The second day, I rushed a neighbor woman who had been bitten by a poisonous snake to the hospital; she died five hours after being admitted, and I sat with her as I helplessly watched the life drain out of her. This was the first of many deaths I was to witness, and one of my first realizations that the environment we were inhabiting was quite dangerous, that a life could be snuffed out instantly by an unforeseen hazard.

A few days later, early in the morning, I opened the door of my house and found a small crowd of people waiting quietly and patiently for me to wake up. They sat gathered around two beds made from wood and goatskin, upon each of which lay emaciated men whom I could tell were extremely ill even after only a quick and untrained glance. They were both barely conscious; I would later find out that they were suffering from advanced tuberculosis. One had lost control of his bowels. I looked from the men to the people who had brought them.

"I'm sorry," I told the crowd, afraid that they might expect me to have a cure for the men. "I am not a doctor."

"We know that," they said, "but you have a car. We want you to take these men to the hospital in Humera." They carried referral papers from the Ada Bai clinic. Humera Hospital, the only hospital within one hundred kilometers, was twenty kilometers from Ada Bai—a trip that took half an hour in my car.

I grabbed my keys and we loaded the men gently into the car along with their relatives. Despite our efforts, both men died a few days later, having suffered terribly. One was buried in an unmarked grave by the hospital gravedigger in a cemetery in town before his wife had even learned of his death. The doctors at the hospital had not wanted to tell her that he had died because, they said, "We did not want to upset her." So I was left to tell her in my broken Tigrinya. I searched with her in vain to find out which of the unmarked graves in the Humera graveyard was his. Finally the gravedigger pointed to a grave and said that the man was under that pile of stones, but I suspect he was just trying to give us some reason to stop looking for the grave—he buried so many bodies he was unlikely to remember who was buried where.

The requests for rides to the hospital and to the market in town continued throughout my stay. If I could be cajoled into providing transport to my neighbors, I could save each person the three to five birr (80 cents to $1) taxi fare that each person would otherwise have had to pay for a place in the crowded taxi, or fifty to sixty birr for a chartered taxi run to the hospital. People's access to cash was extremely limited, and such expenses, not to mention the cost of medicine, food for the patient, and the lost earnings of the family members who stayed in town to care for the patient, were usually prohibitive. I had heard of many people who had died because their families could not afford to pay for them to be transported to the hospital.

Even though I knew that most people were desperate by the time they came to ask me for assistance, this was not always the case, and I found the volume and frequency of the demands for help particularly vexing. I began to think that I could probably spend all day every day driving to and from the hospital, without ever getting to my "real" research. I would emerge each morning from my hut to find between one to twenty people waiting to ask me for a lift to town. Often when I thought that my help would not make a difference or if the patient looked well enough that immediate hospitalization was probably not necessary, I refused on the grounds that I had "work" (interviews and note taking) to do. Most of the referral papers from the clinic were for patients who could not be treated at the Humera Hospital anyway (the hospital had only four junior doctors—none of whom had completed their specialist training—and lacked basic drugs, blood transfusion equipment, and surgical facilities).[5] Finally I convinced the clinic staff to agree to make a note on the referral papers (which were written in English) to indicate whether a case was an emergency that a trip to the hospital might actually help to resolve. I tried to organize the carloads into a more or less regular twice-weekly schedule.

Some of the cases were truly critical. Those who had been bitten by a poisonous snake could bleed to death within a few hours if they did not receive an injection of anti-venom medication (the snake venom acts as an anticoagulant, preventing the blood from clotting). The medicine had to be kept refrigerated and thus was only available at the Humera Hospital. Women with childbirth complications could also bleed to death or the infant could die in the womb if medical care was delayed. In such cases, I dropped my day's research plans (or my night's sleep) and headed into town with the patients and their relatives.

My reticence about going to the hospital every day, or even several times a day, confused many people, who considered my real job to be that of a driver and my responsibility to be to drive them to the hospital or market. Few people considered what I did as real work: I spent my days with paper, pens, and books, visiting people, and, as far as they could tell, hardly exerting myself physically. Real work to them was plowing, cooking, hauling firewood, building houses or fences, herding animals, and tending children. Work such as mine, people reasoned, was not to be taken seriously and could certainly be interrupted for something as urgent as a trip to the hospital or clinic. For that matter, they did not see why I should not be willing to take them to town to do their marketing as well.

My role as ambulance/taxi driver at times played a larger part in my life than I wanted it to, not merely because it conflicted with the research I had come to carry out or because it interrupted my sleep but because very often my efforts were ineffective. I had never been exposed to such great levels of suffering, and at first I felt a responsibility to try to help everyone. I was quickly made to feel my own impotence, as most of the ill people who were brought to me were already too weak to be saved, and I lacked the skills to be able to treat them myself. When people came to me in the middle of the night for rides to the village clinic, I would invariably be obliged to serve as "assistant health assistant" (holding lanterns, fetching medicines and supplies for the health assistant) for several hours before the crisis could be brought under control.

It took several months for me to see the connection between my fieldwork and my ambulance driver job. Over time, however, I realized that the role assigned to me by the community provided an opportunity for people to open up to me, to share some of the most intense and difficult aspects of their lives. The rewards they gave me were often intangible and I only recognized them in hindsight. In exchange for helping people, I was ushered through a door that helped me to become a part of the community. Our shared experiences of suffering, grief, and celebration, in what were often life and death situations, bound us together as friends and neighbors. My closest friends and most important informants were people whom I had assisted with either their own or their family's health emergencies. Relationships that were already close became markedly deeper after we had gone through such an emergency together.

My service to the community, and the bonds that were formed as a result of it, revealed to me an important organizational principle in the constructed community of Ada Bai. I came to understand the significance of shared history and interdependence as a force that bound Ada Bai people together and gave them an identity as a community. As a newcomer who had not shared the experiences of war, flight from Tigray, and refugee camp life, I was not privy to much of the shared history that had bound those living in Ada Bai together by the time they repatriated to Ethiopia. Through my role as ambulance driver, however, I was allowed into their lives to witness the power of such shared history in forging interpersonal relationships. By asking me to help them, people were also offering to bring me into the process of shared history formation. The process by which I became a member of the Ada Bai community, therefore, paralleled in many ways the efforts of Ada Bayans to strengthen their own sense of community.

Liisa Malkki's description of the anthropologist as witness closely resembles my own approach to fieldwork. In outlining two types of fieldworkers (investigators versus witnesses) she points out that the investigator

> sometimes gets deeply caught up in the practice of probing or digging for ever more information and of pursuing hidden, secret, or restricted knowledge in the (sometimes unexamined) belief that the hidden is more fundamental than the things that are more accessible to study—that unearthing a secret yields a "key" or a "code" to unlocking important mysteries about "a culture" . . . The anthropologist as witness is differently

located. Here, the injunction to know "everything" and to find the key to unlock mysteries is not a central (or sometimes even a meaningful) activity. Trying to be an attentive listener, recognizing the situatedness of one's intellectual work . . . and affirming one's own connection to the ideas, processes, and people one is studying are more important in this kind of practice. (1995a, 96)

Renato Rosaldo argues that the social analyst straddles a line between detached outside observer and impassioned internal critic or advocate (1989, 194). These roles are very often not easily separable. I often felt that the more of an "insider" I became, the greater was my felt need to criticize or reject what I saw. My position as witness compelled me to take a moral stand on many issues, particularly those that involved human suffering. This flew in the face of my anthropological training, which had stressed cultural relativism, tolerance, and suspension of judgment. It was particularly difficult for me to study some kinds of traditional medicine when painful remedies were being used on people I knew well. Witnessing the bloodletting, cauterization, and scarification of young children who were suspected of having eye diseases or of being possessed by spirits (when biomedicine would have diagnosed them as having intestinal parasites and acute malnutrition) without voicing my concern, for instance, was almost impossible. Sometimes the contradiction between cultural relativism and my own beliefs about proper treatment only became evident after I had already acted: in a split second I was obliged to choose between their kind of medicine and mine, and all too often I chose my own before I even realized what was happening. I discuss these dilemmas in chapter 5.

I also found it difficult to conduct interviews about food shortages and famine while there was severe hunger in the community. Many studies by applied anthropologists and other social scientists have remarked on the fact that Ethiopians who have undergone an extremely violent war and devastating famine show remarkably few signs of psychosocial distress. Writing about the tendency of migrants to bury those who die along the way, Dessalegn Rahmato observes:

On many occasions the dead are given a quick and simple burial, and the traditional mourning ceremony is dispensed with. So much crying, weeping, and anguished mourning has been done already in connection with the numerous deaths that have occurred in the weeks and months before the journey that men and women are drained of all emotions, and burial takes place in silence and with many people wearing wooden faces. (1991, 156)

My own experience suggested that many Tigrayans found it difficult to discuss painful experiences while they were in the midst of them. For my part, I was reluctant to question people about their own experiences of starvation. I was attuned to the danger of seeming to reduce their hunger and destitution to "interesting research questions," rather than acknowledging them as the human tragedies that they were. Instead of asking someone about their own experience of suffering, I often asked them about hunger in more general terms, as it affected the community and our neighbors, or as it was experienced during the war. This distancing technique helped both my informants and me to feel more comfortable talking about these difficult issues. In so doing, I hope I have not committed the error that Nancy Scheper-Hughes recognizes when she criticizes studies in which "hunger was sanitized and aestheticized . . . [and] also denied" so as to "turn away, we might say, from the plain facts of hunger as a lived experience that consigns millions of Third World people to an early grave" (1993, 132). Most of my information concerning hunger and poverty comes from observing people and interviewing them about child-rearing practices, feeding routines, economic strategies, and rituals concerning healing, death, and birth rather than direct testimony from people about hunger per se.

The people I lived with in Ada Bai were probably more aware of my activist role than I was. I was part advocate and part detached observer, and although they understood that my own power to help them was limited, they knew that I had connections to people who worked in the government and international organizations who might be able to assist them. At times they would ask me to "please tell the government or UNHCR" (the United Nations High Commissioner for Refugees) what they had told me or what I had seen. I usually did as they had directed me if I could, because I felt a moral responsibility to alert those who were in a position to bring help about the precarious situation I was witnessing before disaster struck. In March and April 1994, the village experienced a massive food shortage and several adults and children died from lack of food. My neighbors told me that one man had mixed soil with his last remaining food grains to make the food last longer; in eating the mixture he accelerated his own death. During this time, I was in regular communication by high-frequency radio with the head of the regional Relief and Rehabilitation Bureau in the regional capital, who eventually sent emergency grain rations to the returnees. Likewise, when the borehole pump broke down for six weeks, I made daily trips to Humera with as many jerry cans as I could fit in my car to bring back clean water for my neighbors.

I also harangued the UNHCR offices in Humera and Addis Ababa to provide a tanker to bring seven thousand liters of water a day to the village until the pump was fixed. It was not difficult to decide whether or not to act in these instances. Indeed, I doubt that the people I lived with would have tolerated my questions and given me such rich information if I had not tried to help them. More important, as a member of the community, these actions were part of my overall contribution.

Over the months I began to understand intuitively, rather than in an intellectual sense, the community as a collection of people who share certain responsibilities for each other, who owe and are owed certain debts to others, but who for the most part refuse to act on these debts, seeing such exchange instead as part of the matrix of costs and benefits through which membership in this particular community is woven and made meaningful. Throughout this book, I discuss my own role in the community, as it provided the avenue, and in some cases no doubt the filter, through which I was able to make sense of the processes of emplacement and community construction.

My arrival in Ada Bai followed closely the returnees' own arrival from Sudan. I arrived five months after they did. The settlement I found when I first arrived was very different from the community that I left. For this reason, this ethnographic account is necessarily not only an exploration of certain themes, cultural meanings, and forms of practice, it is also a story with a chronological element to it. However, while the story has a clear beginning, it does not have an ending; this has kept me coming back over the years.

One of the factors that may have contributed to my sense that Ada Bayans' approach to community construction grew richer as time went on may be because the quality of my own research was also enhanced over time as my language skills improved and as people came to trust and open up to me. Despite the fact that my ability to perceive in-depth matters more clearly increased over time, I also think that people grew more reflexive about their physical environment as a locus for home and community when they had mastered the basic challenges of survival.

From Flight to Camp to Ada Bai

The people of Ada Bai were no strangers to migration, war, or famine, and the transitional phase in which I encountered them was surely not the first such experience they had known. Seasonal and distress migration are common occurrences in highland Ethiopia, as annual harvests even in good rainfall years do not usually provide adequate food to support the household for the entire year. As the life histories and personal narratives that make up chapters 2 and 3 show, flight to Sudan was exceptional partly because of the extreme suffering that precipitated it, but also because external actors (governments and international organizations) noticed their movement and stepped in to help. Life in the refugee camps was at times difficult, particularly at the beginning when inadequate food and clean water led to high malnutrition and disease levels. People coped with these problems in much the same way that Alex de Waal describes those who faced famine in Darfur, Sudan, did during the same period: they sought to preserve their way of life for the future (de Waal 1989, 65 and 148). Changes that did occur were often so gradual that they went unnoticed and only became evident once people had left the camps to return to Ethiopia.

Given the refugees' long history of, and familiarity with, migration, repatriation more closely resembled a new move than a return home. The uncertainty of climatic, political, and economic factors in Tigray was chronic, and people had learned to incorporate this tenuousness into their responses to challenges in living. Returnees in Ada Bai had no reason to believe that in coming back to Ethiopia they had migrated for the last time, yet the surest way they knew to make the most of their lives there was to behave as if this was their final destination. I therefore treat repatriation and the processes of social change that follow it as John Davis (1992) might—as being continuous with other forms of social organization and change, involving moments and processes that occur both within established though mutable structures and outside of those structures.

The processes of emplacement and community formation are continuations of the very process of community disintegration (not to be confused with cultural disintegration) that accompanied the initial displacement. In chapter 1, I examine the causes and experiences of flight from Tigray by following the personal accounts of several individuals. Chapter 2 describes refugees' experiences by presenting their own narratives about life in the camps. These testimonies show the resolve with which people clung to their old cultural frames of reference while at the same time adopting innovations to enable them to survive, and thrive, in their new habitations. I discuss the ways that people's survival strategies incorporated both new and old elements of judgment, morality, cosmology, and value. Through the experiences of struggle and suffering (as they described their lives), the refugees formed communities, neighborhoods, and kin networks even in their temporary domiciles, which they would use, to the extent possible, upon coming to Ada Bai.

On their return to Ethiopia, many of these cultural beliefs and practices were called into action yet again, as I show in chapter 3. Specifically concerned with homecoming and the organization of physical space, this chapter develops the theme of the process of emplacement. By emplacement I refer to the organization of the environment into units that have different meanings for men and women, the elderly and younger people. This chapter examines the social space of the Ada Bai returnee settlement with regard to the distribution of houses, the establishment and organization of neighborhoods, and the durability of some, and the flexibility of other, kin and social networks. I argue that the organization of space in the returnee village reflected the residents' choice to develop a community that borrowed some features from highland preflight Tigray as well as from the refugee camps, but also included new innovations that rendered the environment productive and gave it meaning as a home.

Ada Bai was neither a camp, nor a village, nor a city, though it had aspects of each of these types of settlement. It was a social grouping that attempted to preserve the elements of community that people felt effectively safeguarded them from danger, and positioned its members to exploit the benefits of cross-border trade and employment with Sudan and Eritrea, to reap the benefits of the fertile land on which they were settled, and to take advantage of the social services that were available. Ada Bai had characteristics of a rural settlement, but it also had many of the features of an urban area with social services (however limited) and socialization opportunities that did not exist in rural areas.

Chapter 4 examines household economies in detail to determine the ways that family units interacted and developed strategies to meet their basic needs and to further community formation. Based on a survey that I conducted with ten households every day for four months, the data included all resource inflows (wage labor, loans and gifts received, loan repayments) and outflows (items purchased, payments made, loans and gifts extended) as well as consumption patterns. The data collection period spanned from the harvest season to the "hungry season" and demonstrated spending and food consumption patterns. It also showed many of the strategies that households employed to keep from falling below the minimum subsistence level. Principal among these strategies was the use of informal credit and the sharing of household items and cash between households based on the linkages discussed in chapter 3. Although the refugees experienced an overall decline in income and consumption levels, the increased reliance on social support networks (both kin and affinal) helped to provide a social safety net in times of shortage. Such forms of collaboration and cooperation served to forge new, and strengthen old, kinship and other forms of alliances while at the same time forming the basis for a limited form of class-based stratification within the village.

In chapter 5 I consider the rituals involving birth and death as mechanisms of socialization through which the individual was accepted, incorporated, and implicated in the community. Because of the dangerous nature of birth, and the ease with which death came to claim its victims, rituals at once both affirmed life and the individual's role in the community and sought to ward off death and safeguard the spirit for entry into the afterlife. These rituals incorporated the supernatural world as known and passed down through the generations by Tigrayan society, and also embraced aspects of the lived experience that were a result of the returnees' particular historical, economic, and political circumstances.

In chapter 6 I examine the political character of Ada Bai and the relationships between the village and the wider world. Despite their geographic remoteness from centers of political and economic control, Ada Bai returnees were conscious participants in global processes. As a border community living at the intersection between three nations and having had extensive contact with the international humanitarian relief system, returnees' lives were implicated in processes whose influences were regional and often global. A few people received remittances from relatives living abroad. Others worked in the regional sorghum and sesame export trade that spanned Sudan, Ethiopia, and Eritrea. In this chapter I follow the lines leading out of the community to show the interconnectedness of this small village with the world around it.

I focus on the way that returnees understood their own citizenship on returning to Ethiopia. As they negotiated their new place within Tigrayan (and at the national level, Ethiopian) society, people's ideas about their participation in elections and about their relationship to the government and political party changed. In addition, their understanding of the role of international organizations in providing humanitarian assistance changed as well. In general, people became more disillusioned with these holders of power, and felt that their basic needs had not been met in the first two years following their return. They were disappointed and perceived that their lives had been made more difficult than they should have been because they had not been given more assistance on their return from Sudan.

At the same time, vying to gain access to the few resources that were available gave rise to a code of socially acceptable behavior, effectively defining the "good citizen." Faced with a shortage of land and food, residents vied for favor with the political authorities by demonstrating their civic responsibility through such activities as voting in local or national elections, tree planting, ditch digging, contributing to local fund-raising efforts, and assisting the local anthropologist. They were rewarded for these actions with allocations of land and inclusion in the relief food distribution lists. In this sense, establishing a link to the land by gaining access to it and exclusive rights to use it involved the establishment of a connection and relation to place, a relation seen as necessary to assure household food security and therefore economic viability within the new community. These forms of behavior became in effect a social code for upstanding citizens, and those who were excluded from the lists typically complained that their unwillingness to curry favor with the political leaders was the reason they had not been given food or land. I examine public and private discussions that returnees held on the subjects of land and food distribution and on political favoritism. What emerged was the beginning of a stratification of the community based largely on political loyalty and, to a lesser extent, on income differentials.

I conclude this analysis by turning to anthropological and social science discourse on the study of refugees and other forced migrants to show that the prevailing sedentarist bias has served to limit theoretical exploration of such concepts as social change, community formation, identity, and the role of place in cultural studies. The limitations of theory have, in turn, had practical implications in helping to perpetuate the myth that repatriation is—under all conditions—the best solution to forced migration, and that "return" is equivalent to "homecoming" and is therefore not problematic. I argue for more rigorous theory to take seriously the idea that repatriation is in fact a new beginning, one in which people may need significant assistance, and that such assistance should be based on sound anthropological and social scientific analysis that identifies the main obstacles and challenges that people who return typically face in constructing their lives anew.

Repatriation in a Postwar Context

Although relocation overwhelmingly established the context for social change in Ada Bai, it was certainly not the only factor. Residents of Ada Bai faced some of the same challenges of postwar reconstruction that all

Tigrayans—and all Ethiopians—faced. They returned to Ethiopia as victors in a seventeen-year civil war; their army had taken control of the central government in Addis Ababa. With the regime change came new policies of regional autonomy, private investment, and center-periphery relations that the entire nation was grappling with. The new government referred to itself as the Transitional Government of Ethiopia (TGE), and during the period of my fieldwork the people of Ada Bai participated in the first parliamentary elections and in the nationwide debate on the new constitution. Although geographically located in the hinterlands at the edge of the EPRDF's reach, they were also legitimate participants in the new system and they took that participation seriously.

At a more fundamental level, they also shared many of the same challenges that their compatriots who had stayed behind did: they still faced extreme poverty and the threat of famine hung over them all, ironically, like a persistent rain cloud. Thus, although Ada Bai's story is truly its own, it is also in part the story of a people, a nation, and a state struggling to chart a new course in a climate that, while peaceful, still bore many of the same hallmarks of uncertainty that Ethiopians had always faced and which were not specific to former migrants or returnees.

1

Narratives of Displacement

The life histories of Ada Bai returnees are, to a large extent, migration histories. Migration before 1984–85 was a fairly common experience for most Tigrayans: in addition to displacement caused by drought, war, and extreme poverty, seasonal migration of either individuals or entire families to places where there were work opportunities, better land, or support from family was a regular way of coping with recurrent resource shortages. What made the 1984–85 migration extraordinary was its organization and scale, the migrants' desperation, the fact that there was nowhere inside Ethiopia that people felt safe enough to seek refuge or relief, and the length of time they would remain away from their homes.

Similarly, although drought and famine are recurrent threats to Ethiopia's rural population, the famine of 1984–85 was exceptional in its severity and in being largely a by-product—in some cases a deliberate one—of the war between the Derg and the rebel armies in the north of the country. Like the 1973–74 famine, which precipitated the Derg's overthrow of Emperor Haile Selassie in September 1974, this famine was largely ignored by the government, and relief agencies were denied access to the most severely affected areas. This chapter considers the history of the civil war in Tigray, its effects on the civilian population, and its interaction with drought, which resulted in devastating famine. Using personal accounts as well as archival information, I examine the escalation of the military conflict, the progressive social and economic erosion that ultimately led to famine, the various strategies undertaken by the peasants to avert disaster, and their final flight out of Ethiopia.

This information also provides a glimpse of people's lives prior to leaving their homes and introduces several points of contrast, between highland and lowland societies and between returnees and settled communities, that I develop further in subsequent chapters. The distinction between highland and lowland societies in Ethiopia is in many ways more significant than the difference between ethnic groups within the same agro-ecological zone. Highland Amhara and Tigrayan cultures, for instance, are very similar because the basis of economic production is ox-plow agriculture and the crops (wheat, teff, barley, and millet) are the same. Strategies for minimizing vulnerability to famine and the risk of asset depletion are similar (see McCann 1995, 1998, and 1999, and Rahmato 1991). In the lowlands, by contrast, sorghum and maize are the common cereals, with sesame and smaller amounts of cotton grown as cash crops. The soil is soft enough and the terrain flat enough that it can be plowed by machine or by donkey (even camels are sometimes used for plowing).

Much has been made in Ethiopian political and cultural discourse of the cultural unity of people from different parts of Tigray. The Tigrayan People's Liberation Front (TPLF) advocated Tigrayan nationalism to build solidarity during the war. The TPLF's propaganda, education, and mass mobilization exercises trained people to overlook their differences and unite behind the common goal of overthrowing the Derg government (J. Young 1997, 173). However, people living in Tigray Region form a remarkably heterogeneous population. They distinguish between residents of different agro-ecological zones (lowland, midland, and highland); speakers of different languages and dialects (at least seven different languages are spoken—the majority speak Tigrinya, but Amharic, Arabic, Afar, Kunama, Oromo, and Irob/Saho are also spoken); and followers of different religions (Ethiopian Orthodox, Catholic, Protestant, and Muslim) (Hammond 1996a; see also J. Young 1997, 182). The end of the civil war brought a relaxation of Tigrayan nationalism, and people once more became interested in the variation that exists in Tigrayan society. A favorite pastime of returnees in Ada Bai was discussing the particular characteristics of people from different districts within Tigray (see chapter 3).

Prewar Life in the Tigrayan Highlands

The returnees who settled in Ada Bai came from all over Tigray. Most had been highland peasant farmers who supported themselves in the same way that their ancestors had for hundreds of years—through ox-plow agriculture and petty trade. Eking out a harvest on as little as a single acre, households that averaged six or more people remained in a perpetual state of poverty and in most years did not produce enough food to feed themselves. Attempts to gain access to cash through sale of items produced in the home, small livestock sales, and labor migration to areas west and south of Tigray were often insufficient, so people gradually sold their assets until they reached a point where they had nothing else to sell. People tended to abandon their farms only after having sold off their productive assets such as plowshares, seed stocks, and hand tools. The civil war exacerbated the situation, causing some to flee even before they had liquidated all of their property. Those who remained in the refugee camps the longest, however, tended to be those who had lost all of their property and thus had little to return to.

The Political Economy of Famine in Ethiopia

Famine in Ethiopia is generally seen as a result of natural hazards such as drought, flood, and pest infestation. Crop failure is cited as the cause of rising malnutrition and as justification for annual appeals for enormous amounts of food. However, climatic causes are only part of the problem. It was estimated in 2003 that 45 percent of Ethiopia's population is vulnerable to food insecurity, and that four to six million people are chronically food insecure—that is, so poor that they are unable to provide all of their household food needs for the year without assistance.

Tigray is a land of dramatic mountain peaks, dry, rocky soil, and cool air. The region has a stark beauty that comes in part from its near total lack of forest cover caused by deforestation and erosion over many generations. Farmers plow fields littered with large rocks using a single pair of oxen and a wooden plowshare. They often extend their fields up the steep mountain slopes; they know that this practice accelerates erosion, but they believe they have no choice if they are to grow enough to feed their families. Partly because of the scarcity of natural resources, most people do not live in villages or towns. Rather, they spread their houses across the mountain slopes. Many communities were founded on the common use of a particular water source or farming area. From sharing these resources, more complex relationships have developed: a system of land allocation has been established, a single church or mosque has been built to serve the community, and in some places a weekly market provides an opportunity for people from the surrounding area to barter, trade, and socialize. Few of the rural communities are accessible by road, so people must walk long distances to get to the larger towns. Their ties to the people who live close to them are thus very strong.

Famine in 1984–85 was the result of a period of prolonged drought and of government policies explicitly directed at disrupting northern farmers' activities and preventing their access to markets. In the period since 1991, when the war ended, famine has continued to plague Ethiopia, not only as a result of harvest failures associated with drought but also because of

Barley is grown on steep hillsides in highland Tigray.
This crop withered prematurely and could not be harvested for food. Only the stalks could be fed to livestock.

a failure of development efforts and of restrictive policies that have kept
Ethiopia bent on a path of trying to survive through increasing agricultural production rather than diversifying its economic base.

The Development of Tigrayan Nationalist Opposition to the Derg

It is generally accepted by scholars of Ethiopian politics and history that
while the famine of 1984–85 was exacerbated by natural hazards, the civil
war was the main cause of the disaster (de Waal 1991; Clay and Holcomb
1986; Clay, Steingraber, and Niggli 1988; Abbay 1998; J. Young 1997,
130–31).[1] A combination of extreme violence and policies perpetrated as

a by-product of the "scientific socialism" practiced by the Derg regime[2] were intended to cripple local people's strategies for survival, since they were assumed to be sympathizers and supporters of the insurrectionists. The result was extreme political and economic insecurity as well as massive food shortages. Those who fled Tigray did so believing they were fleeing for their lives.

The Derg government was composed of military leaders and university student activists, dominated by the Amhara ethnic group. They advocated a brand of socialism based on collective work, national ownership of all assets, and heavy central control. Despite widespread opposition to imperial rule, not everyone believed the Derg was the best alternative. Almost as soon as the Derg came to power in 1974, several opposition movements, many of them regionally or ethnically based, sprang up. Most were also led by students who had worked with their classmates to overthrow Emperor Haile Selassie but did not share the same vision of Ethiopia's future as the Derg. Many of the opposition leaders who had originally supported the Derg became disillusioned by the heavy-handed tactics of the leadership. As one former student leader explained to me in New York City in 1989, "It was like having the plate snatched out of our hands" to see the Derg turn its back on its original ideals (Hammond 1989).

The Tigrayan People's Liberation Front (TPLF) was established in February 1975. It grew out of the Tigray National Organization (TNO),[3] which had been created by a group of university students based in Addis Ababa in 1972. Members of the TNO spent time in the rural areas attempting to raise peasant nationalist consciousness, assisted by local high school students and teachers (J. Young 1997, 83). In its work, the TPLF sought to create a link between radical student politics in Addis Ababa and the Tigrayan peasantry and to pose a challenge to perceived Amhara domination (J. Young 1994, 75; Tareke 1996, 208). Although its ideological platform was not thoroughly developed during its first few years, the TPLF pursued a Marxist-Maoist line (J. Young 1997, 84).

Despite its seventeen-year control of the central government, the Derg's hold over the north (most of Tigray Region and the northernmost parts of Gondar and Wollo, both inhabited by ethnic Amharas) was never complete. The Derg was more concerned with maintaining control in the capital in the face of strong opposition from the Ethiopian People's Revolutionary Party (EPRP) and other groups and with a border war being fought with Somalia in 1977–78. Its efforts to consolidate power in the urban areas included a campaign of violence from 1976 to 1978 known as the Red Terror, which was led by President Mengistu Haile Mariam and characterized by mass detentions, torture, and executions (often in public). More than ten thousand people were killed by the government during this period (de Waal 1991, 101). The campaign drove intellectuals and other skilled workers from the cities into the regions, thereby bolstering the rebel forces.

Another measure that helped to garner support for the TPLF was its implementation of a land reform system that supplanted the Derg's own efforts. The Derg's land reform, based on its Public Ownership of Rural Lands Proclamation of March 1975, nationalized all land. Ownership was retained by the state and land use was managed by peasant associations, local organizations of farmers who administered an average of around eight hundred hectares. In many parts of southern and central Ethiopia, the reform had dramatic effects (Clapham 1988, 46–47, and J. Young 1997, 181–82). However, in Tigray the reform was largely ineffectual, as the government lacked the popular support it needed to maintain its administrative capacity and the political control it needed to implement the policy. The TPLF began to implement its own land reform during the early 1980s, having instituted *baitos* (ባይቶ), or local governing councils, as alternatives to the peasant associations in the areas it controlled (J. Young 1997, 181–86). The experience of Berhe, an elderly Ada Bai resident who had migrated from Tembien *awraja*[4] in central Tigray, is typical of the effect of the land reform on the peasantry. The following passage is excerpted from my field notes:

> [Soon after marrying, Berhe] and his wife worked on his [deceased] father's land until the TPLF land distribution. They had more than enough for themselves. They built their own house near his father's house and started raising children.
>
> When Haile Selassie was overthrown, the Derg came, but they never had much of a hold over the Hager Salaam *tabia*.[5] The TPLF was active there early on, and instituted its land reform program in about 1969 [Ethiopian calendar—1976 in the Gregorian calendar].[6] When they redistributed the land, his family ended up with only about five hectares (about 20 acres). He says he didn't mind that most of his land was taken away because the *dajazmatch*[7] had always had the right to take it away if he wanted to, so his tenure on the land had been insecure anyway. What he was left with was enough, with his wife selling spices in the nearby market town of Abi Adi. What made a difference was that they did not have as much in the way of grain stores, so when the 1977 [1984] drought came they did not have the grain to fall back on.

Throughout my research, people told me that they considered it essential for each household to have access to enough land to feed itself for the year. Those who had larger holdings claimed not to mind losing the extra portion, but said that, to be successful, any government land reform program must guarantee farmers adequate land and control over their production so that they would be able to produce enough to meet their household's consumption needs. This was true even though most households had never been able to produce all of their own food.

"Draining the Sea to Catch the Fish": Insurgency and Counterinsurgency in Tigray

In his account of the war in Tigray, de Waal notes that "the TPLF, from its inception, fought a classic guerrilla insurgency." It launched its operations from a base in western Tigray, near the town of Endaselassie,[8] and focused its early military activity in the rural areas. Instead of seeking to defend territories, it relied on small-scale but widespread attacks in the countryside on government forces. The TPLF's success in mobilizing support in rural Tigray cannot be solely attributed, however, to its military tactics, as J. Young observes:

> The Derg's weak presence in Tigray in the first years after the overthrow
> of the old regime allowed the TPLF and other revolutionary bands the
> opportunity to establish themselves and encourage distrust of the new
> regime. However, it was the Derg's own policies and heavy-handed
> administration . . . that first drove the educated urban youth out of the
> towns into the arms of the TPLF, and then increasingly alienated the
> peasants. Derg policies and practices which encouraged revulsion for the
> regime were in turn reinforced by TPLF efforts in both the military and
> political spheres to transform disaffection into support for armed struggle.
> (J. Young 1994, 83)

Young characterizes the first stage of the TPLF's armed struggle, from 1975 to 1978, as a period of learning, in which the Front joined forces with its more seasoned and better equipped northern separatist counterparts in the Eritrean Liberation Front (ELF) and Eritrean People's Liberation Front (EPLF), who were engaged in their own struggle for independence from Ethiopia.[9] During this period the TPLF also fought for primacy among the other opponents of Derg rule in Tigray, particularly the Tigrayan Liberation Front (TLF), Ethiopian Democratic Union (EDU), and Ethiopian People's Revolutionary Party (EPRP).

The Tigrayan Liberation Front was a short-lived organization that was based in eastern and southern Tigray. Claiming that Tigray, like Eritrea, was a colony of the Ethiopian state, it sought independence for the region. Active during 1975, it officially united with the TPLF in November of that year, but many of its members continued to have a tense relationship with their new umbrella organization for the next several years (Berhe 1991).

The EDU drew its support from the aristocracy, merchants, and wealthy landowners, and was assisted by the Nemeiri regime then in power in Sudan. Its leaders were Mengesha Seyoum, king (or *ras*, ራስ) of Tigray Region during the imperial regime, and Nega Tegegn, governor of Gondar. Major clashes took place between the TPLF and EDU from 1976 to 1978 in the western part of the region, but after that time the EDU retreated to Sudan and was largely inactive.

The EPRP, active in the eastern part of Tigray as well as in Addis Ababa, espoused a centrist Marxist-Leninist platform that sought a pan-Ethiopian urban-based class struggle rather than a national or peasant-based liberation movement. Many of the TPLF's earliest activists are thought to have come from the EPRP (J. Young 1997, 84).

The TPLF's popularity with the peasantry quickly grew as the movement was increasingly perceived to articulate genuine grievances of the rural people and as it became a viable alternative to the increasingly severe and cruel policies of the Derg. The establishment of the Relief Society of Tigray (REST) in 1978 helped to further strengthen this relationship. REST, or Maret (ማረት) as it is known in Tigrinya, was the humanitarian branch of the TPLF, providing relief and development assistance to peasants in liberated areas.[10]

The TPLF's early military strategy was to attempt to control the Derg army's supply routes, from Asmara in Eritrea and Addis Ababa. This took the bulk of the rebel movement's troops. In the rest of Tigray, small bands of TPLF soldiers moved throughout the region staging small ambushes rather than engaging in direct confrontations with the government army. From the early 1980s onward, however, the TPLF's strength grew almost faster than it could keep up with. Whereas most recruits had come from the towns before then, the rural areas began sending more and more men and women to join the movement. J. Young reports that "so massive was recruitment in the period 1980–1982 that the Front [TPLF] was unable to absorb them all and had to send some to the EPLF for training" (1997, 123).

This surge in personnel enabled the TPLF to increase its attacks on the Derg and to expand its territory. After 1980, the TPLF claimed to control

85 percent of Tigray, but this was primarily in rural areas. The Derg continued to control most of the region's major towns with only a few sporadic interruptions. This made it dangerous for rural residents to come into the towns for marketing, to use social service facilities, or to collect food aid rations, for their feared conscription or arrest by the Derg.

In the early 1980s, the Derg carried out a series of counterinsurgency campaigns aimed in large part at crippling peasants' ability to harbor the rebels by effectively cutting off their access to food so that they were unable to feed even themselves. By the early 1980s, the economic and social disruption of the war was so great that massive food shortages had already begun to affect a significant segment of the population, particularly in TPLF-liberated areas. Echoing the conclusions of many observers, de Waal charges that "by the time the drought struck, the famine was already well under way." He goes on to say that "the counter-insurgency strategy of the Ethiopian army [Derg] was the single most important reason why the drought of 1983–84 became not a 'normal' period of hardship but a famine of severity and extent unparalleled for a century" (1991, 133).

In August 1980 the Derg launched its Sixth Offensive as a reaction to—and a provocation of—the war-related activities of the TPLF. The offensive, which lasted until March 1981, involved a campaign of indiscriminate violence against the civilian population, which was suspected of harboring TPLF rebels. De Waal notes "the logic behind the government's strategy was 'draining the sea to catch the fish,'" a direct response to the guerrilla movement's stated tactics of being able to move among the population "like a fish through water" (1991, 139–41). War crimes perpetrated by the Derg against the civilian population of Tigray (and some parts of Gondar and Wollo) included aerial bombardment of markets, regulation of trade and other civilian movement, destruction of grain stores, killing of cattle and other livestock, burning of crops and pastureland, forced displacement of farmers, and bombardment of villages. One informant in Ada Bai recalled, "If the Derg found a pregnant woman, they would cut her with a knife, thinking that the one inside her might be a boy and might [eventually] fight them." Another woman said,

> During the Derg I remember several things. [In] some of them the Derg was unkind. He killed our people without any reason.[11] He burned houses, churches, and different grains before they [were] harvested. He forced the women [to perform] sexual things [acts] and killed the pregnant women by bullets and sword. He killed the priests when they were praying at the church and some of the baito members of the TPLF ... Everyone during the Derg time was hidden everywhere: under bushes ...

In addition to direct destruction to human life and physical infrastructure, the war also crippled the economy of Tigray. The Sixth Offensive's tactics prevented the normal redistribution of surpluses within Tigray as well as with neighboring regions. Traders and other travelers were required to carry passes to move from one place to another. These passes were very rarely granted, and almost never for travel between government and rebel-held territories. This caused the collapse of the terms of trade: grain became exceedingly expensive while livestock prices collapsed. Markets were held at night in many places, and all markets in a given area were held on the same day of the week to discourage the Derg from bombing marketplaces.[12] Although these measures made it safer for market-goers, they prevented merchants from circulating between markets on different days and resulted in massive increases in cereal prices. Farmers were not able to sell their livestock and other farm products. The offensive created an economic stranglehold on the region, ultimately precipitating the disastrous famine of 1984–85. The area worst affected by the Sixth Offensive was Tembien, in central Tigray; it is no coincidence that three years later a large proportion of the refugees who went to Sudan originated from Tembien.

As a response to the Sixth Offensive, mass internal displacement began. People fled from their homes in search of employment and a safe haven from the bombardments. Most of those who fled during the late 1970s and early 1980s were men whose off-farm income-generating opportunities were severely curtailed by the fighting and the Derg's restrictive trade policies. They would leave their wives and children at home, or would bring them to stay with relatives in the towns for safety. People tended to move westward in a series of short journeys, looking for wage labor or more farmland in the lowland areas to supplement their household's income before finally leaving Ethiopia altogether. Movement to Sudan was for the most part restricted at this early stage to those displaced from fighting in the far western parts of Gondar and Tigray, including EDU members who were under attack in Humera (Clay and Holcomb 1986, 53).

The Seventh Offensive, launched in January 1983, was more destructive than any that preceded it. Aerial bombardments, focusing on the central and western parts of Tigray, were intensified. The towns of Axum, Enticho, and Shire (the latter considered a stronghold of TPLF support) were raided and serious human rights abuses were committed including "summary executions, burning of villages, destruction of grain stores, and the killing of cattle" (de Waal 1991, 144). The attacks in the western part of the region, the only surplus-producing part of Tigray, displaced seasonal workers who had migrated from the highlands of Tigray and Gondar, thereby halting the harvest. De Waal reports that one hundred thousand farmers were forced to evacuate their homes, while 375,000 migrants in western Tigray "were obliged to move to other areas to seek work." In addition, the Derg attacked three centers that had been set up by REST to provide assistance to "famine migrants" coming from Tigray (de Waal 1991, 144). By the end of 1983, seventy-five thousand people had crossed the border to Sudan seeking assistance (de Waal 1991, 195).

In 1984, attacks against suspected TPLF supporters were stepped up. Checkpoints were set up by the government army to detain any "would-be migrants who were suspected of TPLF sympathies . . . several thousand people were detained, and more than six hundred were kept in prison or killed" (de Waal 1991, 153).

In 1984, the Derg also launched a voluntary resettlement program. Officially justified as a famine relief measure, the scheme quickly became forced when it failed to attract the number of volunteers originally antic-ipated. The government rounded up peasants in villages and market areas and transported them to areas in the west and south. Families were sepa-rated, some never to be reunited. Many people died while being trans-ported to the sites and thousands more eventually escaped to Sudan (Clay and Holcomb 1986; Clay, Steingraber, and Niggli 1988; Médecins Sans Frontières 1985). Peasants who had heard about the resettlement operation were afraid to go to the markets or the distribution sites to collect food aid. One woman in Ada Bai recalled the experience of her father:

> My father died during the drought of 1977 [1984]. He went from our village to get [food] aid in the town of Axum, which was controlled by the Derg, but he couldn't [that is, they would not give him aid because he would not stay in the town to be registered for resettlement]. He was sick and died by the case [that is, as a result] of hunger. At that time the Derg was collecting the farmers and villagers when they came from their homes to get aid in the town. He [the Derg] took them and sent them by air-plane to the unknown areas in the southern regions that were called reset-tlement programs [safara tabia, ሰፈራ ታቢያ, "assigned camp" or settlement].

By 1986, when the project was finally abandoned due to intense interna-tional criticism, more than six hundred thousand people had been reset-tled from Tigray and Wollo to these resettlement areas.[13]

The Eighth Offensive, begun in February 1985 at the height of the famine, sought to close the TPLF's and REST's main supply pipelines to

Sudan. These routes were used to import food and weapons as well as to evacuate displaced civilians to Sudan. The attacks came just before the rainy season, when essential food relief supplies should have been moving into famine-affected areas, particularly to those areas that would be cut off after the rains started. From the Derg's point of view, this was a largely successful mission: the roads linking Tigray to Sudan were cut off, and by March and April the cross-border relief effort had been practically crippled.

Further complicating the situation was the erosion of TPLF and EPLF relations, the causes of which are still hazy to most observers, and which officials of both parties continue to be reluctant to discuss. When the Derg blocked the roads between Sudan and the Tigrayan highlands, the EPLF refused to allow the TPLF to use the road through southwestern Eritrea to bring food from Sudan to Tigray.[14] The TPLF had to build another road across the Tekezze River, which was only passable during the dry season. This resulted in significant delays in food deliveries and exacerbated the effects of the famine (Abbay 1998, 127–29).

Despite being explicitly prohibited by the Geneva Conventions, the use of food as a weapon in the war was no secret.[15] The Ethiopian foreign minister at the time was even quoted as saying that "food is a major element in our strategy" against the Fronts [TPLF and EPLF] (David Korn 1986, 137, quoted in Duffield and Prendergast 1994, 61). The starvation of selected groups was seen as strategically advantageous to the government forces. Displacing civilians was considered an effective strategy for eroding the guerillas' base of support. Mark Duffield and John Prendergast, both of whom were involved in the cross-border operation that brought assistance through Sudan to the rebel-held parts of the north, point out, "It has been argued that the purpose of Ethiopian aerial bombardment campaigns during peak famine months was to herd people into government held areas and depopulate Front [TPLF] controlled regions" (1994, 61). Blocking rebel relief convoys and convincing people that the only aid they would receive was in government-held towns were both strategies used by the Derg to gain control over the people who lived in rebel-held areas.

At the highest political levels, there was a blatant refusal to consider the pleas of those officials whose job it was to provide relief to needy people. Dawit Wolde Giorgis, who served in the Derg government as head of the Relief and Rehabilitation Commission from 1983 to 1985 (when he defected to the United States), recalls in his book *Red Tears: War, Famine, and Revolution in Ethiopia* that Colonel Mengistu told participants in a 1983 budget meeting, "The only constraints on the successful implementation of our agricultural policies are natural calamities." When the commissioner raised the subject of the famine in the north with Mengistu privately after the meeting had ended, he was told, "You must remember that you are a member of the Central Committee . . . Your primary responsibility is to work toward our political objectives. Don't let these petty human problems that always exist in transition periods consume you. There was famine in Ethiopia for years before we took power—it was the way nature kept the balance. Today we are interfering with that natural mechanism of balance, and that is why our population has soared to over 40 million" (Wolde Giorgis 1989, 128). Although this Malthusian interpretation is extreme, the identification of population pressure as a root cause of famine in Ethiopia is still pervasive today. Such arguments, besides their cruelty, fail to consider the political, economic, and technological factors that contribute to famine vulnerability.

Natural and Other Causes Contributing to the Famine

Although the war was the principal agent in the creation of extreme famine conditions in Tigray during the mid 1980s, the contribution of natural and other causes must not be overlooked. By most accounts, the multiyear drought started in 1982 with the first failure of the rains. This was accompanied by at least one widespread infestation of armyworm, an insect that can quickly and completely destroy grain crops. Many of the people of Ada Bai, in recalling their experience of the drought, said that the armyworm was a more decisive factor in the failure of the crops than the lack of rain.

The drought was accompanied by a collapse in the terms of trade between livestock and grain. Between 1982 and 1984, grain prices rose tenfold from approximately 20 cents per tin to two birr for the same amount.[16] Meanwhile, livestock prices underwent a corresponding drop:

> Because so many people were selling livestock (usually to merchants,
> traders, or peasant association officials) to buy food and because few
> potential buyers had adequate pasture for animals until the next rainy
> season, the average value of an oxen [sic—reference is to a single ox] fell
> from E$300 to E$60.[17] While grain prices increased tenfold, the value of
> oxen decreased by 80 percent. Thus, crop failure for two years in a row
> left most of those interviewed destitute. (Clay and Holcomb 1986, 60)

The table below shows the magnitude of the crop failure. The statistics were gathered in two refugee camps in Sudan by Clay and Holcomb (1986).

Table 1. Agricultural production information from refugee respondents (in kilograms)

	Wad Kowli Camp	Fau II Camp
Amount of produce needed for family of 6	1,500	1,500
Production in best year since 1974	1,695	1,896
Total production in 1983	420	648
Total production in 1984	22.5	none
Total seed needed (all kinds)	150	210

Source: Clay and Holcomb 1986, table no. 5, 61.

Effects of the War on Migration

If the drought of the 1980s had occurred during peacetime, people would likely have employed the same strategies they had during previous food shortages throughout the twentieth century and before: they would have sought employment in the west and other regions of Ethiopia. As already stated, some rural peasants in Tigray relied on internal migration even during "normal" years to meet household food deficits and as a means of generating cash income. De Waal states, "It can safely be assumed that in a normal year, at least one million people in Tigray and north Wollo are reliant on off-farm sources of income, primarily wage labor and petty trade" (1991, 168). Clapham, citing Ponsi, quotes an estimate of 31,000 interregional migrants moving from Tigray in 1969–70, which was considered a "normal" period (Clapham 1988, 165). He says,

> Though the figures must be treated with caution, and much temporary migration was within the region, they give some impression of the role of seasonal migration in mitigating the unviability of peasant agriculture in the most overcrowded highland areas. For Tigrean peasants, the nearest large source of temporary employment was at Humera on the Sudanese border, where some 100,000 labourers found work. (Clapham, 165)

The Derg's Land Reform Proclamation of 1975 also included a prohibition against private individuals hiring farm labor (Clapham, 157). This prohibition, together with the abysmal rates offered to workers on the state farms and the restrictions on travel, effectively stopped internal labor migration. Prime Minister Meles Zenawi claimed in an interview with Paul Henze that the prohibition affected two hundred thousand Tigrayans and "was a major stimulus of peasant discontent in the province" (cited in J. Young 1997, 93).

According to de Waal's analysis, "The famine was set in train because the migration failed. It failed because of the havoc caused in the area around Shire town [western Tigray] and the adjoining areas by the Seventh Offensive" (de Waal 1991, 146). He goes on to measure the loss of employment opportunities and the subsequent effect on the development of famine:

> A conservative estimate of the impact of the government restrictions is that the available employment was gradually cut in half between 1980 and late 1983. The result of 500,000 people—perhaps one in twelve of the population—being rendered unemployed in a time of poor food availability was disastrous. These people formed a large proportion of the total number of destitute migrants seeking help from REST, the RRC [Relief and Rehabilitation Commission] or voluntary agencies. (de Waal, 168)

In another estimate, J. Young cites former TPLF chairman and current prime minister of Ethiopia, Meles Zenawi, as saying that the prohibition against hired labor affected an estimated two hundred thousand Tigrayan workers (J. Young 1997, 133).

These figures summarize the experience of many Ada Bai residents. Lettemariam's story of her experience prior to fleeing to Sudan is typical of others in the community:

> Before 1977 [1984] my father was working in a different area [in western Tigray] and bringing us money and grain [for] additional food and household expenses. Until I was twenty years old my family had a moderate life but after that, because of the drought, which was happening every three years and the locusts and everything, we became completely empty . . . Before 1977 we came two times to Shire [district], Bademe [village]. We worked for the rich people, me as a servant and my husband as a farmer. We worked in the dry season and returned back to our home in the summer or rainy season to plow our farm in order not to be insulted by one of our neighbors. They could take our farm [if we did not return to plow it]. So when we arrived in our village sometimes we spent half of our money from [wage labor] farming to pay our advance [to start agricultural work on our own land]. Other times we were working in the field [for wages] and on our farmland. Sometimes we were giving [renting out] our land for one half or one third [of the harvest].
>
> When we stayed at Bademe, some of the previous residents of that area were insulting the people who came from the highlands. They were calling us "Hamesien beggars."[18] Also in that area there was the Derg and sometimes the TPLF and the Derg were trying to share [allocate] the farmland, but he [both parties] couldn't do it practically. Then the EPRP

and EDU were visiting that area sometimes. They [the TPLF fighters] came and there was a war between them. Then all of them were dismissed by the TPLF and the area came under the control of them.

The third time [we came from our village in Axum] we plowed at Bademe and sowed different crops: sorghum and barley. It was nice [at first] but later we had a shortage of rain on time and I was very sick [and pregnant] and became anemic continuously for three months. At Bademe there was not any armyworm, but in other parts of Tigray there was a lot.[19]

Faced with these problems, Lettemariam and her family eventually decided to go to Sudan.

The War Front in Humera

While the war in the highlands sought to cripple the TPLF's popular support, in the west the struggle was over control of the fertile farmland. The land in western Tigray, particularly around Humera, is the only part of Tigray capable of producing a grain surplus. Sorghum grown in the area is bought by local traders and sold domestically in the grain markets as well as in areas of Sudan and Eritrea experiencing food shortages (McCann 1990). Since 1996 it has also been purchased by international donors for distribution in food-scarce parts of the country as emergency relief. The area is also potentially (as well as historically) a major source of foreign exchange from sesame, the main cash crop. Before the war, Humera's sesame production was a major source of foreign income. Sesame exports rose from 19,800 tons in 1967 to 84,600 tons in 1974, generating $38 million in export earnings and making Ethiopia the second largest exporter of sesame in the world (Clapham, 104). The private farms drew workers from the Tigray, Gondar, and Wollo regions as well as Sudan and Eritrea; estimates of the size of the seasonal workforce range from one hundred thousand to three hundred thousand per year (Clapham, 104; de Waal, 166; Rahmato 1986; McCann 1990). Wages were relatively high, at ten birr a day.[20] Clapham observes that "these earnings, large by peasant standards, were of critical importance in helping to relieve the effects of land shortage and impoverishment in the areas of peasant agriculture from which the migrants came" (Clapham, 184).

Humera was one of the most important and economically strategic areas of the north, particularly in the early years of the war. When the Derg nationalized all land, it seized control over the large commercial farms in the area and established state farms. This was not done easily. Former Humera landholders reported that they protested the seizure of their lands and the restrictions on hiring labor by killing their cattle, destroying buildings, burning down the Commercial Bank of Ethiopia's Humera branch, destroying their farm equipment, and burning their harvested grain or sending it to Sudan. These protests were largely ineffective, however, and the landowners only hurt themselves and the local economy (J. Young 1997, 93). "According to refugees living in [the Humera] area at the time, they challenged the authority of the new government longer than residents in any other area in Ethiopia" (Clay and Holcomb, 51). The EDU was particularly active there; in 1977 much of the town was destroyed in fighting between the Derg and the EDU.

Migrant workers who had regularly gone to Humera to supplement their farm income with wages were either unable or, given the working conditions and collapse in wage rates, unwilling to continue working. When, in the mid 1970s, the Derg began forcible conscription into the army at Humera, sixteen thousand laborers immediately fled to Sudan. These were among the first refugees from the war.

The state farm operations continued, albeit with a serious shortage of labor. To attempt to increase production, the Derg resorted to forced recruitment of labor. De Waal describes the forced conscription of workers and the conditions in the farms:

> When insufficient volunteers were found, soldiers and *kebele* [neighborhood] guards simply rounded up people from the street. 14,140 "volunteers" were taken in Addis Ababa and about 30,000 in other towns. Their belongings (even their shoes) were confiscated and they were crammed into trucks, without even the most basic facilities or stops for rest or sleeping: the trucks were so overcrowded that they had to squat for the journey of more than three days. On arrival at the army camp close to Humera, the soldiers rushed onto the trucks and dragged away many women, who were raped that night, and many of whom were never seen again by their relatives or friends.
>
> At the Humera state farm itself, no facilities or accommodations were available. Food for the workers was inadequate, and twelve hours of work was enforced each day. No wages were paid. Minor disciplinary offenses were dealt with by detention or beating; offenders were called "counter-revolutionaries." The whole camp was guarded by armed members of the "Production Task Force" who detained or shot dead those trying to escape. In prison, the cells were grossly overcrowded and torture was routine. According to the farm supervisors, 1,626 people died from starvation, disease, beatings and torture, or were shot trying to escape. Several hundred disappeared, including women abducted for sexual abuse by soldiers and officials. Many others fled to Sudan. (de Waal 1991, 167)

Those workers who came "voluntarily" to the state farms were lured with promises of 49.50 birr per month,[21] plus food, medical services, and accommodation expenses (de Waal 1991, 167). Despite these measures, production hit an all-time low of 3,400 tons that year.

In 1980, even more workers were brought to the Humera area. They were kept there for four months, which prevented them from plowing and planting their own plots in the highlands. Wages fell to 2.75 birr per day,[22] from which food and other expenses were deducted. The average worker kept less than one birr per day.

Production rose slightly during 1980–81 to approximately 7,500 tons. It rose further in 1982 to 16,400 tons but then collapsed back to the 1979 level because of a lack of cooperation by workers, inefficient management, and insecurity in the area. Meanwhile, the world price of sesame doubled and the price per ton exceeded $900 for the first half of the 1980s (Clapham, 185).

Evacuating the Region

When famine conditions began to develop, the TPLF tried to relieve the stress on highland communities by encouraging intraregional migration to the territory it held in western Tigray. It offered people income-generating opportunities, including basket weaving and tree tapping for gum arabic (de Waal 1991, 172). This initiative had only a limited impact. With the near complete failure of the 1984 harvest, the severe restriction of the movement of relief food supplies from Sudan because of inadequate funds and government attacks on convoys, and the population's reluctance to go to government-held towns to seek aid for fear of being taken for resettlement, it was clear to the TPLF leaders that more comprehensive action was needed to assist the people. "The TPLF decided that it would be impossible for many Tigrayans to survive if they stayed in the region . . . [they] explained to [the people] that the organization knew that it could not get enough food for everyone" (Clay and Holcomb 1986, 71).

In January 1984, REST issued a statement warning that 1.5 million people were in need of "urgent relief aid" and made reference to an assessment conducted in 1983 that showed that "among the examined children, between 9–10% were found to be acutely malnourished." The organization claimed that by late 1983, the malnutrition rate had risen to 22 percent (REST 1984b). By November 1984, REST's figures were revised to 3.8 million people (including the entire population of Tigray) classified as "drought affected" and three million of those being in need of emergency relief (REST 1984a). Crop failure for the main growing season was estimated at 80 percent in most parts of Tigray, and loss of livestock was described as "in some areas . . . almost total" (REST 1984b).

As what it called a "last measure," REST and the TPLF organized a massive evacuation of civilians from Tigray to Sudan. An estimated two hundred thousand people were escorted out of the region and into the relative safety of Sudan during 1984 and 1985 (J. Young 1994, 92; Duffield and Prendergast 1994, 62; de Waal 1991, 195; Hendrie 1996, 35). The operation was necessary, REST claimed, as a "consequence of our inability to deliver relief aid where the people are, because we are not getting enough assistance from the world community" (REST 1984a). In November 1984, REST reported that fifty thousand people were "at any given moment . . . at our forty checkpoints along the migration route" to Sudan: "In the last two weeks alone, over 25,000 people have entered the Sudan and another 20–30,000 more are poised now, along the border of Tigray with the Sudan, ready to cross; indeed, over 1,200 people are crossing daily through the REST recognised crossing points" (REST 1984a). In January 1985, the UNHCR representative in Sudan estimated that the number of daily arrivals had reached 3,000 (Miller 1985).

Participation in the evacuation scheme was voluntary. TPLF cadres held meetings in the villages under their control to explain to the people their options. All of the respondents in the Cultural Survival study carried out in Sudan by Clay and Holcomb (1986), as well as all of my informants in Ada Bai, claimed that they had freely chosen to go with REST and the TPLF to Sudan; indeed, they credited these organizations with saving their lives during this difficult time, often at risk to themselves and at the expense of "the Struggle."[23]

The evacuation was, by all accounts, extremely well organized. TPLF cadres guided evacuees. Most movement was carried out under the cover of darkness to avoid detection and aerial bombardment by the Derg. The TPLF and REST set up forty relief centers along the way to distribute food and water and provide medical care to the migrants. Most people reported walking for at least one month, and in most cases two, to reach the relative safety of Sudan. Many others were too debilitated to survive the journey. Tsehai recalled that "if people were too weak to travel we would bury them up to their heads so that if passersby saw them they would take them with them." If no one passed by, or if the person died, it was thought that at least their body would be buried and they would be able to proceed to heaven.

Not all of those living in Ada Bai had participated in the evacuation. Some people were absent from their home village when the organizers came to guide people westwards or had stayed on their farms in the hope that conditions would improve. Tesfaye had been working for the Derg as an accountant, statistician, and artist in Mekele. His main works of art, portraits of Marx, Engels, and Lenin, still adorn many walls and buildings throughout the region. A very tall, dignified man with a thick beard and deep, dark eyes, he was quiet and thoughtful and always gave me the impression that while remembering his life he was sad. He recalled the days leading up to his decision to go to Sudan:

[In Mekele] there was a movement underground with a group of Amharic and Oromo speakers. I did not know their aim but if you went with the Amharic speaker, the Oromo would dislike you, and if you went with the Oromo speaker the Amharic speaker would dislike you. In this case, there was a big problem at the office. When there was a nice job and increase of salary, they gave it to their group members.

The office was not paying me enough salary. I worked a lot but did not get enough money and another office asked me to transfer to them but my office opposed me. So all the time I was angry and I quarreled with my chief. Most of the party members were quarrelling even in the bars and restaurants outside the office. There were a lot of groups moving underground. When I complained to them [and requested that they] increase my salary or give me permission to transfer to another office to get a better job and salary, they opposed me. Every day they said, "Maybe you are a member of the TPLF." They arrested me . . . and released me without reason several times.

I was worried that these people after a time might kill me, so I left my job and in 1978 [1984] I left to go to Sudan. I was thirty-seven years old at that time.

There was drought throughout the whole of Tigray. The villagers were coming from their homes and [when they got to Mekele] they fell down in the streets. A lot of people died because of hunger. There was no aid. After a time some of the helicopters and planes were bringing aid and staff. They were helping the people in the Mekele streets. You could find a dead body at every corner because there was no food. Uncountable people died without help. Children, adults, men and women . . . There wasn't any grain at the market. Even the government workers were in a problem. The aid was only for the people who came from the village, not for the town residents . . . there was one Catholic agency named Dom Bosco. This agency was helping the town residents. The lives of the townspeople were saved by the help of this agency. So the workers of the government, they were buying grain from those people [those who got aid from Dom Bosco] because they needed money for flour milling and other house expenses.

I decided to leave my job and escape. I was working hard but there was no improvement of my salary and job . . . I was angry all the time and there were some of the staff [who] did not work [as hard as I did] but they got a higher salary, double what I was earning. I [left Mekele and] walked during the daytime on the way to Addis Ababa via Ende Yesus. Then when I had gone a long distance I found some of the [TPLF] fighters. They took me to their liberated areas of Tigray. During the rainy season there was no way to get to Sudan. So I stayed with them for six months helping drawing and writing in their propaganda bureau voluntarily. They asked me to stay with them but my idea was that I might get a chance to go to a foreign country [Europe or America] if I went to Sudan. So I did not agree to stay with them. But until I left I helped them with maps and charts for their teaching program.

When I was at school I was trying to draw maps and other pictures and when I was employed as a statistician I was watching and learning with craftsmen all the time. From day to day I improved my ability and experience. Even from the beginning my handwriting was very nice so I learned everything through my experience.

For the TPLF I did only [drawings about] the elementary school program, but when I was at Mekele I did portraits of Lenin, Marx, Engels, slogans, and Mengistu Haile Mariam. I didn't make private pictures [for sale]. The charts that I was drawing for the Derg were useful to show them where the TPLF were. They used it for war and it was very important to them. But for the TPLF I didn't draw maps, only the charts of the elementary school programs.

The TPLF never asked me what my work [had been for the Derg government] . . . They saw my handwriting and they asked me for help. I stayed for six months with the others, about three hundred youngsters who came from different areas. They were against the national service of the Derg. We stayed at Kalema, one of the liberated areas of Tigray [in Wolkait] and then [the TPLF] took us by their own truck to Kor Humera [on the Ethiopian side of the border with Sudan]. They dropped us there and we walked to Safawa on foot. We went together. They were asking us to be fighters but we preferred to go to Sudan. No one forced us [to enlist] so they took all of us to Sudan.

Tesfaye's story followed a particular form that was consistent with that of most of the other migration histories I collected. Most of the life histories featured a similarity of detail concerning the evacuation from Tigray. Nearly every testimony was extremely detailed and included information about each place the person stopped or passed through, the treatment they were given by the TPLF, their physical condition, and the difficulties they endured on the trip. Whereas people were more vague about the years in which other events, including their own birth or marriage, had occurred, they were very clear about the events of 1977 (1984). In addition, whereas they often did not like to discuss the suffering they had experienced as a result of the famine in Tigray and conditions in the Sudan camps, they seemed eager to talk about the trek to Sudan.

Listening to their stories, I was reminded of Renato Rosaldo's description of Philippine Ilongot villagers' narratives about 1945, when they were forced to flee inland from Japanese soldiers who were being pushed into the mountains by invading American troops. One-third of the Ilongot population died during that period, and their history came to be conceptualized as being either before or after the time of the Japanese invasion. Rosaldo recalls that "stories were studded with the names of every brook and hill and craggy cliff where people walked or ate or spent the night" (1980, 39). In a similar way, Tigrayans' experience of flight became a major landmark in the terrain of memory, an event that marked the disjuncture between life in the highlands and life in the refugee camp. Places and place names were like the punctuation marks in their narratives, and in the telling "the pervasive cultural impact of human experiences," which although in conventional units of time had not lasted more than eight weeks, became "so laden with significance as to be protracted in retrospect" (R. Rosaldo, 1980, 39). No other experience of migration before or after the evacuation has been accorded as much significance in Tigrayans' life histories.

Lettemariam, whose preflight story I recounted above, described her flight experience to me as we shared a pot of coffee in her house in Ada Bai:

> When I arrived at Sheraro [for medical treatment for the complications with her pregnancy], the medical workers [foreigners] touched me and examined my stomach and tried to check everything. They ordered me [to take] six tablets and one injection daily. On the way, the Derg airplane was coming [i.e., bombing] daily and they [the TPLF medical workers] took us with the other patients to Zelazela in the liberated area.
>
> At that time everyone was ready to go to Sudan because of the drought. [That was in] 1977. [It was] organized by the TPLF. To save his life, my husband said, "I will never go to Sudan. I have only two children and [in Sudan] I heard that there is disease, and I don't want to lose my children."

My leg was swollen. They advised [my husband] and me to eat meat and have milk. I was severely anemic. After a time I delivered [my son] at Zelazela. I quarreled with my husband. I told him to go to Sudan. He refused, even for me [to go]. He took me from the hospital [without the permission of the health workers] and I stayed outside. [He later agreed to take the children and go to Sudan.] But I was not well. When the airplanes came they [the TPLF] took me and carried me with one man to the border of the river [so that I would not be attacked by the planes]. When I became well I was staying with other lactating women and everyone was traveling [together]. I became tired. I was not strong. Then they took me after three weeks by truck with the other people to Wad Kowli [refugee camp].

Another account, by Fatima, a young Muslim woman from the central highlands, is representative of those who were fleeing the war rather than the famine:

I stayed at Abi Adi[24] until 1977 [1984]. I cannot remember very much about when I was a child but I know that when the airplanes of the Derg bombarded the towns and villages, everyone was frightened and worried about them. At that time everyone was spending his day hidden under a bush and coming back at dark [to the town]. He took his food with him that was prepared during the nighttime in order not to be attacked by the Derg.

I went to Sudan because of the war and drought. I was a child in 1977 [1984]. One day I remember there was a celebration of Lekatit 11[25] in the villages surrounding Abi Adi . . . There were a lot of people [congregating together] in those villages, but the Derg helicopters arrived and bombarded the towns and a lot of the population were killed. My father and mother were there. I went to see what happened to them. Then the airplanes arrived [again], and the [soldiers] could see where we were. We were inside one house, a hidmo, made up of stone and mud.[26] The airplanes threw a bomb and a lot of militia and civilians were killed. Even me, I now have a mark on my face made when I hit the wall of the hidmo when the bomb hit it [she points to a large scar above her eye].

After that I was frightened just to go to the market and I planned to go to Sudan with my other friends. My family was worried and they were not volunteering to send me to Sudan. I was their only daughter. So they decided to go with me to Sudan . . .

In our family there was no shortage of food at that time but my family wanted to [go] because I wanted to. Before we went to Sudan my mother was working as a trader selling kemim,[27] soap, and other things and my father was a weaver so we did not have any [economic] problem. We were ruling our own lives at a moderate level.

Before we left, the TPLF told us that on Friday the Derg was going to come to Abi Adi. They said that everyone must be ready to go to Sudan [before then]. Before that happened, we got out of Tembien on Wednesday at midday. For the time being we prepared our private ration [rather than accept rations from the TPLF, REST, or other assistance providers— an indication that the household's food stores were not yet completely depleted].

On the way we crossed Edaga Hiburt near Shire. In the morning the Derg helicopters arrived and we went quickly to hide under the bush. No one was hurt by them. The rest of the trip was at night, so we didn't have any problem [with bombardments] . . . After one month we arrived at Wad Kowli. Sixty-five of us went by the TPLF truck from Gaba up to Kor Humera [on the Sudan border] . . . We told them [the TPLF] that we had family in Sudan at Gedaref, so until the Derg left Abi Adi we wanted to stay there with them and then return back home. But when we arrived at Wad Kowli the REST people told us that we had no permission from the Sudan government to go alone to Gedaref. Everybody had to be organized and stay together [in the refugee camps].

At the end of 1984, the TPLF warned the Sudanese government and UNHCR in Sudan to expect three hundred thousand people to cross the border from Tigray. Even though only two-thirds of this figure actually arrived at the border, UNHCR was only prepared to receive fifty thousand refugees. The subject of the arrivals from Ethiopia sparked an enormous debate within the United Nations and humanitarian aid circles. Because neither the Ethiopian nor Sudanese government would declare a humanitarian emergency and request international refugee assistance, the United Nations claimed that those coming out of Tigray were drought victims rather than refugees. The Derg would not acknowledge that the people were fleeing war, and it forced aid organizations to keep silent about the fighting by threatening them with expulsion from Ethiopia.[28] The Sudanese government was at first reluctant to appeal for international aid as it did not want to bring attention to its own inability to respond or to be drawn into the Ethiopian conflict (Minear and Deng 1992). Finally, the TPLF and REST, which sought assistance for the migrants, were not considered legitimate entities; the UN, as well as many donors and NGOs, had a strict policy of only working with recognized governments, and it was unable to enter into funding agreements with any rebel movements. Only after unsuccessfully attempting to close the border to new arrivals from Ethiopia did the Sudanese government request assistance from the United Nations. UNHCR agreed to provide assistance only as a "special case," still refusing to admit that the influx fell under its mandate (de Waal

1991, 195). By 1985, half a million displaced Tigrayans were living in relief camps both inside and outside Ethiopia (de Waal 1991, 172).

The evacuation from Tigray to Sudan was intended to be temporary. It was assumed that the refugees would return to Tigray in April 1985 to begin preparing their land for planting in June. In fact, nearly one-third of the refugees returned to Ethiopia after one year (Hendrie 1992). During the 1992 TPLF anniversary celebrations, TPLF leader and then president of Ethiopia (later prime minister) Meles Zenawi[29] recalled the evacuation and first repatriation:

> Conditions favored extinction. There cannot be a test worse than this. Man dies, man is born; a village is razed, a village sprouts; but when a people perish, that is a final loss!
> . . . Then we let the people—from Raya [Southeast Tigray] to Adiabo [Northwest Tigray]—go to Sudan. Only at night for fear of bombardment. In Sudan, no food was readily available. There, too, people starved. Some died while waiting for food . . .
> Then hoping the rains would come, we asked those physically fit to return to Tigray—to the land of fire, to the land of bullets, to the land of death, to the land of famine . . . The TPLF told them to plow the land again. The physically strong then flocked back to Tigray. Foreign observers objected to the return of famine-stricken and weakened people to a battle zone. [But the peasants replied] "There cannot be Tigrayans without Tigray; no Tigray without Tigrayans. Whatever the price could be, we grip the land, we grip the mountains—however rough they may be! And we struggle for those mountains; we die and win for them! That is our plan." (quoted from *Weyan*, the TPLF newspaper, March 1992, in Abbay, 132–33)

The terrestrial metaphors and liberal use of place names in Meles's statement were a common feature of TPLF nationalism, which sought to bind Tigrayan identity to the soil and the topography of the region.

The evacuation of so many people from central Tigray who had been an important source of support for the TPLF soldiers and the diversion of resources to implement the operation made the rebel movement militarily vulnerable. A quick return from the refugee camps to Ethiopia was considered important to keep people self-sufficient and to provide much needed logistical support for the rebels.

Almost all of those who returned to Tigray in 1985 went back to the houses and plots of land they had left. They resumed planting on their farms. Little analysis has been done of their experiences following repatriation. Those who chose to remain in Sudan did so because they were too poor to return, were afraid to return while the war was going on, or had heard that their homes or land had been taken over by someone else. They stayed in the refugee camps until 1993, long enough in most cases to lose their access to farmland and other property in their areas of origin, and long enough to develop new strategies for coping with their lives in a fragile and uncertain environment.

Postwar Famine Politics

The Ethiopian famine of 1984–85 is considered something of a milestone in international humanitarian aid and journalistic circles. Conditions of starvation were the worst that had ever been captured by video cameras, and the level of human suffering shown on the nightly news sparked an outpouring of sympathy and support from governments and the public throughout the developed world. The Band-Aid/Live-Aid projects, organized by musician Bob Geldof, raised an estimated $75 million for famine relief. Most "experts" who were in the business of providing assistance to refugees and the internally displaced had never seen anything so bad on such a large scale. Epidemiological reports written in the decade following the emergency attempted to derive lessons from the experience of providing assistance in the Sudanese refugee camps. Journalists, too, have referred to 1984–85 as a benchmark of just how bad things could become, of the worst kind of famine imaginable.

In 1999, while working for the United Nations Emergencies Unit in Ethiopia on yet another food shortage emergency, I was continually asked by journalists who were visiting the country to cover the food shortage whether they could expect conditions to be as bad as they had been in 1984–85. They seemed disappointed when I told them that, although the food crisis facing Ethiopia in 1999 was severe and was the worst that the country had faced since 1984–85, it was not on the same scale as the earlier emergency. Indeed, since 1984–85, aid practitioners have been careful to avoid using the term "famine" except in situations in which the rate of hunger-related deaths has spread out of control throughout large areas of the country. The justification for such a conservative use of the term "famine" is that it if it is only used in extreme cases, donors and journalists may take more notice when the term is used.

This might seem to be a reasonable position, yet in recent years many of the emergencies that the humanitarian assistance community refused to call "famines" may have been just that. In 1999–2000, the UN and the donor community congratulated themselves for having helped to avert a famine in Ethiopia, yet many experts, including a team from the Centers for Disease Control, found that the crude mortality levels in some parts of the country, particularly pastoral areas, were three times the cutoff mark used to define an emergency (Salama et al. 2001).

Assistance providers, policy makers, and academics argue about the definition of famine, often for reasons that have more to do with protecting one's job or defending an organization's professional mandate than disagreement about what constitutes hunger. Some believe that famine should refer to a situation in which there is widespread death due to starvation; others argue that under those terms a famine may never be labeled as such until it has passed, and that malnutrition figures, morbidity statistics, and even indicators of destitution should be considered as evidence of the existence of famine. Because vulnerability to famine is not evenly distributed throughout a country, "national famine" is a virtual impossibility. In 2003, the Ethiopian government estimated that eleven million people needed 1.4 million tons of food aid. The numbers were significantly higher than those of 1984–85 (when it was estimated that seven million people required one million tons of food aid) yet many in the international community were reluctant to use the term *famine* for fear of giving the impression that it had allowed the situation to escalate out of control.

Whereas the famine of 1984–85 was exacerbated by the civil war and the government's attempt to cover up the level of need, later emergencies have developed more as a result of deepening vulnerability caused by a combination of the failure of development initiatives, inability to adapt to increasing population pressure on a largely agrarian-based economic system, and the effects of natural hazards. The new Ethiopian government has not tried to cover up food shortages, and in fact has accused donor governments of not responding early and robustly enough to stave off disaster. Many senior officials in the EPRDF government were active in the rebel movement in Tigray during 1984–85 and claim to continue to be haunted by that experience. Prime Minister Meles Zenawi repeatedly refers to that period as "our Holocaust." In addition, REST has continued to work as a nongovernmental organization, albeit heavily supported by the TPLF party mechanism, to promote disaster mitigation, rural development, and relief assistance. International observers agree that this more cooperative and proactive attitude on the part of the EPRDF and Tigray regional administration has been an important factor in stimulating timely response.

2

Life in the Sudan Camps

I was not able to obtain a visa to travel to the refugee camps in Sudan during my fieldwork, despite the intervention of the UNHCR Sudan Country Representative on my behalf. Americans were not welcome to visit the country at that time, since the United States had criticized the Islamic government's suspected close ties to terrorists and the continuation of the civil war in the south of the country. In reconstructing conditions in the refugee camps, therefore, I have had to piece together information from a variety of sources. I spent one week in Geneva going through UNHCR's Documentation Center and Technical Support Section archives. I also was given access to the Médecins Sans Frontières–France archives on eastern Sudan, held in Paris. In Addis Ababa, I combed the holdings of the UNHCR Regional Liaison Office (now referred to as the Ethiopia Branch Office) and UN Emergencies Unit for Ethiopia's (now known as UNOCHA) extensive library of unpublished documentation. In New York, I reviewed all of the press articles in the archives of the *New York Times* and the New York Public Library between 1984 and 1993 on refugees in Sudan.

Information from these sources was valuable in conveying a sense of the challenge the emergency presented to international donors and relief workers, but said little about the experience of those who were its main players: the refugees. Clifford May, writing in the *New York Times Magazine* about relief workers in Africa (including Sudan and Ethiopia, where he spent ten months), lamented, "At times, the life seems cloistered. Relief people mainly know only other relief people." May asked a nurse working in a camp for internally displaced persons "which Ethiopian had made the deepest impression on her . . . She stuttered and stumbled and finally said that none stood out. Although she treats scores of people every day, the translated conversations seldom went beyond basic facts and symptoms" (May 1985d).

This aspect of emergency assistance has not changed much since the mid 1980s. Relief workers still spend most of their time with other relief workers and rarely develop friendships with those they are there to help, even though many refugees and other aid beneficiaries work in camp hospitals, schools, and other social service facilities. Language barriers and the near-constant atmosphere of urgency in which work is conducted may prevent international and local staff from getting to know each other well, to say nothing of relations between aid workers and beneficiaries. Whatever the reasons for the gap in understanding between refugees and their providers, the result is that refugees are often cast as helpless victims—as bodies to be fed, healed, or buried. The testimonies of journalists and relief workers reveal little about how refugees themselves made sense of or understood their lives in the camps, and thus gave me only a very partial view of their history.

Returnees to Ada Bai were eager to tell me about their lives in the camps after the emergency had passed, but they were more reticent to ask about the dark days immediately after their arrival in Sudan. People did not want to be equated with being "famine victims," and were reluctant to describe themselves as once having been so desperate. I found it difficult to ask about such experiences until I had spent several months in Ada Bai, and even then I often had to work my questions into more general discussions about child rearing, religion, or food security, by asking about generalized conditions of hunger in the camp during the first few months or about the kinds of illnesses that people suffered from. People seemed to prefer to answer questions about the community's experience rather than their own.

In this chapter, I draw from aid agency reports, epidemiological studies, journalists' accounts, personal memoirs, and the refugees' own voices to paint a picture of life in the refugee camps. The variety of sources, each rich in its own, more or less limited, way, also shows the particular limitations and focus of each type of documentation. A story emerges of refugees' efforts to overcome crisis and their attempts to make a temporary home for themselves.

Wad Kowli Refugee Camp

Refugees from Tigray arriving in Sudan between late 1984 and early 1985 were exhausted, emaciated, sick, and weak. In 1986, UNHCR estimated that 402,000 out of the 677,000 Ethiopian and Eritrean refugees living in Sudan were receiving food and medical assistance (Mebtouche 1987). The rest were living in Sudanese cities and towns, supporting themselves through petty trade and farm labor. Unlike other places where refugees integrate more easily into local communities in the host country because of ethnic or linguistic ties, these Ethiopian refugees settling in towns did not share such connections with the Sudanese. Although there were many different crossing points from Ethiopia into Sudan, one of the largest of these was Wad Kowli camp, situated at the confluence of the Atbara and Bar el Selaam Rivers seven kilometers west of the Ethiopian border. At the height of the crisis, in February 1985, Wad Kowli hosted one hundred thousand Tigrayan refugees (Médecins Sans Frontières, or MSF, 1985).

Conditions in the camp were appalling, as neither the Sudanese government nor the UNHCR had been prepared for the arrival of so many people in such a weakened state. Although increased mortality is generally expected during the first months of a refugee emergency, the rates reported in eastern Sudan skyrocketed out of control. From January through March 1985 monthly crude mortality rates (CMR) in the camps were reported to be 16.2 per thousand, nearly twice the rate of the famine-affected sedentary populations within Ethiopia (recorded at 8.8 in Shoa Province between October 1984 and January 1985), and eight times the baseline mortality rate (CDC 1992). Far worse, however, was the mortality rate for those who were internally displaced: the U.S. Centers for Disease Control and Prevention (CDC) cites unpublished data from MSF which indicates that at Korem (in southern Tigray) monthly crude mortality rates were between 60 and 90 from October through December 1984, and at Harbu (in Wollo Region, just south of Tigray) the CMR was found to be 147 (CDC 1992).

Overall, the U.S. Centers for Disease Control estimates that 9 percent of all refugees in eastern Sudan died during the first twelve months following the initial refugee influx. Despite the fact that malnutrition was the precipitating cause of death, most deaths were the immediate result of communicable diseases, which spread quickly as a result of the weakened resistance of the population (CDC 1992). The CDC reported after the emergency had passed that "in eastern Sudan in 1985, inadequate amounts of food (1,360–1,870 kcal/person/day) were distributed to Ethiopian refugees during the first five months after their arrival in the camps.[1] Malnutrition rates, as well as mortality rates, remained high during this period. In addition, a severe measles outbreak in the Sudanese camps added to the high mortality" (CDC 1992). The disease wreaked havoc in Wad Kowli. The CDC reported that "in early 1985, the crude, measles-specific death rate ... reached 13/1,000/month [13 deaths per 1,000 refugees per month]; among children less than 5 years of age, the measles-specific death rate was 30/1,000/month.[2] Over 2,000 [total] measles deaths were reported in this camp from February through May 1985." The authors note that the measles morbidity rate of 33 percent is probably low as many mild cases went unreported since people were reluctant to seek assistance from the clinics unless absolutely necessary (CDC 1992).

High morbidity was not confined to the Wad Kowli camp. In addition to the measles epidemic, between 25 and 50 percent of all deaths in the four major camps in Sudan were caused by diarrheal disease (CDC 1992). Cholera, which spreads rapidly and can quickly lead to death if untreated, broke out in camps where there was an inadequate water supply and where conditions were especially crowded. "During [1985], two adjacent refugee camps in the Sudan reported a total of 1,175 cases of cholera with 51 deaths . . . over the course of a 2-week epidemic" (CDC 1992). Cholera was also reported in Ethiopia, but both the Sudanese and Ethiopian governments refused to recognize the outbreaks—doing so would have affected their agricultural export markets (May 1985b and 1985c). Malaria was a major problem among the refugees, most of whom had traveled from the Tigrayan highlands, where malaria is not endemic, and therefore had decreased immunity to the disease (CDC 1992). Compounding these problems, acute respiratory infections (including tuberculosis) were also a major cause of death, and outbreaks of meningococcal meningitis were reported (CDC 1992). The chart shows the relative significance of each of the major causes of death at Wad Kowli in February 1985.

The severity of the situation was not immediately clear to statisticians and epidemiologists. Nieburg et al. (1988) report that, "In January, the prevalence of acute malnutrition in children less than 5 years of age was 26.3%; in March, the rate was 28.4%." The implication was that there was a "relatively stable nutritional situation." However, when figures on child nutritional status, camp population, and mortality were consulted together, it was discovered that "during these two months, almost 13% of the children in the camp died, mainly from measles and diarrheal diseases . . . Many malnourished children in the first survey, who had died, were 'replaced' in the second survey sample by surviving children whose nutritional status had meanwhile deteriorated . . . the elevated child mortality rate masked diminished nutritional status in the population" (Nieburg et al. 1988).

Returnees' Recollections of the Grim Days in Wad Kowli

At first, grain rations were given to refugees in wet form: each person received a cup of porridge at least once a day. The weakest individuals could not digest the food they had been given (which included white flour,

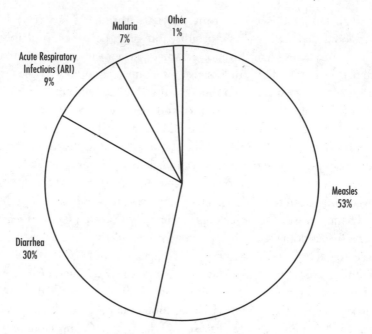

Cause of Death, Wad Kowli Refugee Camp, Sudan, February 1985
Source: Centers for Disease Control, 1992.

to which they were unaccustomed) and they perished in spite of the availability of food. Medical care was provided by international NGOs (Médecins Sans Frontières–France, Save the Children–UK, and the International Committee of the Red Cross) with funding from UNHCR and other donors.

Returnees' descriptions of the days and months following their arrival in Sudan help to give a human element to the quantitative findings of the epidemiologists, but they paint no less disturbing a picture of the suffering they endured. Returnees found discussing those days extremely difficult; nearly all had suffered the loss of a child, a parent, or a sibling, and the pain of their losses often showed in their faces as they described to me their experiences, even if it was absent from their words. Most people preferred to discuss life in Wad Kowli in general terms, and few were willing to recount their own stories of loss. When I asked one old man to describe his first impressions of the camp, he put his hands to his face in agony at the memory: "Death was uncountable there," he said. "The refugees became sick from . . . the climate and the food . . . There was [deadly] diarrhea." Another woman shook her head as she recalled, "At Wad Kowli, so many people were dying I can't explain it. So many people died every day that you didn't even want to go to the graveyard. You simply dumped people in the grave and left."

Alternative Interpretations of Death

Many of those who did mention the death of a close relative did so in passing, as if to gloss over the difficult details of the death, to give the impression that the death of their loved one had been no more important than the death of anyone else. I once showed several of my neighbors photographs taken by a *National Geographic* photographer of Tigrayans both in Sudan during the 1984–85 famine and back in Ethiopia during the early 1990s after the change of government. The point of the article had been to contrast the intense suffering of the 1980s with the remarkable recovery that Tigrayans (and others living in the Horn of Africa) had made ten years later. People were unwilling to look at the photos of suffering. "Why do you want to see that?" they asked me. They were much more interested in the photos taken of strong farmers hard at work and at images of the Tigrayan highlands.

Still, in quiet moments people would recall their dead relatives and offer their own explanations of why and how they had died. As they attempted to make some sense of what they had endured and the reasons that many had not survived, their explanations tended not to match those of the foreign epidemiologists or the journalists. Diseases, rather than being spread by germs, were thought to be caused by the intervention of spirits and other supernatural forces. While many people indirectly attributed the deaths to sickness or starvation, others said that they were sure that the primary cause of death was a spirit, most commonly the Evil Eye, or *buda* (ቡዳ).

Belief in the Evil Eye is common throughout East Africa; while the belief has local variations, spirits (known as *tebib*—ጠቢብ) carrying the Evil Eye are generally believed to be capable of possessing a person through biting, pinching, hitting, or establishing direct eye contact with the victim. Once resident inside a human host, the tebib is said to make the victim ill and eventually cause his or her death. People believe that the spirit can be exorcised, if detected early enough, by traditional healers who use herbal remedies, special incense (potash, bits of bone, or rubber tire), and prayer to coax the spirit from the victim or to get the victim to reveal the name of the person who passed the spirit to him or her.[3]

At Wad Kowli, people shared the conviction that overcrowding caused illness to spread, but the vector of contagion was attributed to spirits rather

than to biomedical explanations. The Evil Eye was said to have been particularly dangerous in the camp during the early days because people were
ordered by camp administrators to stay together in tents with people
whom they did not know.

Gebre Selassie was about seventy when I met him. He had come to
Ada Bai with his daughter and her family, he said, in order to die in his
own country. He described to me how one of his daughters had died in
Wad Kowli:

> In 1978 [1985] my girl who was 12 years old died by the case of diarrhea.
> But I don't believe that was the reason—she was sick only for three
> days, from Friday to Sunday. She was killed by the tebib [the spirit
> which carries the Evil Eye]. I could not find a *habesha medehanit* [ሐበሻ
> መደሃኒት, the generic term for traditional medicine]. [People from] my
> woreda were not there. They were all at Girba [another refugee camp
> nearby]. I was living with Keyih Tekeli people [those who had come from
> Keyih Tekeli, a place said to have many tebibs]. [Another child] my boy
> [also] died by the case of diarrhea like the others. It is the worst thing to
> live with unknown people.

Tsehai, who ran a small tea shop in the marketplace, loved to tell me
about the spirit world. She would lower her voice as if she were telling
me a great secret, her eyes sparkling and a smile tugging at her lips
as she described a belief system that the political establishment had
forbidden. She said many women had died in childbirth because they
had been bitten by the Evil Eye. There had, Tsehai recalled, been many
Sudanese tebibs in Sudan. I asked whether there were spirits or magic
powers that Ethiopians had learned from the Sudanese. She replied that
in Sudan there were powerful wizards there who could bewitch you or cure
you. She recalled:

> Some of the refugees sometimes became crazy. Maybe it was because it
> was a desert and [we were] sitting under a bush. We were living in a tent
> and this disease was unknown there [by the clinic staff]. Anyway, by our
> culture we called it *ganin* [ገኒን, also known as *jinn*, ጂን]. We found it at
> Sudan [not in Ethiopia]. They tried [to cure it with] medical treatment
> but there was no improvement and they [the sick people] were living with
> the other community members together in one tent. They were living
> about eight people [in one tent] whether they were sick or healthy. To
> some extent some of the patients were using habesha medehanit [to treat
> the possession effectively] and we heard that [those people] were bitten by
> the tebib.

The attribution of supernatural causes to explain death, particularly that of women or children, is not uncommon in Tigrayan society, as in many cultures in the Horn of Africa, or for that matter in cultures throughout the world where literacy and education rates are low.[4] Tigrayans consider pregnant women to be particularly at risk of being possessed by spirits. Young children are also thought to be susceptible, since they are too young to speak, cannot reveal the identity of their attacker and thus are more difficult to exorcise the spirit from. Most young children and pregnant women wear leather pouches—containing ashes or herbal mixtures, or with small written prayers sewn into them—as amulets around their necks or under their arms to ward off evil spirits. Supernatural causes are most frequently attributed to deaths that are not easily explained or in which biomedical attempts to heal the afflicted person have been ineffective. Death by starvation, which was often accompanied by tuberculosis, pneumonia, measles, cholera, or dysentery, was often said to be caused by spirit possession because, in the acute final stages of life, it seemed that no amount of feeding or medication could save the person. I watched several parents in Ada Bai agonize over their young children who gradually wasted away despite their attempts to feed them nutritious food, including milk fed through a feeding tube while also being treated with drugs as inpatients at Humera Hospital. To these sad and frustrated parents, spirit intervention seemed the only reasonable explanation for their child's death, particularly since biomedical attempts to treat the child had proven ineffective. Some people even blamed the biomedical health care facilities for having given their loved ones the sickness, an accusation that, given the generally poor sanitary conditions of the clinics and hospitals, may not have been misplaced.

Not surprisingly, the response of many people to the perceived threat of spirits was to move their families to other camps or to less crowded areas within Wad Kowli (if they could find them). This helped to minimize the health threat by relieving the congestion in the camp, even as efforts to provide better and more comprehensive nutritional and health assistance also improved the general health of the refugee population.

Early Repatriation, 1985

The poor conditions in the camps encouraged people to return to Tigray as quickly as possible, even though the war was continuing. Farmers who had left their land were eager to sow their fields, knowing that if they missed the planting season they would not be able to feed themselves and would have to remain in the camps for another year (May 1985b; Heiden 1992, 169–75). The Tigrayan rebels also had found it extremely difficult to fight in areas that had been depopulated by their supporters, on whom they had previously relied for food, shelter, and recruits (May 1985a; de Waal 1991). In May 1985, REST organized the repatriation of 154,000 refugees from Sudan, against the advice of international organizations that were afraid the refugees were not strong enough to return, that conditions were not safe, and that return would render the former refugees inaccessible to aid workers who were unable to work inside the war zones in Tigray (Hendrie 1992). David Heiden, a doctor working in the camps, recalls the preparations of the refugees to return: "Many of the children wore feeding center arm bracelets, and when the mothers saw Will [a doctor working with Save the Children] checking, they tore the bracelets off" (Heiden 1992, 173). The mothers clearly felt that keeping the children in the feeding center was not as imperative as their need to return to their farms. The lack of understanding on the part of international aid workers of the refugees' perceived need to return to their farms is indicative of the mistaken notion that refugees were helpless victims incapable of providing for themselves, or that they had nothing to return to.

After the first large-scale repatriation of 1985, REST continued to assist smaller groups of refugees to return through the end of the 1980s. Refugees' faith in REST's commitment to promoting the well-being of the civilian population remained high, and most who were strong enough to make the journey chose to return home. Participants in the repatriation operation returned, for the most part, to their original homes, and REST provided relief food and agricultural inputs to help them resume their productive activities. Some of those I interviewed in Ada Bai had participated in that early repatriation, but had remigrated to Sudan again when fighting near their home intensified. Those who opted to stay in Sudan later said they had been too ill to travel, had been afraid of continued war and hunger, or had wanted to avoid forced resettlement or being conscripted into the government army (Clay and Holcomb 1986, 104; Clay, Steingraber, and Niggli 1988, 44–45). These refugees were determined not to return to their home areas inside Ethiopia until the Derg government had been ousted.

In April 1986, the Sudanese government decided to close the Wad Kowli camp. The camp's water supply during the dry season was extremely limited because the Atbara River had dried up, yet during the rainy season the camp was often cut off from the town of Gedaref and it was impossible to get supplies to the refugees. In addition, the camp was said to be situated too close to the Sudan/Ethiopia border to be secure. UNHCR, following the 1969 OAU Convention Governing Specific Aspects of Refugee Problems in Africa (Article II, paragraph 6), recommended that "For reasons of security, countries of asylum shall, as far as possible, settle refugees at a reasonable distance from the frontier of their country of origin." The Sudanese authorities were concerned that the camp might be used as a staging area for rebel troops going into Ethiopia, a suspicion that proved correct, as volunteers from the camps regularly enlisted in the TPLF.

In just ten days, the camp was dismantled and its residents were moved to Safawa, a reception center from which it was expected the remaining refugees would be repatriated in short order or else integrated into agricultural production schemes for refugees in Sudan. At that time the Sudanese authorities and international refugee assistance organizations were willing to try to help refugee settlements to become self-sustaining through providing them with their own farmland or else allowing them to work on the large commercial farms around Gedaref and Kassala. This approach was never successful: refugees were not allocated adequate land to make self-sufficiency feasible and competition for employment with Sudanese host communities was exacerbated over time (see Kibreab 1989).

Safawa: A New Start

Most popular notions of life in refugee camps resemble the scenario I have described thus far. Camps are imagined to be places of misery, over-crowded and dirty, with masses of sick and dying people, helpless people who depend on handouts from relief agencies and host governments to survive. However, in situations where refugees continue to live in camps for several years, the syndrome of dependency and helplessness eventually gives way to entrepreneurial ingenuity, which helps refugees to become engaged in trying to maximize their opportunities, both economically and socially. Over time, refugee camps become more like settled villages than communities in crisis, even though they may continue to face difficulties associated with their displacement.

Refugees moving to Safawa found more assistance available to them than they had had at Wad Kowli. They were given more generous rations of food, closer to the 1,900–2,100 kcal per person per day standard that is internationally recommended. They had access to free medical care—provided by international relief agencies—of a quality they had never had, and could not expect during their lifetimes, in Ethiopia. They also received clothing, blankets, plastic sheeting, soap, and other household supplies on an irregular basis. Many people in Ada Bai said that once the emergency days of the first year had passed, material conditions in Sudan improved so much that they felt that they were better off in the camps than they could ever expect to be in Ethiopia.

Not only were the rations more generous in Safawa but the repatriation of some of the refugees and the movement of others between camps provided opportunities for refugees to obtain multiple ration cards, a practice that camp officials were largely powerless to stop. Additional ration cards were even bought illegally from camp officials in exchange for cash or a portion of the ration, or were given as partial payment to refugees who worked for the Sudanese authorities in the camps. Although officially prohibited, the refugees considered access to extra cards to be essential to ensure that the household had enough food to eat and to sell, so that they could afford clothing and other items that were not included in the food basket.

As important as the monthly ration was to household survival, it was inadequate to sustain the refugees. Everyone depended on cash income from farm labor, trading between refugee camps or from towns to camps, or from small businesses inside the camps. The following testimonies indicate how households made ends meet in the camps.

Tesfamariam, who married his wife in Safawa, relied on a combination of multiple ration cards and income from trade to support his family. He and his wife (they did not have children at that time) had one ration card each. They bought another four cards from other refugees for one hundred Sudanese pounds each. In addition to feeding themselves, however, they were obliged to support his wife's father, uncle, and sister for six years, and his own brother, who was convalescing after having been stabbed in a fight, for one year. To help support the household, Tesfamariam worked as a daily laborer for three years, until he had saved enough money to trade cattle, goats, and sheep between Safawa town and the Safawa camp (known by Sudanese locals as Kura Zem Berma, or Safawa II). With the money he earned from selling animals, he bought a donkey and cart with which to sell water, wood, and sand, and left the animal trading business, which he said was too risky because if an animal died while in his care (as happened to him once) he was responsible for absorbing its entire cost. However, the monthly grain rations had to be shared with the donkey as well, since there was no grazing area around the camp. The six rations were not always enough for both the household and the beast, particularly when the ration size was reduced because of delayed or missed deliveries. This was a frequent phenomenon. Tesfamariam told me, "There was never enough extra to sell. We ate everything." Others, however, said that they did sell a portion of the ration to get money to buy vegetables, coffee, spices, or nonfood items, particularly if their ability to raise cash income through employment was limited.

Although trade was necessary for their survival, most trade by refugees between camps and towns was illegal and carried with it risks of being caught and punished by the Sudanese authorities. Bekele, who went to Sudan before the 1984–85 famine to look for work, had a particularly hard time:

> I stayed at Tawawa, Gurja [both of which are refugee camps close to the town of Gedaref, and] Port Sudan. I worked as a trader, buying kerosene and clothes from Port Sudan at a cheaper price. I would sell kerosene in Tawawa to the distributors and the clothes to the traders. That was in 1977 E.C. [1984 G.C.]. The [retail] price of sugar was very high so I decided to bring sugar from Port Sudan. I bought thirty-six sacks and when I passed the Kilo 80 area of Port Sudan to load them by truck to take to Gedaref, the security police caught me. They took all the sugar. They whipped me fifty times and put me in prison for five years.
>
> While I was in prison [they put us to work] . . . I was carrying salt at the seaport. At midday every day the prison car took us from the port for lunch. One day when I saw the car coming I found a stick and put it in the water at the border of the sea to use as a [post]. I jumped into the water and held onto the stick until after the car had been gone for a few minutes. Then I got out of the water.
>
> I saw a Beni Amer man [a member of the Beni Amer ethnic group, which lives along both sides of the Sudanese-Eritrean border] and I asked him to give me some of his clothes [Beni Amer men wear distinctive clothing: a loose pair of white cotton trousers and a waistcoat-like vest]. He gave me some, and I took off my prison uniform and buried it in the sand. I put on the new clothes and went to the bus station. I found one bus driver who I knew before. I went with him from Port Sudan to Gedaref.

Bekele then went to Wad Kowli, where he registered with the other new arrivals as a refugee and soon married a young girl who had migrated from his home area. He supported her and her family by working on the commercial farms for daily wages.

Bekele's story is not unusual; refugees often found that their efforts to earn an income brought them into conflict with the Sudanese laws, which they did not understand very well and often were obliged to break even if they did understand them in order to have enough cash to support their families. A 1988 UNHCR report acknowledged the problems facing refugee workers, warning that there was no protection available for refugees who were agricultural workers and no "redress for unfair practices." The workers only had power against exploitation during the sesame harvest period when "shortage of labour and crucial need for timely harvesting" gave the workers some bargaining power (Drucker 1988).

Women were particularly vulnerable to punishment and exploitation from Sudanese security forces as well as others, since their main sources of income—brewing alcoholic drinks, selling cigarettes, and prostitution—were illegal activities. Meseret, a feisty woman who had worked for many years as a prostitute and brothel owner before marrying her current husband, recalled those days with bitterness:

> If [the Sudanese authorities caught] us, they poured our sewa [sorghum beer] onto the ground and they took our container and arrested us and took us to the police station. Then they made us pay money to the court. I was arrested six times and punished [with a fine of] forty thousand Sudanese pounds. In those days also [the police] terrorized us with a knife to try to kill us and they insulted us.

I asked her whether women were ever forced to have sexual relations with the Sudanese police:

> Yes. They forced us. They even killed [a prostitute] sometimes if she refused them. Doing sexual things by force was common in Sudan and this thing was not happening only to prostitutes. It was even happening to women who had husbands. They forced them to do sexual things and afterwards they quarreled with their husbands and arrested them [the husbands] without any reason . . . [We reported these things to REST], but the police would reply to REST that "this is a Muslim country and is ruled by sharia [religious rule of law]. Drinking and prostitution are illegal," so they [REST] couldn't do anything. They tried to help us but they couldn't do anything. It was not our country . . . [Life in Sudan] was hard, with arrests, insults, and killing. Even there were Ethiopians working as guards for the prostitutes daily. They got money from them [the prostitutes] without working. During the day she did what she wanted and at night she spent with him [the guard]. They [the guards] could kill them [the prostitutes] and [they] stole their gold sometimes . . . every prostitute hid their property or gold underground where nobody could get it easily.

Whenever possible, refugees tried to resolve conflicts and to maintain order themselves without having to rely on the Sudanese authorities. The

TPLF, through REST, established a political structure in the camps for administration, conflict resolution, political education, and community support. Houses were grouped according to the *woreda* (county) from which the refugees had come. Three representatives from each woreda reported to a *zoba* (zonal) council, which was also composed of three members. Each of the five zoba in the camp reported to the political cadre responsible for the camp, who was code-named "08," indicating his role as administrator. The entire system was known as *serit* (ሰሪት),[5] and closely followed the system that had been put in place in TPLF-held areas in Tigray (and later in Ada Bai). The chart shows the structure of the system:

Refugees reported that the effectiveness of serit was limited because it existed as a parallel system to that of the Sudanese, and decisions could easily be rendered meaningless if one of the parties referred the case to the Sudanese authorities. Thus, the system was generally not useful in adjudicating cases between Sudanese and Tigrayan parties.

Rebuilding a Social Order

Increased access to food and cash in Safawa helped people to strengthen relationships with kin and neighbors, to repay debts, and to resume participation in savings and burial associations. Refugees were more free to focus on those aspects of life that, in the face of impending starvation and death, had been left neglected: young men and women got married, children were born and enrolled in schools, and both men and women developed trades and businesses to support their households. Households shared meals, and neighborhoods celebrated saints' days, children's christenings, and other festivals together. Travel between camps, and from

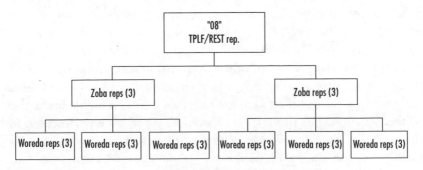

Organizational chart for the Relief Society of Tigray as seen from the refugee camps, 1984–1991

camps to the larger cities in the area, increased. Preexisting connections between individuals and families were reestablished. In addition, new alliances between people who had not known each other in Ethiopia but who came from the same part of Tigray, or who came to know each other through their shared experiences, often of suffering or of working in the camps, were developed.

Assefu, a single woman in her mid thirties who had a ten-year-old son living with her in Ada Bai and a teenage daughter who worked in Khartoum as a housemaid, recalled that living conditions were "good in Sudan because we used to eat together and share." Contrasting those days with her life in Ada Bai, she said, "But now we live like we did in the highlands . . . even though we are close together, it is as if we were [physically] dispersed because no one has enough to share." Sharing, as I discuss in chapter 4, was considered one of the most basic principles of community cohesiveness. Inability to share signified an absolute failure to participate in the life of the community; it was a source of embarrassment and humiliation to have to deny a neighbor in need a request for food, cash, or other assistance. Inability to share among households living in close proximity to one another led people to consider that the community had become more individualized.

Changing Patterns of Marriage

A sign that conditions in the camps were returning to "normal" was the resurgence in the number of weddings. As a result of having been displaced to Sudan, being separated by the war, and having lost so many people during the famine, many people found themselves widowed, divorced, or separated from their spouses. Many of those who had left their spouses behind in Tigray or whose spouse had joined the TPLF army did not expect to see them again, and thus sought new husbands and wives in Sudan.[6]

While some of the rules surrounding marriage were relaxed in the context of the refugee camp, others were maintained: men were not as likely to insist that their betrothed be a virgin as they would have been in their home areas, and they were not expected to pay as high a bride price to the woman or her family as they would have in Tigray. However, for the most part, men and women continued to seek partners who had originally come from the same area in Ethiopia. For example, a man from Adiet in central Tigray would try to find a bride who was also from Adiet. He would consult the elders from that area in the camp for assistance in determining whether the family was reputable and to represent him in the marriage negotiations if he had no relatives in the camp.

Couples drew up written contracts, known as *wi'il* (ውዕል), before their marriage to guarantee the resources that each would be expected to bring to the union, as well as to stipulate the arrangements that would be expected if the marriage ended in divorce (*fetih*, ፍትሕ). The wi'il was negotiated between the bride and groom's respective marriage parties, and was often the subject of heated debate. I attended one wedding in which the wi'il had not been finalized prior to the ceremony. The festivities were called to a halt as the groom and his friends tried to get the bride's relatives to accept his offer. While he wanted to include household items that had belonged to his first wife (who had died in childbirth), the bride's family wanted a commitment of cash. The bride did not take part in these negotiations, but remained hidden inside her parents' house until a settlement had been reached.

Witnesses from both sides signed their names or marked the wi'il with a thumbprint. The paper was submitted to the baito for further signature, which gave it the status of a binding legal document. The TPLF had promoted the adoption of the wi'il as a way of simplifying disputes involving divorce and to give women rights to property and a share of their husbands' asset base.

Those who could not afford a wedding of any kind often chose to live together without a formal ceremony, though they would usually draw up a wi'il and have their marriage blessed by a priest or shcik. Men and women saw the necessity of having a spouse to help them take care of their household and other relatives. A reputation for industriousness was the paramount quality that each looked for in the other, and this superseded the family name and even in many cases the physical beauty of the betrothed.

In addition to those who had been separated from their spouses, many weddings involved children who had come of age in the refugee camps. Many of these marriages were arranged by parents who found it difficult to support their children and thus sought to relieve the burden on the household by encouraging their children to marry as soon as possible and thus establish their own household. Although the financial cost to the households hosting the wedding could be considerable (celebrations were typically held at both the bride's and groom's parents' houses), in the long term people said it was worth this financial outlay to ensure that their son or daughter would be well looked after and that they would not have to support him or her in the future.[7]

So eager were parents to marry off their children that often the daughters were sent to live with their husbands while they were still young. This practice, common among poor households in the highlands, was continued in the camps. Several women reported to me that, having been married as early as nine years old, they had run away from their first husbands because they had been afraid of them, and only later remarried, often to men whom they had had a hand in choosing.

One day, while I sat drinking coffee in her house with Selamawit—who at eighteen was one of the younger mothers I knew—she surprised me by telling me that she had been married to another man before her marriage to Hagos, her current husband. She compared her first and second marriages. She told me that she had married her first husband when she was twelve. Her father had come to Sudan with her alone, and felt that he was not able to take good care of her on his own:

> So when the man asked him he gave me to him. [The groom] sent his friends to ask since he had no parents there. I knew him in the refugee camp. He was also from the same woreda. It happens a lot like that, that a man marries a woman from the same woreda. I don't know why. They say, "They come from our own people, so it is good." My family knew his family [in Tigray].
>
> He was very big [older]. He wanted to take me [i.e., to have sexual relations], but I said no because I was young and afraid. So I stayed for two years [after the wedding] with my father. I went to [my husband's] house but I was afraid so I came back. I didn't even stay for a month. I was too afraid. I came back for two years. I just ignored [my husband] after that. He got married to another.
>
> If your husband gave you clothes or gold [as an engagement present before the wedding] and you were a virgin [when he married you], he cannot take anything else from you [more important than your virginity]. So I kept those gifts [when I left him].
>
> Hagos [her second husband] knew that I had been married before so it was not a problem that I was not a virgin. We did a wi'il with his materials and my materials. He had no relations but preparations were done by my father and his friends. We did not know Hagos's family, only Hagos himself. It was not a big celebration, just our friends. We had only one celebration. He did not have anyone to prepare the feast for him so I prepared it, and we called his friends to my house. We lived together after that right away. I [had been with] him before [the wedding].
>
> His presents to me were less: one dress [in the first wedding she had received two]. It was partly because I had been married before and partly because he had a plan to give me more later. My father gave money again.

Divorce had been common in Tigray, but most people agreed that the incidence of divorce increased in Sudan. Either the man or woman could petition the local woreda representatives to have their marriage annulled. Where previously there had been a social stigma attached to marrying a woman or man who had been married before, especially if that person had children from their earlier marriage, in the refugee camps such aversions were relaxed. People told me that it was quite common for both men and women to be married as many as three times before some members of the community would begin to think of them as being promiscuous or to question their virtue. It was also not uncommon for women who had been prostitutes to marry and regain their respectability.

Decisions to Repatriate

Although by the beginning of the 1990s refugees had enough to eat and had rebuilt their social networks in the camps, most still held fast to the idea that one day they would be able to return to their homes in Tigray. Indeed, the desire to return had become an important mechanism for maintaining identity and social relations in the camp. The Sudanese government's policies of encouraging refugee communities to become self-sufficient and independent from humanitarian assistance by providing them with small plots of land had been largely ineffective, as refugees had not been granted access to enough land and other resources (such as fuel-wood and access to markets) to make this objective possible (Kibreab 1990 and 1996). At the same time, most Tigrayans were distinct from the Sudanese (as well as from many Eritrean refugees) in their religion, language, and customs and thus found it difficult to assimilate into the host society. These differences between refugee and host were most pronounced among older people, who felt more dissociated from their home communities and preferred to be buried in their birthplaces. Youngsters who learned to speak Arabic and were sometimes able to take advantage of educational and employment opportunities together with Sudanese of the same age were less concerned with returning.

Refugees' stated desire to return to their homeland cannot be understood outside the political context in which they lived. The refugee camps were extremely politicized places, and people's everyday lives were influenced at every step by their contact with the TPLF and REST—or with the Ethiopian Democratic Union (EDU) in some of the other camps. The

TPLF recruited soldiers from the camps, and solicited contributions of food, cash, and other items from the refugee population for the war effort. Because the TPLF had helped people to escape from the war zones of Tigray during 1984–85, most people felt a bond of loyalty to the movement. Toward the end of the war, they waited for the TPLF to tell them when they should prepare to return to Ethiopia.

This political reality complicates any discussion of the nature of "voluntary return." Accepting the language of the 1967 Organization of African Unity (OAU) Convention Governing the Specific Aspects of Refugee Problems in Africa, signed in Addis Ababa, UNHCR and the international community have adopted the following principles:

1. The essentially voluntary character of repatriation shall be respected in all cases and no refugee shall be repatriated against his will.
2. The country of asylum, in collaboration with the country of origin, shall make adequate arrangements for the safe return of refugees who request repatriation.
3. The country of origin, on receiving back refugees, shall facilitate their resettlement and grant them the full rights and privileges of nationals of the country, and subject them to the same obligations.
4. Refugees who voluntarily return to their country shall in no way be penalized for having left it for any of the reasons giving rise to refugee situations. Whenever necessary, an appeal shall be made through national information media and through the Administrative Secretary-General of the OAU, inviting refugees to return home and giving assurance that the new circumstances prevailing in their country of origin will enable them to return without risk and to take up a normal and peaceful life without fear of being disturbed or punished, and that the text of such appeal should be given to refugees and clearly explained to them by their country of asylum.
5. Refugees who freely decide to return to their homeland, as a result of such assurances or on their own initiative, shall be given every possible assistance by the country of asylum, the country of origin, voluntary agencies and international and intergovernmental organizations, to facilitate their return. (OAU 1969)

The first clause in this article suggests that the decision to return is an individual one, and that the international community is obligated to ensure that the decision to participate in organized repatriation is freely made. This principle fails to distinguish between deciding to return to one's country of origin and deciding *the best time* to return. It also does not concern itself with refugees who return when they are told by their community leaders that they should do so or when the option of remaining in the refugee camp is no longer available.

In this case, most people did want to return to Ethiopia. Older people said that it was much better to die in their homeland than in a foreign country; others wanted to be free from the constraints of Sudanese law and culture (as they saw them) or to be reunited with family members. Despite this, they did not consider the decision of when to return to be a matter that they should decide individually. Rather, they believed it best to act as a group.

Most people told me that they had been waiting for REST to tell them when conditions were ready for their return, and that they had participated in the 1993 repatriation operation because they understood that the TPLF was organizing it. The international humanitarian community and the government of Sudan were intent on closing the refugee camps and suspending assistance as quickly as possible. If the Tigrayan refugees had chosen not to return to Ethiopia with their neighbors and relatives, they would have become stateless, as Sudan had refused to grant them permanent residence status and the camps were to be closed.[8] At the same time, people had come to rely on the community dynamic they had developed while living in Sudan and did not want to give it up. Furthermore, although they may not have been familiar with the text of the legal convention quoted above through which their protection was framed, they did expect that there would be some assistance on the other side of the border to help them to return. Thus, while the decision of Tigrayan refugees to repatriate was not forced, and they did not do so under duress, the decision making process was more communal than individual.

In any repatriation operation that involves UNHCR assistance, there are a series of steps leading up to the repatriation. Information campaigns are conducted throughout the refugee camps to let people know about the options that exist for them, the conditions in the country of return, and the process of repatriation that they can expect. Refugees are then asked to sign a voluntary repatriation (VolRep) form that certifies that they are electing to return to their country of origin of their own free will. Finally, refugees are organized for transport and then assisted to return. They are medically screened before repatriation and those receiving medical care, such as TB patients, are given medical reports and medicine to carry with them to their country of origin.

It is unclear to what extent the information campaign included promises of assistance in Ethiopia. UNHCR, REST, and Ethiopian government officials claim that it was made clear to people that there would be no assistance available to them once they had repatriated. Returnees say they had been led to believe that there would be assistance for them in the resettlement sites. Items that they claimed were promised included oxen and plows, food, free medical care, and cash grants. A few people told me they had heard that there would not be any aid agencies operating in the settlement areas, but that they could not imagine such a thing to be possible, so they had assumed that at least one organization would be there to help them. Most were bitterly disappointed to learn on arrival in Ada Bai that only minimal assistance was available. Lettemariam, a woman in her late thirties whose youngest daughter died (probably from tuberculosis) shortly after arriving in Ada Bai, told me that the TPLF leaders had told the community that everything they had in Safawa would be available in Ethiopia and that they had decided to come on that basis. "I am angry now," she said. "These people [the TPLF] are our brothers and our sons. They lied to us. If they knew that things would be different here, they should have told us. Then those people who couldn't work or support themselves could have stayed in the Sudan."

Others had a more sympathetic view. Berhan, a woman in her forties who lived near my house with her husband and three children, was one of the poorest people I knew. She and her husband were both often too sick to work, suffering from an undiagnosed illness that they treated with traditional medicine and visits to the local holy water spring. Despite the difficulties she faced, she said,

> They [the TPLF] took us to Sudan and they did whatever they could.
> And they brought us back. There is hunger [here in Ada Bai] but it is a
> short-term problem. But it is not their fault. We try not to blame them. It
> is the fault of the administrators here. We heard all those good things in
> Sudan. When we first came it was raining and all our things were spoiled.

In her charitable view of things, she did not see the administrators of Ada Bai, whom she knew, as being the same as those representatives of the TPLF, whom she saw as leaders of the movement. To her, disappointments were the result of local corruption rather than dishonesty by the movement's leaders.

The disappointment that returnees felt upon settling in Ada Bai resulted from the realization that the social order had been disrupted once again and that they would be expected to negotiate a new order in Ada Bai.

Without the benefit of welfare and assistance organizations, they would have to provide all that they needed for themselves. The uncertainty that accompanied the need to place themselves within a new community even as they constructed that community complicated these processes and made the first months following repatriation stressful and difficult.

3

A Patchwork of Emplacements

With this chapter I return to the opening scene of this book, in which returnees disembarked from trucks amid the wide open space of Ada Bai. Faced with an unknown wilderness, they were compelled to create something, a home, from virtually nothing. Their raw materials included their "cultural baggage": the experiences, beliefs, and customs that they had been taught in Tigray or had acquired in Sudan as well as the physical challenges and limitations of the space into which they had moved. Yet the results of that construction were more than the products of these raw materials. As Carolyn Nordstrom says, writing about the return of displaced Mozambicans following the civil war:

> When people look out over a land that should resonate with meaning and life but that now stares blankly back . . . they are left with the choice of accepting a deadened world or creating a livable one. It is the imagination—creativity—that bridges the abyss, if not to reconstruct the past, to make the present livable. (1997, 190)

Creativity was the web that tied together the returnees' various resources, influences, and experiences to produce a community and way of life that were larger than the sum of their parts. This chapter examines these creative processes and the quality of the connection forged between person/community and place/landscape, the symbolic meanings and new, reworked practices that sprung from returnees' engagement with their new environment.

Implications of a Rejection of Sedentarism

A sedentarist reading of culture ties person and community to place in such a way that the removal of place—displacement—has the effect of stripping the individual or group of their culture and identity (Malkki 1995b, 508). To challenge this notion is not to deny that people have strong attachments to the places they inhabit or that their identity is derived in part through particular relations of emplacement. In the context of displacement and repatriation, questioning sedentarism need not invalidate the facts that such movement may be traumatic, that people may miss the places from which they have moved, and that returning to these areas may be their ultimate goal (Stefansson 2003). What is at issue, however, is the *assumption* that place plays a particular, generalizable, and predictable kind of role in community construction and identity formation across cultures. The quality of the relation between person, community, and place within the specific context of postwar Ethiopia is the focus.

Much has been written about the ethnographer's relation to place, to his or her field site and to the ways in which that site is delimited (Clifford 1997; Appadurai 1988; R. Rosaldo 1989; Feld and Basso 1996; Strathern 1988). Throughout the first two-thirds of the twentieth century, ethnographic study was largely synonymous with analysis of a single, particular village or place. The principle defining the boundary of a culture was its geographic location and relation to other similarly bounded entities. Historical, ethnic, political, and other types of continuities that bind people together into communities were given secondary consideration, if they were thought of at all. Despite the primacy of place as the most important defining criterion of a culture, however, the nature of the group's relation to that place remained largely unexamined. The nature of habitation, of the use of space, and the understanding of emplacement by those who occupied the place were not addressed as valid research questions.

More recently, culture has been disassociated from place. The notion of a culture as a geographically bounded unit has gradually given way to a vision of locality as a node within a complex web of influences brought by regional and global flows in information, money, goods, and people. Communities without geographic referents, or whose physical location is less of a defining influence than are other variables, have forced a reevaluation of cultural definition. Even the most physically remote societies have come to be considered as being linked to global power processes through the media, transnational economic and political influences, diasporic connections, and even displacement, and are transformed by these relationships (Appadurai [1996]; Appadurai and Breckenridge 1988; Clifford 1997; R. Rosaldo 1989; Malkki 1992 and 1994).

Many of the contributions to discussions on changing definitions of culture, however, seem to get lost in a labyrinth of reflexivity. They offer sweeping statements about the significance of place to all cultures, or to the ethnographer's perspective, as if there can ever be one universal ethnographic perspective. However, the anthropological subjects' own ideas about their involvement in emplacement processes—as both actors and subjects—are largely ignored.

In this chapter I examine the processes by which people in Ada Bai used physical space to organize themselves socially. Through emplacement, returnees addressed what they saw as the main challenges to a viable lifestyle: to create "safety" in a world that they initially regarded as dangerous. Unknown space was considered dangerous and could cause hunger, sickness, and death. Their activities during the first two years in Ada Bai were aimed at making the unknown and previously uninhabited place known, at taming the wild and making it a cultivated place. Examination of their experience reveals the importance that people attributed to their physical surroundings in defining the community and making life "livable."

The Expectation and the Reality of Return

In comparing returnees' expectations prior to return with their actual experiences, articulations and grievances emerge that give one a sense of how they approached the enormous task of emplacement. In this context, emplacement connotes the opposite of displacement; that is, the act of forging a relationship between person (individual or collective) and place. A great deal of the literature on repatriation, including that on Tigrayan and Eritrean refugees in Sudan, focuses on the decision to repatriate—on the information that the refugee uses to make the decision, his or her expectations of return, and the extent to which decisions to repatriate are negotiated with other household and community members (Dolan 1999; Gmelch 1980; Habte-Selassie 1992; Kibreab 1996b; Koser 1997; Makanya 1994; Walsh, Black, and Koser 1999; Pottier 1999; Rogge 1994). While representations of the homeland made by the group in exile are informative, they are often colored by "diaspora politics," nostalgia (the "imagined homeland"), inaccurate information on the conditions in the place of return based on gossip and rumors, and deliberate misinformation from community leaders and others who have a vested interest in encouraging or discouraging repatriation (Rogge 1994, 32–34; Clifford 1997). Returning migrants often find that they must radically alter their image of the homeland once they arrive. This adjustment may lead to intense disappointment, resentment, and sometimes even anger on the part of the returnees toward government officials, aid organizations, or local or host communities (Akol 1994). This was true in Ada Bai in 1993; it was also true of returnees with whom I spoke in 1994 in Rawayan—one of the other settlements in the Humera area. I also found the same tendency in Gondar, Amhara Region, during 1995, when I interviewed ethnic Amhara returnees in a transit center outside Gondar town to which they had just been repatriated from Sudan.

Most returnees settling in Ada Bai in 1993 expected that life in the settlement would be similar to that which they had known in the refugee camp, with plenty of assistance from the REST, the United Nations, and international nongovernmental organizations. Instead, they were confronted by a place without aid agencies and with very limited government services, and by the enormous task of emplacement that lay before them. They were daunted, and commonly complained that "not knowing the place" made life more difficult for them. A song verse, frequently sung by girls in Ada Bai while they worked, shows the contrast that they felt about life in Sudan versus their new life:

> *Mishet ne'mehetu* መሽት ነመሐቱ In the evening the good day has passed.
> *Safawa haletu* ስፋዋ ሐለቱ Safawa was good.

In the same sense that a good day cannot be relived, the song expresses resignation that the days of bounty in Safawa cannot be brought back and that it is time to make the best of life in Ada Bai.[1] Others, however, did not accept the change so easily. One man told me bitterly, "I named my son for Meles Zenawi [president of the Transitional Government of Ethiopia from 1993 through 1995, and later elected prime minister] but he [the president] has thrown me under a bush without any shelter."

Space, Place, and Landscape

Much of the literature on place and landscape either lacks precision or refers to uses of these terms that are not appropriate for this particular study. I will not delve into all of the ways in which these terms appear in the literature. Edward Casey (1996; 1997) provides an exhaustive phenomenological discussion of the meaning of place and its relation to space, landscape, person, and community. His analysis provides a detailed historical and philosophical road map to the study of place based on his reading of nearly every major Western philosopher who has written on the subject. For the purposes of this study, however, definition of terms is necessary.

I use the term *space* to refer to geographical topography that is new and unfamiliar to the people in question.[2] Because it has not yet been incorporated into the realm of the known landscape by those who have come to inhabit it (through use, practice, and the accumulation of familiarity), space is considered expansive, dangerous, and largely unknown.

Place in my analysis refers to any kind of space that people, through their everyday lives, use, appropriate, and reflect on, thereby generating meaning through practice and association. In the process of place-making, meaning is generated through the particular relationship between physical place and individual and/or collective subject. This connection to place I refer to, with Feld and Basso (1996), as a *sense of place*.

I take *landscape* to refer to the collection of meanings associated with the place that are produced through both interaction with that place in everyday practice and reflection on that place through imagination, visualization, narration, performance, and even policy formulation. Landscape is intimately tied with community self-conception, for as Nordstrom, citing Watts (1992, 122), says, "Landscapes are ways of seeing—seeing not only outward to culturally constructed realities, but inward to ideas and ideals of self and identity" (1997, 179). As this chapter demonstrates, landscapes are experienced differently by different people. Because every person's perspective is unique, and landscapes are best seen as fluid scenes that are constantly changing (Appadurai 1996), emplacement within the environment is also best understood as a continuous process of making one's place in the world.

Ada Bai residents constructed their landscape by implicating themselves in a physical place through everyday use and practice. This echoes Carolyn Humphrey's observations of a Mongolian sense of place:

> Landscapes are more in the nature of practices designed to have results: it is not contemplation of the land that is important but interaction with it . . . The Mongols do not take over any terrain in the vicinity and transform it into something that is their own. Instead, they move within a space and environment where some kind of pastoral life is possible and 'in-habit-it.' . . . However, this is not a pre-reflective or spontaneous existence, but one recognizing human choice and agencies, which are conceived as interrelated with and subordinate to the agencies attributed to entities in the land. (1995, 135)

In part, Ada Bayans' use of the land was a response to the kind of resources the area offered. In the hot lowlands they had returned to, for example, they were not able to grow the same crops that they were accustomed to in the highlands and so they had to learn to grow sesame and sorghum. At the same time their use of the environment was based on real choices, in which opportunities for the construction of meaningful places within the landscape were functions of the needs and interests of the people who lived there.

"Emplacement" as I use it here refers to more than a process of naming or particularizing space. Ada Bai residents were involved in emplacing their environment in such a way as to make it feel like a home. This involved the interworking of place, identity, and practice in such a way as to generate a relationship of belonging between person and place. Emplacement involved the gradual expansion of places that people considered to be familiar and safe from the raw material of a space that was unfamiliar and dangerous. The dangerous places delimited the edge of the Ada Bai landscape. These localities obtained the qualities of being safe or dangerous through use or visitation, through interaction rather than perception. This corresponds with Peter Gow's notion of landscape as lived, as an active relationship between place-making and narrative, rather than merely as representation (1995, 52–53) or objectification found in maps, paintings, songs, or poetry that characterize the Western concept of "landscape" (Humphrey 1995, 135; Gow 1995, 60).

Emplacement was defined differently by men and women, farmer and trader, children, adults, and the elderly. Indeed, at one level the experience of emplacement is an individual one. Yet the boundaries of creativity or innovation may be dictated by social habits, customs, and prohibitions to make emplacement a social, shared experience as well. Different senses of place can be more or less grouped by kinds of places (household, town, and field) and by types of users (youth, women, and men).

Setting Boundaries: Local Leadership's Efforts to Shape a Community

When I first arrived in Ada Bai, the locus of the settlement and the center of social activity was the area where the clinic, grain warehouse, and local administrator's house were located. Men in particular would pass by this area at least once a day to exchange the latest news and gossip. Women tended to congregate around the clinic and the well, chatting as they waited for their turn to bring the children into the clinic for examination or to fill their jerry can with water. The clinic was a small collection of buildings located between the main road and the dry riverbed that ran along the southern edge of the settlement. Houses in this part of the settlement were sprinkled over a network of small hillocks that had been carved by groundwater from heavy rainstorms making its way down to the riverbed. The slightly raised terrain of the houses helped them to catch the passing breezes, thereby cooling them from the afternoon sun, and the relative abundance of trees, mostly acacia, provided welcome shade.

I was given a house plot on the same hillock as the administrator's house, with the explanation that it was the safest place for me. The administrator's guards would be able to keep an eye on me (I assumed that they meant both for my purposes and for theirs). I hired Negash, a respected builder, to construct my one-room house for approximately U.S.$80. The house was very sturdy and had a small shade, or *das*, which extended out from the front door to provide a cool place to sit out the hot midday sun.

As I came to know my neighbors, I learned that everyone who lived in that area was from Axum awraja. Many had fled from Tigray in the same TPLF-escorted group and had lived together in the same part of Safawa camp. Others had joined the neighborhood later on, having migrated to Sudan later or returned to the refugee camps a second time after repatriating to Tigray in 1985 and being displaced all over again by war or famine. I saw some significance in the fact that Ada Bai's political center was in the Axum neighborhood, since Axum is considered the historical birthplace of Ethiopian Orthodox Christianity and the symbolic heart of the Ethiopian Empire.[3] However, I may have been reading too much into this as none of the Axumites or other residents of Ada Bai indicated that this was significant when I asked them about it. It was sometimes difficult to tell whether symbolic connections and associations that I made were shared by those whose lives I was researching—people's silence about a particular issue could mean either that they did not see it in the same way or that the association was so obvious that it was not worth remarking on.

All Ada Bai residents had been given house plots, measuring no larger than 16 by 20 square meters, together with others from the same part of Tigray; in addition, these corresponded to the neighborhoods or residential groupings that had been in place in Sudan. Although most people maintained cordial relations with others in the settlement, they said that they thought it was better to live together with the people who came from the same area of Tigray (particularly the same woreda) because then "you know who your neighbors are." Strangers represented potential dangers associated with thievery, spirit possession, and disease.

There were two exceptions to this pattern. One was the small Muslim population (60–80 households) that lived together in two neighborhoods of Ada Bai, regardless of where in Tigray they had come from. Each of these areas had mosques, small straw huts with relatively large courtyards. Although Muslims and Christians were cordial with one another, a certain degree of mistrust was generated by the differences in religious and cultural practices, particularly the prohibition held by both religions against eating meat that had been slaughtered according to the tradition of the other religion. Prohibitions against marriages between Christians and Muslims also served to keep the two groups distinct, although they often did attend each others' funeral and wedding ceremonies when provisions had been made for slaughtering a smaller animal (a goat or sheep rather than an ox) according to the other religion's customs (the prayer invoked prior to the slaughter, and the manner of incising the throat, was different for Muslims and Christians). In the two Muslim neighborhoods, a common religion served as a more significant factor in binding households together than area of origin, although the latter was often a secondary factor in household location within the neighborhood. Muslims also tended to build their compound fences around several houses, even if the households were not related through kinship ties. Compounds included space for praying outside and latrine/shower areas for washing prior to prayer.

The other distinct neighborhood, Safawa Hade,[4] was made up of people from all parts of Tigray who had lived together in Sudan in Safawa I (the older part of the refugee camp) before the opening of Safawa II (when the Wad Kowli camp was closed). There was a barely perceptible level of discrimination against those from Safawa Hade. Those who lived in the neighborhoods corresponding to a single awraja sometimes said that the Safawa Hade people mixed more easily with people from all parts of Tigray and had "looser" morals. Such suspicion may be attributed to the perception that the people who lived in Safawa I had not shared the same history during their flight and early days in Sudan, and that they sometimes had had to compete with each other for relief resources in the camps.

The first houses to be constructed in Ada Bai were generally extremely modest straw huts. Because they had been built quickly and the men who brought the materials from the forest did not always know the best places to find wood and straw, the walls of the houses were thin and in many places transparent. Whereas the interior walls of Tigrayan highland stone houses (*hidmo*) and more permanent straw houses were covered with mud and limestone, in Ada Bai the straw was left uncovered. Many people opted to build simple square houses with sloped roofs, reinforced with their plastic sheet, rather than the round straw *tukul* (ቱኩል), which was more watertight and longer lasting but also required more intensive labor inputs and a greater number of, and longer, building poles.[5]

In February 1994, the camp administrator informed the village that those residents who lived in the eastern end of the village, near the clinic, would have to be moved two kilometers to the east and to the north, to the other side of the road, away from the river. The resettled houses would extend the village to the north. Each household would be responsible for moving itself and for absorbing any expenses incurred by the move. The reason for the move was never made completely clear to the residents of the settlement or to me. Some people said that they thought it was a measure to keep the houses away from the river, which during the rainy season (June–October) would be a mosquito breeding site. Others said that a master plan for the village was being developed, and that the marketplace should form the core of the town, so the move was an attempt to orient the community around the marketplace. Nearly one-quarter of the village population were directed to move their houses. Although some grumbled among themselves, particularly those who would have a hard time meeting the expense of building a new house, no one refused to move.

I was given a house plot in the new Axum neighborhood together with my former neighbors, again near the administrative (or *baito*) headquarters. By this time, however, a local civilian had been elected to take the TPLF administrator's place.[6] He lived in his own house with his family rather than near the baito office, so my sense of being watched over by the local leadership was mitigated to some extent. I again hired Negash (who had become my regular handyman, more because I wanted to support his malnourished infant twins than because my house needed improvements) to rebuild the round side walls of my house in the new site and then we recruited thirty men to carry the roof of my first house on their shoulders all the way down the road to the new site. I bought a twenty liter jerry can of sewa to thank them, as they refused to accept money for their services.

Those who relocated took more time and care to build their second house than they had the first. Men began to collect the wood and long straw for building early, searching carefully for the straightest limbs and the strongest straw. Because most of the surrounding area was under cultivation, the men had to travel long distances to find these materials. Although the second houses tended to be larger, they were still one-room constructions made from wood and straw. Men worked alone or with their sons, brothers, or close friends to frame the house and thatch the roof.

My neighbors relocating the roof of my house to the new house plot.

They used very few, if any, nails; the supports of the house were tied together with thin strips of rubber (known as *jamaica*) taken from old tires, and the straw was sandwiched between the wood pieces to form the walls. The houses usually had only two small windows placed near the base of the roof, to allow for cross-ventilation. These windows were high and small enough to prevent passersby (particularly those who might be carrying the Evil Eye) from looking into the house and kept the inside of the house dark and cool during the day. Once the basic shape of the house was completed, the men brought mud from the riverbed and, together with their wives and other family members (not necessarily from the same household), mixed it with straw to create a plaster-like substance to cover the interior walls. Finally, they returned to the riverbed and brought limestone, known as *nora* (ኖራ), to whitewash the walls.[7] Wives and children remained in the old houses until the new ones were finished, or else slept at the new site under a *das* (ዳስ), or shade, adjacent to the house. Once they had moved into their houses, they continued to carefully build additional components of the household place, including a cooking stove known as a *magogo* (ምጎጎ)—used for baking the *injera* (እንጀራ) flatbread eaten with every meal—built by women out of stones and mud and designed to maximize fuelwood efficiency by keeping the wind out of the fire. Shelters for young animals, chicken coops, and grain and animal feed containers were also constructed. The more accomplished house builders were regularly visited by their neighbors, who wanted to admire their work and pick up pointers for their own houses. A well-built house would last at least five years.

Sons learn how to build houses from their fathers.

Finally, men built fences between their household plots, sometimes encircling only their own house and sometimes including one or two other houses of close kin or friends. The decision to build fences around the houses was a subject of heated public discussion. At a town meeting, a motion was made to ban fences on the grounds that they were fire hazards and that, if a house caught fire, the fences would prevent people from getting to it quickly to extinguish it. The suggestion was quickly overruled by the assembled crowd, who argued that the fences helped to keep thieves out of, and animals in, the compounds at night. Although some fences clearly did serve these purposes, most were either not closed on all sides or lacked doors. It seems likely that the fences served another purpose: to clearly demarcate "household" space from "outside" space, and to lay claim to the immediate land around the house so as to be able to use it to shelter animals and to grow vegetables (tomatoes, potatoes, and onions), cotton, and spices during the rainy season. Fences also tended to mark the edge of a household's territorial claim: visitors were expected to announce themselves at the gate before entering. To approach the door of the house without alerting the occupants of one's arrival was considered extremely rude.

Another public debate concerned the practice of growing vegetables, or *hamle*,[8] in the house plots. Some people argued that green plants attracted mosquitoes, and should not be allowed as a public health measure to reduce the spread of malaria. "It is better to leave [i.e., not to grow] the hamle," said the man who had raised the issue for discussion. "We do not know this place; that is why we and our children are dying." In addition, he wanted improved services to render the new place habitable. "We should press for more medical workers and also have better sanitation," he said. For this man, it was better to minimize the risks that he knew, such as the tendency of mosquitoes to congregate around green plants and standing water, so that he would be better able to cope with the hazards that existed in the new place that he did not yet know. Others said that hamle was an essential part of the rainy season household diet (a season when many families have exhausted most or all of their grain stocks and are awaiting the next harvest), and should not be banned. The community decided in favor of the gardens, leaving the decision of whether to plant to the individual homesteader. The control over household space was, in the final analysis, unquestionably that of the household itself and thus was not subject to community regulation.

Administrative and public decisions about where and how to organize residential space on a communitywide level set the boundaries for returnees' creation of household places. Except when disagreement was aired in public debate, most people felt that such regulations were reasonable and worked within them. Rather than create uniformity, the limits implied by the rules allowed ample room for improvisation and innovation.

Household Space as Women's Space

As in most societies (Engels 1972 [1884], M. Rosaldo 1974, Lepowsky 1993), the household space was largely the domain of women in Ada Bai. Association with this particular space was defined through women's work. Women were responsible for cooking, cleaning, and for all regular water hauling for the needs of the household and the domestic animals that sheltered there at night.[9] If the rains failed, the well dried up, or the borehole pump broke down, a woman's husband or other male relative might agree to assist her by fetching water with his donkey and cart, if he had one.[10] A donkey could carry a maximum of two 20-liter jerry cans on its back; with a cart it could pull a tank with a 220-liter capacity. Otherwise, if she could afford it, a woman might buy water from the young boys who circulated through the village on their donkeys selling forty liters of water for two birr (U.S. 40 cents). The water was carried by the animals in saddlebags that had been fashioned from old inner tubes and plugged with maize husks.

A woman also bore all child-rearing responsibilities for the daughters, as well as for sons until they were five or six, when the father might begin to teach them farming, shepherding, and other useful skills. Then the boys would go off into the woods or out to the fields to assist their fathers. Boys might start herding animals on their own when they were seven or eight, particularly if the household was labor-poor or needed money from shepherding other people's animals.

The organization of the house interior was strikingly uniform throughout Ada Bai, and seemed to have been developed in the refugee camps, where most people lived in *tukuls* (ቱኩል, straw houses) for the first time.

Zenash prepares coffee outside her house with her daughter.

The house, generically referred to as *geza* (ጌዛ), typically had at least two beds made from wood and woven leather strings or metal, one placed on either side of the door. A third bed might be near the back of the house if the structure was large enough and many people lived there. At night the household members would pile into the beds, one adult to each bed together with up to three young children. On very hot nights the beds were often brought outside; men in particular would sleep outside while the women would usually sleep with the youngest children inside.

A wooden table was arranged, also near the back of the house, with all of the woman's kitchen utensils. The utensils were arranged as if, it seemed to me, for an exhibition. The large metal and enamel plates for injera[11] stood on end at the back of the table. In front of them tall thermoses or pitchers were placed, and the arrangement moved toward the front of the table, with plastic or metal plates leaned up on their sides (reminding me of a display of fine china), then shorter glasses and cups, and finally the tiny Chinese tea cups (*finjal*, ፊንጃል) from which coffee was drunk several times a day. Many of the larger dishes were rarely, if ever, used. Other anthropologists have suggested that the prominence of the dishes may be a statement to visitors about the household having sufficient food. Because the food stocks themselves are generally hidden, this seems unlikely. Rather, some of the dishes had intrinsic value (large pots and kettles could be rented out for large feasts), and the display of a multitude of attractive and clean dishes signified the woman's worth as a homemaker and a cook, and thus contributed to her reputation as a good wife. A household's wealth could be judged by the number and type of dishes on display.

Stacked at the head or foot of the beds were metal boxes and suitcases containing clothing, medicines, important papers, family photographs, and other *mezakerta* (መዘክርት), or souvenirs, that people had collected throughout their lives and carefully stored away. Additional clothes hung in bags and suitcases from the rafters of the house (to prevent them being eaten by termites or nested in by mice or rats), together with farm and building tools, seed stocks, and kerosene lanterns. The few chairs or wooden benches the household owned were set up in front of the beds, to protect them from wear due to people sitting on them during the day. Under the beds, hidden by the blankets and usually covered with plastic sheeting to keep the rats out, were the precious quintal sacks of sorghum that the family relied on for their staple food throughout the year. Additional sacks of grain might be hidden under a plastic sheet outside the house under the shade or in a trusted relative's house.

Organization of the interior house space varied little from one household to another, as women followed the same pattern they had used in Sudan. A woman's house was judged by how tidy it was, and how well she had adhered to the standard house layout. In arranging her house, then, she strove for "re-emplacement," to arrange her house in exactly the same way that it had been in the refugee camp. I learned this lesson well when, in setting up my own house, I left the dishes piled in stacks on the table. My neighbor came and, with a click of her tongue intended to scold me slightly, rearranged the dishes for me, standing everything on end so that it conformed to every other house in Ada Bai.

The woman's control over both the organization and function of the house gave her authority. She had control over the use of all food and significant cash resources. While her husband might keep some of the household's income, derived from the sale of farm goods, for major purchases of livestock, building materials, or renting land, she managed the day to day economics of the household. She was in most cases the keeper of the key to the front door, if there was a lock. Inside her house a Christian woman usually did not cover her head and only wore a *netsela* (ነጠላ, a shawl made from white, usually homespun cotton and often with a colorful banner woven into its edges) when working in the sun or going out of her compound. Muslim women were more circumspect and would usually tie a scarf around their head to cover their hair even inside the house, and would always wear a netsela when going outside.

Muslim and Christian families' diets differed somewhat: Muslims were more accustomed to eating such things as dates and fruit drinks, but the basic elements of the daily food basket were the same (meat was slaughtered according to different rituals for each but otherwise was cooked in the same manner). In other respects Muslim and Christian domestic activities did not differ significantly. Muslim women did, however, pray in the house because they were not allowed to enter the mosque.

The woman's comfort in her own house and those of her close friends and relatives was derived from the place and her role in it. Outside the familiar safety of her compound, a woman would often become withdrawn and appear ill at ease. I often observed Ada Bai women in the marketplace, at the political administration office, or in Humera town looking lost, their sense of composure absent as they sat silently slumped in their seats, their netsela covering their heads and most of their faces. When I asked my female friends why they had been so quiet in these places, they would say, "That is a man's place," or "I don't know that place." One day, after my best friend Tibbletz had begged me several times to take her to Humera, I stopped in front of her house and invited her to come along. She was surprised, and for a moment she hesitated, as if she had not expected me to take her requests seriously. Finally, after checking with her husband to make sure that he would be able to feed and water the animals at the end of the day (she was childless, having lost both a son and daughter in Sudan), she put on her netsela and got into my car. In town, this normally proud, gregarious, and cheerful woman became quiet and unsure of herself. She brightened when we ran into a man she had known in Sudan who was running a vegetable stall in the marketplace. For a moment she grew lively, and then as we moved on she withdrew again. That evening she told me, much to my surprise, that this had been her first visit to Humera. In subsequent months, as the "big city" became more familiar to her and she discovered one of her father's brothers who lived there, she became more comfortable. She had added Humera to her repertoire of known places; she had fit it into her landscape of familiar, and thus safe, places and it ceased to intimidate her.

Ada Bai women were interested and amused by my life, which defied their own gendered boundaries. To them, I seemed to roam all over the village, as I regularly visited people in every neighborhood to conduct interviews or gather other data. Despite my wandering ways, however, I spent the vast majority of my time in women's places: in households or the clinic. When I would return from a day of interviews, my friends would tease me, asking me whether I had been drinking sewa with the men in the marketplace (women also drank sewa, but unless they were selling it to men in their own sewa house—a small shop that they rented to serve the drink—or drinking it at a public celebration such as a wedding, christening, or saint's feast, they would only drink it in their own houses). They wanted to know whom I had seen and where I had been. They would venture out of their neighborhood only rarely, to visit a relative or someone in another neighborhood whom they had known in Sudan, to ask for a service (that is, from a midwife, priest, or traditional healer), or to go to a public building or place (that is, the market, church, or clinic). It was expected that no married woman would leave her house without a specific destination in mind. She would never visit a man who was not a relative on her own, although men frequently visited both married and unmarried women in their homes. Unmarried teenage girls who milled around the marketplace with their girlfriends looking for amusement were frowned upon but still tolerated.

The Men about Town

While women laid claim to the house as their domain, the town was seen to belong to the men, even if some of those spaces were created by women to serve the men. Landmarks in men's landscapes included the restaurants, teahouses, and sewa houses that were sprinkled throughout the marketplace. Sewa houses were identified by a simple red plastic cup (or in some cases an empty beer bottle) placed upside down on a stick in front of the seller's own house or, more commonly, in front of a house that she had rented in the marketplace to serve her customers. Restaurants were similarly identified by a plate hanging outside the door of the house.

The men's domain also included the baito offices, and, for Muslims, the mosque. The baito had one woman representative (who was a single Muslim who lived with her younger brothers). The other members of the baito, however, were all men between the ages of thirty and forty. Some had served in the TPLF as soldiers, while others had been administrators or other noncombatant workers within the movement. They had been elected by the community, and most had family living within the community, but their qualifications for leadership were measured by their commitment during the war to the revolutionary cause. Older men, who in the highlands before the war would have expected to hold positions of leadership and be accorded the highest respect by the community, were held in lower esteem. This was a source of some consternation to the elders, who lamented the changes, but also accepted them with resignation as part of the price of the war. Most older men considered themselves lucky to have lived through the war and famine to be able to return to Ethiopia.

For men of all ages, spending part of the day in the marketplace was a habit, a means of gathering information on the local, regional, and national news and gossip. It was also where business deals were hatched, although they would likely be sealed in the privacy of one of the men's houses. Younger men—who being unmarried and living with their fathers were not relied on as household heads to support their families—would often sit in the marketplace to watch the tractors and ancient Land Rover taxis come and go, taking note of guests, newcomers, and the acquisitions neighbors had brought from Humera or further afield. Men often congregated in the marketplace or outside their friends' houses to listen to the nightly news on the radio, broadcast at 7 p.m. in Tigrinya and 8 p.m. in Amharic (those few men who had learned Amharic in school or in the workplace often listened to both).

With the exception of the mosque, these places were not exclusively for men; women often served the tea and almost always served the sewa. Women, however, were only expected to be present in the marketplace if they had a reason; loitering was frowned on. Waiting for a ride to Humera, for instance, was a valid excuse for sitting in the tea shops; obtaining consent from the baito to seek free treatment for a sick child at the Humera Hospital was a good reason for coming to the baito offices. Women who were seen to be hanging around the shops and offices too much were viewed with much aspersion, and were often quietly accused by both women and men of being prostitutes (*shirmuta*, ሽርሙጣ). Some women even criticized members of the Women's Association, which was used for political mobilization and had frequent meetings, for spending too much time outside their households. Such accusations, were never, however, made in the presence of the members.

Likewise, men who ventured into the marketplace late at night (after 9 p.m.) or who stayed there late were suspected of having been with a shirmuta. A respectable man would never go to a known prostitute's house or place of business in the evening, even though by day these houses served tea, sewa, or food and were not considered off-limits. In this regard, place definition was temporal; a place could be one thing during the day and another at night, and access to that place held very different meanings at different times.

During the daytime, men's and women's places were defined more through their uses than through prohibitions about who could spend time in them. The Tigrayan work ethic, an important aspect of Tigrayan ethnic identity, prescribed that men and women should remain close to their workplaces, but differential use and authority was prescribed by men's and women's social roles (Bodenhorn 1995). Women were expected to remain close to the house unless their domestic responsibilities required them to go, for example, to the marketplace, water collection site, or clinic. Men's places included the house compound outside the house itself, where they often worked with the animals, chopped wood, carved new farm implements, or improved the house structure. Their places extended to the wilderness or forest, where they went to fetch wood, work in their fields, haul water, or obtain other items necessary for the house or to sell for cash. Both public and domestic spheres were open to men and women as long as they were working or had a legitimate purpose in being there. Judgments about those who violated customary use of space were framed by both men and women. Often the criticism a woman received from breaking the rules was greater from other women than it was from men.

Children's Spaces

Children's safe and known places spanned both male and female domains.[12] Very young children (younger than age four) tended to stay with their mothers in the residential compound and house or at the houses of neighbors. Boys five years of age or older tended the household's sheep, goats, and cattle in fields close to the village where water was available. Some enterprising families offered their sons' shepherding services to other households that did not have a child to work for them: the child's family was paid three birr per month (approximately 60 U.S. cents) for each animal the boy tended. Thus, at an early age, boys' safe space was enlarged from the house to the field. Boys brought their animals to central grazing and watering areas, keeping one eye on their animals while playing football, hunting for wild fruits and greens, or swimming in the river with the other shepherd boys. The riverbed (*jirba*) became a place for social interaction with boys of a similar age from all over the village, who might not otherwise have seen one another if they had remained in their homes.

The eldest son was often tasked with fetching water using two 20-liter jerry cans, or saddlebags made from old tires, loaded onto a donkey. The boy brought water to his mother's house first, then refilled his donkey's load with water to deliver for sale to other houses. This helped ease the work burden of the boy's mother, who otherwise had to carry the jerry cans unaided on her back from the water point to the house, a distance of up to one kilometer.

The mobility enjoyed by young boys stood in contrast to that of mothers and daughters. The mother tended to remain close to the house; she was responsible for child care, cooking, cleaning, and tending suckling or ill livestock that could not graze with the rest of the herd. The mother's social network usually consisted of her immediate neighbors who were real or fictive kin (extended family who came to be thought of as closer relatives). Young girls tended to stay close to their homes as well, helping their mothers with chores and playing with other children nearby. Girls were less likely to herd animals, but when they did they tended only those animals that stayed close to the house, such as goats and sheep. However, girls often went uninvited to other houses in the immediate area, and in general were more mobile than their mothers.

The space in which children felt at ease as part of their personal landscape tended to narrow as they matured and became more tightly bound to the social rules of the adult world. Several of my young informants had to relinquish elements of their childhood landscape when they married.

They made the adjustment with some awkwardness, and girls in particular were often embarrassed to talk about their married lives. Girls were more tied to the home once they married, and were less able to visit their friends, linger in the marketplace, or chat at the water source. Younger married men had less free time to loiter in the tea shops; their associations with other men became more rooted in kinship as well as in the likely benefit to be derived from sharing resources or labor on a particular project for the benefit of their household.

Sacred Spaces

Religious spaces in Ada Bai had rigid rules based on gender. The Ethiopian Orthodox Church had strict rules for keeping men and women separated during worship. In most parts of Ethiopia, the typical Orthodox church was a round building with three "layers": the inner sanctum known as Beytelehem (ቤተልሐም), or "Holy of Holies", which held the *tabot* (ታቦት), a replica of the Ark of the Covenant that symbolized the Church's connection to the original Ark, which Ethiopian Orthodox Christians believe is kept in Axum. Only the caretakers of the tabot, one or two priests, were allowed to enter this inner sanctum. The second chamber, the Beytemekdes (ቤተመክደስ) encircling the inner sanctum, was for priests and other clergy, all of whom were men. Finally, the outer sanctum was designated for the worshipers, with men and women's spaces divided into two semicircular chambers.

In Ada Bai, the church was named for Abune Aregawi, an Ethiopian archbishop believed to have particularly potent healing abilities and to have come from Tigray. When I asked about the significance of the name, people told me that the church in the refugee camp had also been called Abune Aregawi, and that they had brought the tabot first from Tigray during the war and later to Ada Bai with them. It is likely that the choice of saint was related to the refugees' desire to maintain an active tie to the Tigrayan church.

The traditional design of the church noted above had been modified since the community could not afford to build such an elaborate structure. This church was a very simple square building. It had two rooms, one for the tabot and one for the priests. All of the parishioners stood outside the building. Those who were considered pure gathered in the church courtyard, with men and women usually sitting on separate sides of the courtyard from one another.

Blood was considered a symbol of impurity. All menstruating women, all men and women who had had sexual intercourse in the past twenty-four hours, women who had delivered babies who were not yet baptized (and who might not have fully healed from childbirth), and others who were considered impure were expected to remain outside the church fence, an elaborate wooden construction built by contributions of wood and money from each neighborhood.[13]

Behind the church and at a distance from any houses or other public buildings was the cemetery. This place was also accompanied by several restrictions. Only men were allowed to enter the graveyard to bury a body. Women were expected to sit on the hillside above the grave. I was told that women were considered "pure" and the sight of the dead body would endanger them. This was confusing, since it was often women who dressed dead bodies in preparation for burial.

When there was no funeral going on, it was considered extremely improper to walk in the cemetery. Anyone who was seen doing this was said to carry the Evil Eye and to feast on dead bodies. I learned this when I suggested that I might do a rough mortality calculation by counting the graves each month. My research assistant, horrified, warned me that the potential costs of being seen wandering through the graves would certainly outweigh any advantages from counting the piles of stones that marked each grave.

Christian and Muslim dead were buried in separate sites. Because the Muslim community in Ada Bai was so small, they used the graveyard of the Muslims who had lived in the area prior to the repatriation. Muslims and Christians would attend each other's funerals, though they would usually sit several meters away from each other.

The separation of the living from the dead, and the practice of burying the followers of one faith together, was based partly on religious principles of purity and danger. In addition, the belief that it was better to be situated among "one's own people" than among strangers, both in the land of the living as well as that of the dead, lent importance to the sanctity of the burial place. Relatives of those who had died in Humera Hospital went to great expense to bring the bodies back to Ada Bai for burial rather than allow it to take place in one of the cemeteries in town.

The importance of burial places was most dramatically demonstrated to me when a friend whom I had taken to a hospital in the Eritrean town of Tesseney, one hundred kilometers away, died in childbirth. The woman's husband, who had accompanied us, first decided that we should attempt to drive her body back to Ada Bai that night. However, we were advised that bandits were regularly attacking lone cars driving at night on the road, so we decided to wait until the next day to bury her. The intense heat made it necessary to bury her early the next morning rather than drive the body back to Ada Bai. The body was dressed at the hospital by two women whom we had brought with us. A debate then ensued about where to bury her. Local clergy decided that she should be buried in a cemetery that had been established for Ethiopian Tigrayans in Tesseney town rather than together with other Christian Eritreans (most of whom were ethnically, religiously, and linguistically similar to her). A hastily arranged funeral was attended by over one hundred Ethiopian Tigrayan mourners who were residents of Tesseney, none of whom had ever met her. A modest feast of bread and sauce made from beans was held in the Tigrayan community center for her husband and our small group (two midwives from Ada Bai and three hospital attendants) before we returned to Ada Bai.

Naming the Place

Whereas the process of home-making in Ada Bai involved re-creating a house that was historically, physically, aesthetically, and practically similar to the dwelling in the refugee camp, place-making in the wider physical environment was more a process of fashioning a new space to fit the practical and spiritual requirements of everyday life. Unlike some other cultures' experiences of emplacement (Morphy 1995, Basso 1988), returnees did not have the benefit of having ancestral connections to their new homes or of mythology or folklore that included this place in its imagery. With the exception of those few who had worked there before as farmhands, residents of Ada Bai had only minimal knowledge of the history of Humera and Wolkait (the name given to the area when it was administered by Gondar Region), based on its reputation and battle stories heard during the war, rather than any sense of personal history that connected them to this place.

Despite the fact that returnees had not had a chance to develop a very rich connection to, or to differentiate, the various kinds of places in Ada Bai, the process of place-making began as soon as they arrived. My analysis of this process follows closely the words that people use to describe various places and their relations to them. In his discussion of the importance of language, and place names in particular, to understanding subjects' understandings of their places, Keith Basso writes:

Whenever the members of a community speak about their landscape—
whenever they name it, or classify it, or evaluate it, or move to tell stories
about it—they unthinkingly represent it in ways that are compatible with
shared understandings of how, in the fullest sense, they know themselves
to occupy it. Which is simply to note that in conversational encounters,
trivial and otherwise, individuals exchange accounts and observations of
the landscape that consistently presuppose [and therefore depend for both
their credibility and appropriateness upon] mutually held ideas of what the
landscape actually is, why its constituent places are important, and how it
may intrude on the practical affairs of its inhabitants. Thus, if frequently
by implication and allusion only, bits and pieces of a common worldview
are given situated relevance and made temporarily accessible. (1988, 101)

Usage of place names in Ada Bai varied from person to person and context
to context. It revealed different understandings and ways of using places
as markers of signification according to the gender, age, and situatedness
of the speaker.

Tigrayan place names often refer to topographical features, functions,
or the religious significance of the area: Edaga Hamus (Thursday Market),
Hager Salaam (Place of Peace), Adigrat (Land to the Left), and Endaselassie (Place of the Trinity) are all names of towns in Tigray. Humera is
said to be named after the homar tree that grows in the area.

Songs celebrating the accomplishments of the TPLF often used the
images of Tigrayan mountains and rivers as everlasting symbols of Tigray:

> I am not your only vanguard.
> All the rivers and mountains are proud of you
> And are your vanguards wherever you go.

TPLF commemoration songs also commonly invoked several locations in
Tigray in rapid succession, thereby highlighting their essential unity in the
face of a common oppressor.

> Fighter, Fighter, Fighter
> [To] Muglat, Senkata, Wukro, Gokhad
> Amdo, Shire, Wukro [a second town by the same name]
> Maraya, Axum, and Adwa
> You went fast.
> After you dismissed the enemy in these areas
> [You went] to Korem and Maichew.[14]

This use of place names from throughout the region was intended to make
all Tigrayans feel included in the Struggle and to show that it had been

fought for every community in the region. For Ada Bai residents, these songs had a special significance, since the town was a microcosm of Tigrayan identities, a melting pot of people from all over the region.

Different farming areas were named after large landowners who owned them prior to the Derg or after topographical features that helped to identify them. Many of these names predated the arrival of the returnees to Ada Bai and were learned by Ada Bayans from the local population and the local government.

Taming the Wilderness

In addition to the unfamiliar city, the "wilderness" or *berekha* (በረኻ) was also an unknown space to women and was thus considered dangerous. Wilderness generally was described as the area that lay beyond the farthest houses and beyond the land that ringed Ada Bai and was used by most of the population as a latrine site, and particularly that which was out of the range of sight from the settlement. Women rarely went to the latrine area on their own, preferring to go with one or more other women. Every evening at dusk, several women could be seen squatting daintily, their skirts spread around their feet to ensure privacy, chatting away as they relieved themselves. Men could be seen several hundred yards away, equally deep in conversation but facing away from the women.

On the rare occasions that women were compelled to go to the berekha, they would never venture out alone. A woman might accompany her husband to the farmland to help weed the crops, or go with other women to gather firewood (although this was increasingly being done by men who had donkey carts to carry larger pieces of wood) or to look for a lost animal, but they mostly left such tasks to the men. Even a single woman who had her own plot of land would usually look for a man to cultivate it in exchange for a portion (usually half) of the harvest, or would hire a man to do the work for her if she had no close male kin. The berekha was thought to be a place full of snakes and other dangerous animals. These fears were well-founded: extremely poisonous snakes were abundant, and during my stay there several people died from snakebite. In addition, newspaper reports from the capital that several farms in the Humera area had been destroyed by elephants were confirmed to me by men who spent time in the berekha.[15]

In addition to snakes and wild animals, bandits or *shifta* (ሽፍታ) were widely feared. The Humera area (or Wolkait as it was known during imperial times and is still referred to today by many) was famous in Tigrayan history and legend as a refuge for murderers, thieves, and other criminals. During the imperial regime, state control over western Tigray/northern Gondar was tenuous, and shifta reportedly escaped punishment for their crimes by fleeing to the lowland areas. The Wolkait people living in the lowlands were generally discriminated against by both Amharas and Tigrayans for their presumed tendency to commit crimes; people also remarked on their extremely dark skin, Negroid features, and "kinky" hair (to distinguish themselves, people would reach for their own hair and twist it when referring to a Wolkait person, whose short hair was tightly curled).[16] Rahma, a woman who had lived in Ada Bai prior to the returnees' arrival, recalled the dangers that the area posed then:

> [Life] was very hard. People would come here at night and demand money, gold [women's jewelry]. They came often. We were three families [living in the same area]. Half of our food would go to them. Half of what we bought was for us, half was for them.
>
> If you did not have what they wanted, they would give you an appointment and if you did not give them [what they had demanded] when they came back they took young animals, or if you had some gold they took it. They were Wolkait people.
>
> Before the returnees came, there were six families [living in Ada Bai]. Now we feel safer. [Even now, however] when some go out for harvesting, Wolkait people come and demand that they be fed. But even though they would steal your property, they would never rape the women. Those who stood up to them were beaten [but it was the] men only.

None of the stories told by Ada Bai residents of the potential dangers posed by Wolkait people acknowledged that the highland settlers were living on land that had traditionally belonged to, and been used by, the Wolkait. Highlanders tended to trace the ancestry of the Wolkait to black Sudanese people, or to migrants from Nigeria who had settled in the area, whom they were considered to closely resemble. This line of reasoning denied the Wolkait their legitimate claim to the land by casting them as foreigners, as non-Ethiopians.

Occasionally, cars and trucks traveling from Ada Bai eastwards to the Tekezze River were attacked by shifta looking to rob the driver and passengers, and occasionally the truck's cargo as well. Yohannes, a trader from Ada Bai whom I had interviewed often, returned from a journey to central Tigray one day and told me that the truck he had been sitting atop had been ambushed. The man sitting next to him had been shot in the shoulder and bled to death before the truck arrived in Ada Bai, the closest clinic. The man had had to be buried in Ada Bai. The story spread through the village like a grass fire. Although these occurrences were not frequent enough to discourage people from traveling by road, they did help to perpetuate people's fear of the berekha and the shifta whom, they believed, lurked therein. I often heard of trucks and buses being attacked along this road as well as the main road between Humera and Gondar. These vehicles were thought to be better targets than faster-moving Land Rovers and Land Cruisers. Even these vehicles often traveled in convoys, and left early in the morning, in the less-than-scientific assumption that bandits usually struck after midday.

Emplacement through Practice

Men's sense of the berekha reflected their familiarity with it. Rather than being an unknown space, they were able to differentiate between the parts of the landscape based on their more intimate and frequent use of it than women's. Men's closer ties to the land outside the village were based in their role as farmers. One of the main reasons that those who came to Ada Bai chose to do so was to obtain access to farmland, or *mereyt* (መሬት). Years of TPLF propagandizing had convinced people that community ownership would guarantee them access to land, and would thus help to prevent them from having to become refugees again.

Because the decision to repatriate refugees from Sudan was made without ample time for preparation, and returnees arrived as the planting season was beginning, the local authorities were unable to identify and allocate sufficient farmland to every head of household. The woreda administration, which was responsible for identifying parcels of land that the baito council would then allocate to individual households, was still trying to sort out land entitlements and claims for the restoration of farmland that were being lodged by the landholders who had been run off their farms by the Derg. In the absence of a national or regional land use policy, the woreda used the Investment Codes of Ethiopia and Tigray.[17] Officials were unable to identify large tracts of unclaimed land close to Ada Bai, and had no resources to compensate landholders so that they could allocate their land to the returnees.

It was very difficult, well-nigh impossible, to determine who should receive a piece of this limited land when all were in need and all were demanding it. The baito faced the choice of either allocating smaller plots to more people or targeting those who were most in need of farmland, giving full allocations to fewer people. It chose to do both. Some households were allocated smaller plots than they were entitled to. In addition, selection criteria were devised to identify the people who were most in need of land. The evolution of this set of criteria gave rise to what I call a "new code of good citizenship" whereby people mapped themselves into their new community by behaving in strategic manners to maximize their chances of being allocated land.

In the Tigrayan highlands, access to land, whether by residence (*diessa*, ዴስአ) or inheritance (*risti*, ርስቲ), or temporary use by arrangement with the owner of the land (*chiguraf-gotet*, ኺጉራፉ ጎተት) defined farmers as members of a particular community. Writing on the relationship between land tenure and community identity in highland Eritrea, where risti was practiced, Kibreab says:

> Land was perceived as serving as a lineage dating back many centuries which nurtured links with the past and the future. Persons without land were viewed as lacking roots, lineage, or heritage. That was the rationale of prohibiting permanent alienation of land. (1996, 159–60)

Likewise, land under the diessa system tied people to a particular community not only through the individual plots allocated to all residents but through communal adjudication of common resources such as grazing land, water sources, and fuel lots (Kibreab 1996a, 159; Bruce 1976; Bauer 1985 [1977]). The removal of these rights amounted to an annulment of one of the principal features by which the individual identified him or herself as a member of the community. Loss of land meant displacement from the physical environment inhabited by the community. Lacking this tie to his or her community of origin following repatriation, the returnee was faced with carving out a new identity in a new community through obtaining access to land. Positioning oneself to be recognized by community leaders in order to receive land was thus a deliberate act of emplacement in the returnee settlement.[18]

The Ada Bai baito chairman told me that 593 households did not receive any land in the first year following repatriation. In distributing land, able-bodied men who could clear and farm the land themselves had been favored; this left female household heads, the elderly, and the disabled, all of whom would have rented out or arranged to have a sharecropper work their plots, at a disadvantage.

Much of the land allocated to Ada Bai households during the first year was at a place called Endadutch, located fifty kilometers from Ada Bai on the Sudan border. It was said by some Ada Bayans that this land had been tilled by Sudanese squatters during the war, and that the government had wanted to reassert its claim to the area by having returnees farm there.[19]

The land, however, was simply too far away from Ada Bai for most returnees. To get there, they had to spend an entire day walking or pay for a three-hour tractor ride, which most could not afford. They then had to sleep in abandoned army and state farm barracks for a week while they plowed, planted, weeded, or harvested. The few who farmed their plots at Endadutch claimed that their harvests had failed because the fields had become waterlogged and birds had eaten the sorghum seeds from the stalks. In highland Tigray, where the fields were located closer to the homesteads, sons were regularly sent to keep watch over the fields with slingshots and whips to crack in the air to scare the birds away. Such maintenance was not possible with plots being so distant from the settlement.

There was also an area of land allocated to Ada Bai farmers closer to the settlement. In the first year, people complained that the land was not cleared, and that they would be unable to clear it in time for planting. "It is like a forest, it is berekha," my closest neighbor, Hagos, said to me. "We are afraid to go there even during the day." He was referring to the perceived danger of marauding bands of shifta. He said that in order to clear it, the men would have to go together in groups, but even then it would take two months to clear the trees from each plot, and three to four months to clear the roots. No one seemed to think that the benefit of being able to keep the wood that they cut, either for building, burning, or charcoal production for sale, was significant enough to make it worth their while to clear the plots, perhaps because the approaching rainy season did not leave enough time to make charcoal from all of the wood.

Whereas women tended to see all land outside the village as berekha, men made a distinction between berekha and mereyt, as is made clear in Hagos's statement. Land that was suitable for farming (mereyt) was land that had been cleared and prepared for plowing and planting. This also made it safe, as the farmer had gained control over it. Because most plots were grouped together, farming was a social act as well, one that bound the man into a community of farmers. Women did recognize their own household's mereyt as part of the safe landscape (even if it was surrounded by dangerous berekha), however, particularly if they had helped with the weeding or other farmwork.

Men "made safe" and cultivated not only places that were allocated to them, they also appropriated land on their own. Many of those who did not receive land in the first allocation went out into the berekha and found empty plots for themselves. Though this was illegal and the land was subject to seizure at any time, they plowed these patches of land with their donkeys, sowed seeds, and brought home what was in many cases a substantial harvest. Often the land was situated close to the Rawayan River, at the edge of Ada Bai's settled area, or near another river farther away. While some people farmed in groups, those who were not able to do so chose to farm on their own, thereby single-handedly taming the wilderness.

Place Names in Tigrinya

In addition to the separation of the environment into safe places and dangerous spaces, Ada Bai residents, like all Tigrinya speakers, disaggregated place further depending on their relationship to it. The Tigrinya language has many different terms to refer to senses of place. *Bota* (በታ) refers to a generic place to which a person does not have an explicit relationship, and is defined by Leslau (1976) as space. One's country—either the nation from which one came or the general area in which one was born—is referred to as *hager* (ሀገር). When used to refer to the specific place in which a person was born, the term *hager seb* (ሀገር ሰብ)—meaning "place of my people"—is used. *Addi* (ኣዲ) meaning land, but usually referring to one's own farmland, is also used, although farmland is also known as *hirsha* or, as we have seen, *mareyt* (መሬት). When people spoke of wanting to be buried in their birthplace, they used the terms *hager seb* and *addi*. These were considered more personalized terms than *woreda* or *tabia*, which were more anonymous administrative terms to refer to physical locations and areas.

Thus, to ask Tigrayans about the processes of homecoming, or home-making, is difficult. The physical house that one lives in is a geza, but one need not feel the kind of attachment that the English term home implies. In patrilineal, patrilateral highland Tigray, men often live in the same village for their entire lives, and women live in the village of their parents until their marriage, when they go to live with their husbands in their village (often quite close to their own birthplace). Home is thus consistent with the idea of hager seb, the place of one's people. In the context of migration and return, however, hager seb may refer to a place that the returnee has not seen for years, if at all, and may be a place that he or she will never see again. The sense of attachment that one feels to the place of one's people over time becomes secondary to a sense of attachment to a new place. Just how long that transformation takes is a question I will return to later.

By discussing the different uses of space in Ada Bai, I hope to illustrate how emplacement is an ever-changing set of practices employed in various ways by people at different times to create a more or less coherent social landscape. In this sense, landscape and place are never inert or unchanging (Bender 1995, 3).

Most of the practices outlined in this chapter were more visible during the first part of my field research, when necessity dictated that returnees quickly construct at least a provisional sense of the place, and when returnees' attention was overwhelmingly focused on ensuring that their most basic needs were met. Deliberate manipulations of space, taming the wilderness, helped them to feel more comfortable, and less threatened, by their surroundings, and more able to meet the challenges of feeding their children, curing their illnesses, and ultimately building their community. Later on, as basic needs were more easily met and people came to "know the place," other kinds of attachments developed between Ada Bai and its residents. As I have returned to Ada Bai in subsequent years, the physical and social landscapes have continued to change, as have the meanings that people have associated with certain places.

4

The Household Food Economy

uring the early months of 1994, I heard the following adage nearly everywhere I turned in Ada Bai:

Izzih addi hamaque iyu: mai yellen, ihili yellen, mereyt yellen.
እዚ አዲ ሀማቅ እዩ፤ ማይ የለን፤ እኽሊ የለን፤ መሬት የለን፤
This is a bad land: there is no water, there is no grain, there is no land.

I could not argue. The borehole pump that provided the only clean water to the settlement had been broken for six weeks and there was a severe water shortage. The first harvest had been a near total failure for the few people who had been allocated land, and the nine-month ration of grain that everyone had received when they first arrived in Ada Bai had been eaten or sold long ago. I heard this complaint so often partly because some people thought that I could do something for them, that I had connections to officials in the Ethiopian government or the United Nations and could bring them help. I had seen enough people with nothing in their houses, however, to know that they were not drastically overstating their case.

More than a list of things they did not have, the expression was a statement of their feelings that the place had failed to provide the most basic and essential ingredients for life, that it was inadequate as a home. Water, food, and land, both in Ada Bai and in the highlands, were their principal needs and the focus of much of their attention. Communities in the highlands were originally established in places where these three elements were available. In complaining about the inadequacies of Ada Bai in these terms, returnees were saying much more about their attitudes toward having been settled there, and about the essential components for a "good place," than they were about the shortages themselves.

During that period of food and water scarcity, several incidents demonstrated to me the level of desperation of Ada Bai residents. One morning, a single woman came to my house with her three young children to ask not for injera or money, as she had sometimes done in the past, but for a ride to Humera where she could find more people to beg from. She said there was no food in Ada Bai, so people did not have enough to give to her and her children. A few days later I saw her back in Ada Bai and asked her how her luck had been in Humera. She said it had been good, and that she was planning to spend a few days a week there in order to get what she needed for her children.

Another day, I went to eat with Tibbletz and Ambachew only to find a change in plans. I often contributed food to their household and we ate together, sitting outside in the cool evening air drinking coffee and trading stories and jokes. On a typical evening, three or four neighbors would stop by to chat with us. That night, rather than eat outside the house where we normally did, Tibbletz beckoned me to come inside and wait for the other visitors, who were mingling outside in the compound, to leave before we ate. "We don't have enough to feed everyone who comes here," she explained. "It is better to eat where they cannot see us so that they will not ask for any."

Rules concerning the treatment of guests dictated that anyone who came into the house when the family was eating should be invited to sit down and eat. Even when feeding the guest meant that the family would not have enough to eat, the invitation was offered. During times when food was not in particularly short supply, the visitor who was offered food (unless he or she was a family member or close kin) was expected to first decline the offer to share the meal. This gave the hosts the opportunity to save their food. If the host insisted that the guest share the meal, then it was considered rude for the guest not to eat something.

When food scarcity set in, rather than abandon the custom of inviting visitors to eat with them, households found other ways to avoid the oblig-ation of issuing an invitation and feeding the guest. Often, the woman serving the meal would serve her guests small portions, but would leave as much food as she could (without appearing to be stingy or rude) in the pot for the family to eat after the guest had left. An old priest known for speaking the truth regardless of its social propriety once advised me, "If you are eating meat you must eat the bones first because the smell of the meat is sure to bring a guest, and when he comes you will tell him, 'Oh, you have come too late: we have finished the bones.'" Then, presumably, one could get away with giving the guest only injera and meat broth. This was, however, a reversal of normal eating habits, in which the sauce was usually eaten first and the bones eaten afterward. The priest's words prompted another man who was sitting with us to tell a parable:

> One man regularly came to a house at mealtime. One time he came as [the family that lived in the house] were washing their hands to prepare to eat. When they saw him they hid the pot and said, "Oh, you have come too late. We have just finished eating. When he had left they brought out the pot and ate, but the man had suspected that they were tricking him so he hid outside and when he saw them start to eat he came back and said, "Why did you deceive me?" expecting that they should still feed him.

These examples of manipulations of the rules of etiquette were instances of innovation born from conditions of scarcity. Unlike other descriptions of creativity (Turner 1969 and 1974; R. Rosaldo 1989; Lavie, Narayan, and Rosaldo 1993), cultural creativity and innovation in Ada Bai were undertaken with a great deal of reluctance and with a view toward changing the social order as little as possible to meet the perceived demands of life in the new environment. Rather than changing or suspending the rule itself—in this case, refraining from offering food to a visitor—the individuals concerned tried to manipulate the situation so that the circumstances, which would typically call for the invitation, did not materialize. Such practices, which might have seemed of minor importance, helped people to maintain their social system in the face of such threats as hunger, disease, or crop failure. This was part of their attempt to preserve their cultural practices and principles of sociability in the face of threatening circumstances.

In Ada Bai the principles of neighborliness, and thus of community formation, began with the household. So, too, strategies of innovation or adherence to cultural practice could be seen most readily at the household level. In this chapter, I examine the household food economy to explain how households were able to survive in the face of extremely scarce resources and in an environment that was not yet well known to them. They did this through diversified attempts to obtain access to food and cash and varied consumption patterns, but also through complex patterns of mutual assistance that involved kin, neighbors, friends, and wider units of social organization.

Economic Practice as Emplacement

Household economic activities were among the most important set of strategies that returnees employed in the process of emplacing themselves within their new environment. Through agricultural production, wage labor, buying and selling, and interacting with one another, the people of Ada Bai forged community networks that helped root them to the new place. As this chapter shows, activities aimed at maximizing the economic well-being of the household resulted in the recoding of social relationships, the creative use of household labor, and the efficient use of resources available within the new environment. Over time, these practices became more and more effective, gradually building household and community-level food security and laying the groundwork for a viable future in the new place.

Emplacement in this sense involved more than a mere collection of "survival strategies" or "coping mechanisms." Such terms tend to imply that the family's principal objective is to survive; the terms are commonly used in food security analysis to refer to the resilience of a community in meeting its basic subsistence needs. Returnees' primary goal during the first year after repatriation was basic subsistence, as it had been in the period leading up to their flight from Tigray a decade earlier. As they became successful at "knowing the place," they were better able to look beyond bare survival toward the accumulation of assets that would provide not only a safety net but a comfortable position from which to look toward the future. The techniques employed by the people of Ada Bai after the first year in their new place can more properly be thought of as "resource maximization strategies" whereby people tried to reap the most possible from their efforts. To do this, they drew from the natural environment, their proximity to labor markets in Sudan and trading ties with Eritrea and Sudan, the social capital existing within Ada Bai, their political position as returnees, and other opportunities.

The Highland Economy

To appreciate the distinctiveness of the lowland economy of Ada Bai, it is essential to discuss the differences between it and the highland economy:

> To a peasantry living in acute destitution and imminent danger, survival considerations are always paramount, and every peasant learns the techniques of survival as part of his/her everyday experience. These techniques may be crude or ingenious depending on the frequency of disasters experienced by the peasantry, the perceptions of the people and the stock of accumulated knowledge having to do with the production and survival, the resources (natural and social) of the community, and the social relations and communal values existing at a given time. (Rahmato 1991, 163)

The Tigrayan highland economy was oriented toward basic subsistence. Rural households were concerned with eking a living out of an environment filled with obstacles that minimized agricultural production, hampered trade, and offered few opportunities for employment. The economy was diversified out of necessity, and limited in its potential.

My own experience with the highland economy in Tigray is based on several periods of fieldwork carried out between 1993 and 2002. From July to November 1993, I evaluated a soil and water conservation project in the rural areas of Agame awraja, in northeastern Tigray for the Adigrat Diocesan Development Action (ADDA), an NGO run by the Ethiopian Catholic Church.[1] I also spent three weeks in the Tigrayan highlands during November 1999 participating in the annual preharvest crop assessment conducted by the government and the international community, and worked in the northern Amhara highlands (which are socioeconomically very similar to Tigray) extensively between 1995 and 2002 as a consultant for NGOs, the United Nations, and the United States Agency for International Development.

The time I spent in Agame coincided with the 1993 post-*kiremti* harvest season.[2] This was a particularly poor harvest, the rains having failed toward the end of the growing season. The barley, the main crop in that highland area, had dried prematurely and could only be used for animal fodder. Household cash supplies were extremely short and people were already beginning to predict that they would need relief food within a few months. They were relying more heavily on off-farm income, such as fuelwood sales, food or cash for work schemes (run by the government to provide employment to vulnerable people in exchange for public works construction), and employment in the towns, than they would have if the harvests had not failed.[3]

Markets in Agame were extremely sparse, occurring weekly in the larger towns. I slept in villagers' houses while I carried out this work, and often in the evening friends and kin who were on their way to or from a market would arrive to sleep. They often brought news from the market and sometimes purchases that had been ordered by the household. Holt and Lawrence (1993), citing Nägeli's study from North Gondar, say that peasants would walk up to three days each way over steep mountains to get to the market. Such treks, I observed, were made only once or, on rare occasions, twice a month. Those who lived closer to the market might go every week.

At the time of the Derg's seizure of power in Addis Ababa, there were only two extensive ethnographies of Tigray, neither of which was widely published. The first was John Bruce's dissertation, "Land Reform Planning and Indigenous Communal Tenures: A Case Study of the Tenure 'Chiguraf-Gwoses' in Tigray, Ethiopia" (1976), a legal study of land rights and institutions governing land use in northeastern Tigray. The second was Franz Bauer's *Household and Society in Ethiopia* (1977),[4] carried out in Tembien, central Tigray, which examined the household as a unit and its life-cycle from formation to dissolution. Both studies were conducted during the last days of the imperial regime. Extensive field research in Tigray was not possible during the civil war; the government restricted the movement of people, particularly foreigners, throughout the country and forbade most research in the areas where conflict was ongoing. Several studies were carried out during the Derg's rule in the highland areas farther to the south that were not directly affected by fighting (Hareide 1991; Rahmato 1991; H. Pankhurst 1992; Pausewang et al. 1990). Research done in areas to which people had been resettled also helps to provide a picture of highland economics as settlers were interviewed about the conditions in their areas of origin (Clay and Holcomb 1986; Clay, Steingraber, and Niggli 1988; A. Pankhurst 1989). Since the Ethiopian People's Revolutionary Democratic Front (EPRDF) came to power, clearance for research has been easier to obtain and more studies of the Ethiopian rural highland economy have been published (Webb and von Braun 1994; Holt and Lawrence 1993). These studies point out that most of the highlands were food deficit throughout the 1980s and early 1990s, that the few surplus-producing areas did not usually send their surplus to the nearest deficit areas, and that peasants relied on a wide variety of practices to meet their household food and cash needs. Holt and Lawrence estimate that in 1993 an average highland household of 4.2 people required 9.9 quintals (990 kg) per year to meet its minimum subsistence and planting requirements (one quintal being set aside for seed), a figure they say is in general agreement with peasants' own estimations that they needed 10.2 quintals (1,020 kg) per household per year.[5] As noted by the Relief Society of Tigray:

> Average yield/hectare [in the highlands] is around 5 quintals, and is so minimal that it cannot support a family for the whole year; a family of six members can feed for 6 months at the rate of 500 g per day per head. This means that the farmers have to find other means of income for the remaining 6 months . . . This will include off-farm employment, seasonal migration to surplus-producing areas, petty trade, etc. (REST 1993, quoted in Holt and Lawrence 1993)

In addition, food aid became a regular staple of the household food economy. Holt and Lawrence's study found that 99 percent of the households in forty-nine villages they surveyed in central, southern, and eastern Tigray had received food aid from 1988 to 1992. Sixty-one percent of the sampled population had received grain rations amounting to an average of two quintals per household.

While there is no doubt that this assistance was needed, and that in some years (for the purposes of this study, particularly 1989, 1991, and 1994) the provision of food aid probably helped to avert widespread migration and starvation, the repeated provision of food aid created a sense of dependency in many parts of Tigray as well as in other parts of Ethiopia. In an attempt to curb dependency, the Transitional Government of Ethiopia in 1993 issued a National Policy for Disaster Prevention, Preparedness, and Management that stipulated that 80 percent of food distributed should be on a food-for-work basis. Only those unable to work (the elderly, disabled, children, and those too weak to exert themselves physically) would be eligible for free food rations. Community work projects typically consisted of such projects as hillside terracing, water resource development, and feeder road construction and maintenance. Although this model was difficult to implement in many parts of Ethiopia, in Tigray it was largely successful, at least in part because the TPLF was involved in community work mobilization during the war and campaigned in local areas against dependency.

Coping Mechanisms as Essential Features of the Highland Economy

Webb and von Braun (1994) have argued that the coping strategies of Ethiopian highland households fall into three categories, employed more or less successively as the conditions of economic insecurity worsen. First, peasants embark on risk minimization, ensuring against risk "in an environment of limited credit and insurance markets" by focusing their efforts on "savings, investment, accumulation, [and] diversification" (1994, 56). Second, highland households become involved in risk absorption, characterized by "drawing down of investments, calling in loans, searching for new credit," and restricting consumption of food and nonfood items. At this stage, Webb and von Braun say, "the number and variety of potential income sources available bec[a]me crucial to survival" (Webb and von Braun, 56). Finally, when "normal systems of survival" collapsed, peasants resort to extraordinary means to survive. They eat famine foods (roots, wild plants, wild animals); sell their remaining assets, many of which are necessary to maintain their productive base (oxen, plows, farm equipment); send members of the household to look for work or welfare from kin or in towns, and finally migrate from their homesteads or reduce daily activities so as to conserve energy (Webb and von Braun, 56).

My own experience suggests that the availability of credit and insurance opportunities may not have been as great as Webb and von Braun suggest. Except where aid agencies provided agricultural or small enterprise credit, interhousehold credit was extremely limited, and in times of hardship became even more so. Rahmato notes:

> There is reason to believe that rural money-lending dries up in times of serious food shortages, as the risks of lending are very high—borrowers might die of starvation, or permanently migrate elsewhere—and the credit worthiness of peasant borrowers falls sharply owing to their distressful conditions. (1991, 164)

Because of the absence of credit opportunities (particularly so where the war was being fought and local administrative structures were either weak or nonexistent), regular access to cash through market activity or employment was even more important than Webb and von Braun indicate.

Webb and von Braun's analysis may be more useful as a conceptual framework for understanding categories of coping mechanisms than as a step-by-step description of the measures people took to keep hunger at bay. Informants who explained to me what they had done to minimize risk in the months leading up to their migration from Tigray said they employed several practices at once, often from more than one of the categories Webb and von Braun identify. In addition, many of the practices that these authors attributed to risk taking (eating famine foods, for example) I would associate with earlier stages of insecurity. For instance, Agame residents typically relied on eating *beles* (በለስ), or prickly pear, for two months prior to the harvest, even in years of relatively good harvest. Nicknamed by locals "the poor man's breakfast," beles was considered a famine food but was also part of the regular household economy, and was figured into projections by households of how long they could expect their food stocks to last.

Mesfin Wolde Mariam accepts James C. Scott's idea of the "safety first" principle in explaining subsistence production, in that the farmer chooses to minimize the likelihood that disaster would strike his family rather than maximize the return on his production. He notes, however, that this principle assumes that the farmer is able to produce enough to guarantee his subsistence, an assumption that in Tigray was highly questionable (Wolde

Mariam 1984, 94; Scott 1976). Instead, the Tigrayan farmer appeared to be scrambling throughout most of the year just to attain the subsistence level.

Webb and von Braun's attempts to explain coping in the Ethiopian highlands as a form of social behavior that is continuous with other forms of "regular" action echo J. Davis's (1992) notion that responses to disastrous events are consistent with other more "comfortable" expressions of social organization. As Holt and Lawrence point out,

> Coping is the stuff of everyday life . . . Frank famine is the rare event when coping absolutely ceases to work—when customary market and employment options are overwhelmed, accessible kinfolk are in no position to help, and people are driven to try to sell the oxen and other capital on which their productive life depends. (6)

To a certain extent, Tigrayan coping strategies in the face of disaster had already been incorporated into the corpus of social practice through years of battling with chronic poverty, drought, and food shortage. However, where chronic malnutrition is the "normal" state of affairs, there is a sense in which the population is living through a long, drawn-out kind of vulnerability that becomes a low-grade, constant famine.

Dessalegn Rahmato's analysis of survival strategies in Ambassel awraja, North Wollo, is apt for the Tigrayan highlands as well: "It is tragic but true that the two major elements that are essential to the well-being of the peasant mode of production, namely political and social stability on the one hand, and environmental constancy on the other, have often eluded the peasantry of the region" (1991, 164). Rahmato groups the "elements of indigenous famine survival" into four "sequential series of activities": austerity and reduced consumption; temporary migration; divestment of assets and crisis migration (which includes mass migration, mass death, and wide-scale dislocation of communities). Rahmato's description of each of these processes emphasizes cultural conservatism. In the austerity and reduced consumption phase, gender roles within the household are preserved: "Women are entrusted with the management of all immediately consumable food resources, men are responsible for managing other assets of the family and for entering into reciprocal arrangements with other families for purposes of mutual support and exchange" (1991, 165). As the crisis unfolds, the woman's role is enhanced because the household's main activity is to obtain and responsibly allocate food. Throughout the ordeal, the objective is similar to the Sudanese of Darfur in de Waal's analysis: "Their central aim during the famine was to preserve the base of their livelihood, so that they could return to a normal or acceptable way of life after the famine" (1989, 141).

During the divestment and asset disposal phase, households chose which assets to liquidate on the basis of which were most expendable and would hamper postfamine recovery the least. When migration did occur, it was often to areas nearby (even within the famine-affected area), rather than to far-off places where the chances that the household would lose its land and property rights in the home area were greater (de Waal 1989, 172–73).

Coping Strategies in the Lowlands

If, as I have argued, the process of emplacement was carried out in Ada Bai through the myriad forms of everyday practice, then the economics of the household unit should show many of the ways in which the physical environment was used to create the building blocks of community. The foundation of such a construction was the household. I have also argued that the overriding concern of all households in Ada Bai was their own economic survival. In this sense, I think they were not very different from those who remained in the highlands, or probably from those facing chronic famine in Sudan, Bangladesh, or North Korea. Food insecurity has a way of becoming an obsession for those whose experience of it is chronic. Strategies to establish linkages with other households, particularly nonkin, or collectivized institutions were often based at least in part on determinations of the potential economic benefits that the individual household might achieve through them. Even where such maximizing strategies were not in play, the consideration of whether the household could afford to participate in other forms of social organization was always in the minds of the actors.

This may seem like an overly materialistic reading of Tigrayan society. I do not mean to say that all household decisions in Ada Bai were based on economic maximization (or risk minimization), but, as Holt and Lawrence state:

> The premise . . . is that the law of demand and supply operates in the rural
> Ethiopian context, that farmers respond rationally to perceived ways of
> securing and maximising income, and that their first priority is access to
> food. No social custom interferes significantly with this process, and the
> morality which underpins sharing between families, as well as support for
> the destitute within the community, may also be seen as an insurance
> policy against misfortune for any family. A family's economic ties may well

extend further than the immediate village, especially in the seasonal movement of farm labour to better-favoured areas, and in the husbandry in the lowlands of livestock borrowed or contracted from highlanders. The elements of the food economy are simple relative to more urbanised and industrialised countries: complexity lies in the way in which people negotiate opportunities at the margin in a context of overall poverty. (6)

The fact that Ada Bai residents' daily lives were primarily dedicated to avoiding the clutches of starvation meant that social relations, and thus community construction, were rooted in these practices. The household food economy was the locus for social formation just as it was the foundation of survival.

The Household Food Economy in Ada Bai

Self-sufficiency, the ability of the household to attain enough food to eat and adequate cash to meet its basic needs on a regular basis, was the primary goal of returnees in Ada Bai during the first two years following repatriation. It was also a preoccupation of assistance providers and development agents working in chronically food-insecure areas of Tigray and other parts of Ethiopia. Most of these agencies, however, did not work in the lowlands because it was assumed that returnees could easily become self-sufficient through farming and wage labor, Yet the question of what self-sufficiency consisted of in the returnee settlements, as in the lowlands in general, was not well understood. Although there was a great deal of information about the cost of living in the highlands, based on household and food economy analysis (Holt and Lawrence 1993; Webb and von Braun 1994), as well as data from other sources, no such information existed for the lowland areas. Thus, estimations of how much food and cash was required to support a household, and where these assets came from if not from aid, were based on rough guestimation. Even less clear were the means by which households interacted with one another, though exchange of cash, food, labor, and other forms of mutual assistance, in their efforts meet their own basic needs. With such a shortage of accurate information, government and aid agencies could argue that that their assistance was not needed. Without this information, however, it was impossible to monitor returnees' progress in achieving self-sufficiency and economic integration.

In the language of emplacement theory, not knowing the details of what people were doing to make ends meet obscured the ways in which the geographic and social landscape gained meaning through economic practice. Examination of returnees' livelihood strategies provides crucial insight into the nature of emplacement, and helps to ground this theoretical tool. Emplacement in Ada Bai is not merely the creation of affective ties to a place; it is a central organizing principle on which life (in all its manifestations) in a new place becomes possible. Understanding the economic opportunities and constraints of households shows how the environment was rendered usable. The degree of success that returnees achieved in meeting their basic needs is to a large extent a measure of their abilities to emplace themselves in their new home.

Using Household Economy Analysis to Track Integration

Although I had been in Ada Bai for a year, I realized that I still had little idea of the basic requirements a household needed to survive in the settlement. I therefore devoted four months to studying the particular food economy of ten households, tracking resource in- and outflows as well as daily food consumption habits. The study followed Ethiopian calendar dates, beginning on 1 Hidar 1987 (mid-November 1994), when the sorghum harvest was beginning, and finished on 30 Lekatit 1987 (mid-March 1995), in the middle of the hungry season.

My goal was not so much to gather quantitative, statistically significant data as it was to understand the kinds of decisions that the household made in the course of "making ends meet." When did people decide to sell off their food stocks or animals? At what point and how did people borrow from each other, and how were debts repaid? How did households change their spending and consumption practices from one season to the next? Did these levels change dramatically in response to fluctuations in income levels? By gathering household economic data from a small group of people, I expected to be able to track the data more closely and to supplement the household survey information with more in-depth discussions with the respondents about the choices they had made. Although I had a research assistant who went to all of the households every day, I attended at least three of the interviews each day myself, rotating between the households and spending up to an hour in each house discussing other issues with the respondents.

Each of the ten households included in the survey was well known to me before the study, either because they were in the same neighborhood or because I had done a significant favor for them in the past, such as bringing a sick family member to the hospital in Humera during the middle of the night. However, none had ever received any financial assistance from me.

In selecting the respondent households I attempted to represent the economic and social diversity of the community. Two of the households were female headed (one with a man who came and went periodically but did not share most resources with his wife, as he had remarried and spent most of his time with his new wife). Two were Muslim; eight were Orthodox Christian (including one headed by a priest). Nine households had farmland that was either allocated to them or rented from another landholder (in exchange for half the harvest). Two had regular supplementary income from a skilled trade (one was a tailor and one was a weaver). The average household size was five people. Table 2 provides a demographic profile of the ten households.

Based on my knowledge of the households before the start of this study, I hypothesized that the group could be divided into three terciles based on their relative economic strength. The terciles were not marked by dramatic differences: all were very poor and preoccupied with meeting their basic economic needs. Three of the households (HH 1, 2, 7) showed initial indications of representing the poorest stratum of the community because they had so few belongings in their houses and had a general lack of purchasing power. I predicted that four households (HH 3, 4, 5, 8) would represent the average household economic status in Ada Bai, and three would have a slightly higher economic standing in the community than

Table 2. Demographic profile of the ten sample households

HH number	Number of members	Male or female head	Religion (C = Christian; M = Muslim)	Land farmed (hectares)	Nonfarm sources of regular income*
1	5	M	C	1	None
2	3	F	C	0	None
3	5	M	C	1.5	Sell Water
4	3	M	C	2	None
5	3	M	C	1	None
6	6	M	M	1	Tailor
7	3	F	C	1	Sell Sewa
8	6	M	C	2	Sell Water
9	9	M	C	5	Orthodox Priest
10	7	M	M	2	Weaver

* Not including wages earned infrequently on commercial farms.

the others (HH 6, 9, 10) because they had more cash, livestock, or a supplemental form of income besides farming. I did not include any very wealthy households in the group, as I felt that such representation would give the impression that people were better off than they really were. At any rate, there were very few such households in Ada Bai.

Before beginning the survey, I collected baseline information from each of the households. This included such information as the age, education, and training of each household member; number of household members who were chronically ill (and thus dependent and incapable of contributing their labor to the household); estimated monthly income; assets (food, cash, animals, other property); amount of any remittances from relatives working outside the community; resources shared with other households; size of landholdings, planted crops and yields; outstanding debts; schedules for repayment; and amount and date of last receipt of food aid. This information provided some indication of the type of savings and collateral that a household could use to augment its income, as well as any anticipated extraordinary expenses that might influence decision making or resource use.

None of the households had many assets. Four (HH 1, 3, 6, 7) had no livestock at all save a few chickens (which people were reluctant to count because, they said, the chicks die very easily before they begin to lay eggs or are ready to be eaten, as well as the fact that they basically raised themselves, surviving on food scraps and greens in the neighborhood). These households also had very little property that they could sell if they needed to. The other households (HH 2, 4, 8) owned one donkey or goat with the exception of one (HH 9), which had seven sheep and two goats, and another that had two cows (HH 5), one of which was lactating.

Most of the households (except for the two that were female headed) owned at least one metal bed (valued at 200 birr each). Other durable property included metal storage boxes (100–150 birr), oil drums for holding water (150 birr), watches (100–200 birr), tape recorders (500–700 birr), radios (100–200 birr), and (in the case of a few of the women) gold jewelry (from Sudan, at 30 birr per gram). Two households (HH 5 and 8) reported at the start of the study that they had recently sold furniture or tape recorders to cover their household expenses.[6]

As might be expected, households tended to underreport their holdings at the start of the study, particularly the size of their cash and grain reserves. Such underreporting was revealed when households were forced to draw from their reserves in order to meet household expenses. Some people claimed that they had either "forgotten" to report the full amount

Weaving is a trade typically reserved for Muslim men. This man has set up his loom in the shade outside his house.

of their resources, had not realized that they had more than they initially reported, or thought that what they had was too insignificant to be worth mentioning. One woman who had underreported her grain holdings at the start of the study later said, "I consider anything less than a half a quintal (50 kg) to be insignificant. What is it? It is only enough to feed my family for a few days." Such sentiment was widespread, but after we stressed that we considered even one cupful of grain to be important and promised repeatedly not to share information about their stored assets, people were more forthcoming and detailed about their holdings, expenditures, and consumption. Indeed, our daily visits became something of an occasion, with everyone in the household contributing to the daily report on income, expenditures, and consumption. Young children would remind their mothers, "Don't forget about the sugar you bought this morning!"

During the study returnees in Ada Bai did not receive any external food aid, though oil was distributed in early April 1995 by the Relief Society of Tigray on behalf of the regional Disaster Prevention and Preparedness Bureau as part of a grain and oil relief package that had been promised the year before (the wheat was distributed in May 1994) to provide assistance to those most affected by the 1993 crop failure. The last time a month's grain ration had been distributed to the most needy prior to the study had been two months before the start of the survey.

Confidentiality and the Importance of Appearing Destitute

The returnees, no matter how great or small their resource base, went to great lengths to hide their resource holdings from both their extended relatives and their neighbors in order to discourage them from asking for loans or gifts. They also hid such information from local authorities so as not to be excluded from distribution of relief aid. Returnees commonly felt that the baito's decisions about who should receive aid were unfair and that those in need were often screened out if, for instance, they owned animals, had what local officials considered to be expendable assets, or were engaged in work that was deemed more profitable (in many cases defined as carrying more social prestige) than farming. They reasoned, much like those in the highlands who were slightly better off than the poorest of the poor, that if they did not receive food aid they would have to liquidate the few assets they had and would soon become as needy as their poorer neighbors.[7] Our assurances of confidentiality and the respondents' awareness that we were not directly associated with any aid organization—as well as the fact that my research assistant was a returnee himself who was known and trusted by the community and not linked to the political leadership—allowed us to collect data that was very likely more reliable than that which might have been obtainable by other aid workers in the area. Our credibility was also enhanced by our refusal to discuss the survey with households that were not included. Sometimes people who saw us going to the same houses every day inquired about our work or "dropped in" to the respondent houses when we were there. We would suspend the interviews in the presence of the visitors, resuming our questioning after they had left. Respondents told us later that they had appreciated the fact that we did not ask questions when others were present, and quickly realized that we did not discuss our findings with others in the community.

Administering the Survey

In most of the male-headed households, the information was initially provided by the man, but later on the woman assumed the role of chief respondent. Not only was the woman more likely to be in the house (her domain) when we came, but she also had a better idea of her household's expenditures than her husband did. In a few cases, where the man earned income from a trade, the woman was not always aware of how much he had earned; in such cases the man would provide the data. Information collected included wage earnings, money or goods obtained through sale, borrowing, and gifts, as well as all expenses (itemized), loans, and gifts given. Meals eaten the previous day were also recorded.

Once the daily recall part of the study began, people reported their incomes and expenditures with more accuracy than they had in the baseline study. Had there been serious levels of under- or overreporting of either resource in- or outflows, I would have been able to identify them in the data supplied in the questionnaire. It is likely that as people came to trust us not to share the information with others, they became more willing to reveal the full extent of their asset holdings. In addition, I continually monitored and analyzed the data throughout the study period so that I could promptly clarify questions and inconsistencies concerning the data. Most of these arose from misunderstandings about how to characterize certain transactions that did not neatly fall into one of the questionnaire categories.

The small size of the sample and the variation between household types prevented the use of most forms of statistical analysis of the data. When I aggregated statistics from the ten households as a group, my intention was merely to give the most basic indication of trends. In most cases, I treated households as independent entities. In at least one case, this may have confused the data. Toward the end of the four-month study I realized that, based on the reported expenditure and consumption habits, Household 2 might really have been considered an auxiliary part of Household 1, since the female head of HH 2 shared most of her and her children's meals with HH1. They worked together on household tasks and pooled most resources, and the former relied on the man and teenage boy in the latter household to help her and her teenage son with farming and other tasks that required heavy manual labor. This was an example of an

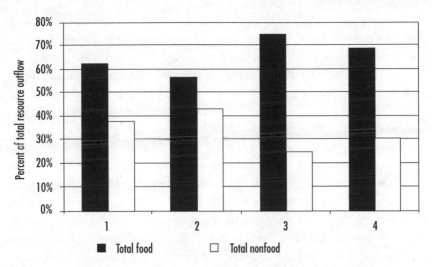

Food and nonfood expenses expressed as percent of total household resource outflows

invented kin network; although the two households were not related, having lived together in the refugee camp and then in the returnee settlement, over time they had come to think of, and refer to, one another as close kin.

Expenditure Profiles

In analyzing the data on resources flowing out of the household, I made distinctions between food and nonfood expenses, loans extended and repaid, and gifts given. Chart 3 shows the levels of food and nonfood expenses expressed as percentages of total household resource outflows over the four-month period.

Most households in the community got nearly all of their nongrain food from the market (unlike in the highlands, where households also grew lentils and vegetables, and produced butter, meat, eggs, and honey). Sorghum in most cases was the only crop grown (though some people grew corn and a few small crops in their house-plot gardens during the long rainy season: these crops were usually consumed immediately after being harvested and were not a factor in the four months studied, since it was not the rainy season). Because of this heavy reliance on the market, per person food expenditures did not change greatly from month to month unless there was an unusual event such as a celebration (HH 2 and 9 hosted funerals for extended family members) or a family member became sick and required hospitalization or other expensive treatment including special high-calorie foods (HH 3 had a sick two-year-old child who spent three weeks in the hospital with his parents caring for him before he finally died).

Food expenditures were also influenced by changes in the nonfood expenditure levels, which were subject to significant increase during harvest season. In all of the landholding households, nonfood expenditures were much higher (recorded on an individual household level at between 20 percent and 70 percent) during harvest time than later on in the year when the harvest was finished. Most of these nonfood expenditures were attributed to the costs incurred by the harvest: purchase of grain sacks, repayment of loans obtained during the growing season against a promise of repayment at harvest time, and payment of workers. Other major expenses included clothing and shoes, items for which people did not have enough money at other times of the year.

The main sources of income during the first month of the survey were occasional wage labor (paid at a set daily rate) on the large commercial farms around Ada Bai and the sale of farm products at the local market or in Humera. During the month of Hidar (month 1), the returnees' recorded rate of borrowing was extremely high, as they had to cover the costs of harvesting and repay debts incurred during the cultivation season. Expenses were limited to basic food and nonfood items. Data from the first month also suggested that income earned at harvest time was insufficient to meet the cash and food needs of the sample households. Some households reported selling expendable assets such as tape recorders, bicycles, and sewing machines in order to meet their cash needs.

Households whose nonfood expenses were very high one month tended to reduce their food expenditure levels the next month. This reduction in food expenditure levels (in most cases by consuming cheaper and less nutritious kinds of foods rather than by missing meals altogether) revealed an important strategy to recover relatively quickly from the increased cash outflow required by the harvest, a strategy that may have enabled them to reach the next harvest season without encountering serious food shortages.

Cost of Living in Ada Bai

Despite the obvious limitations of such a small sample size in producing generalizable results, I believed it was still worthwhile to examine the monthly per-capita cost of living as reported in the ten households. Table 3 shows average per person and total expenditures in the four major

Table 3. Average per person cost of living (in Ethiopian Birr)

Month	Total food purchase	Total nonfood purchase	Debt repaid	Gift given	Total resource outflow
November	31.40	28.00	7.20	1.40	68.00
December	28.80	48.80	15.80	1.00	94.40
January	20.40	10.20	13.80	1.40	45.80
February	26.40	19.80	8.80	.40	55.40
Average	26.75	26.70	11.40	1.05	65.90

categories. Special notice should be taken of the increase during months 1 and 2 (November and December) due to increased farm expenses and the cost of such items as clothing.

These totals are only crude estimates of the cost of living per person in Ada Bai. Actual per person expenditures varied widely, and were influenced, among other things, by a household's food stores before the start of the study, farming and nonfarming income-generation activities, and the amount of available cash and credit.

Income Levels

Chart 4 shows the aggregated sources of income for the ten households. I defined income as a combination of wages earned and items sold. Harvest figures were for sorghum.[8] The table shows that after the first month the level of borrowing dropped dramatically, reflecting the fact that people borrowed early in the harvest season to cover their costs. Their income then rose during and immediately after the harvest, as farm products were sold quickly to pay off the household's debts and to purchase household items that people had gone without for a long time. For the most part, people were unable to store their grain until the price rose (usually several months after the harvest season) because their creditors demanded immediate repayment.

The sharp drop in borrowing after the harvest (after month 1) may have been more a function of the dwindling availability of credit than lack of demand for it. Respondents reported that it was much easier to find people to lend them money before and during the harvest than in later months. Many lenders advanced money against the promise of a certain amount of the farmer's harvest (usually at significant advantage to the lender). Because households had to repay their debts as soon as the harvest became available, rather than wait to sell it until January or February (when prices

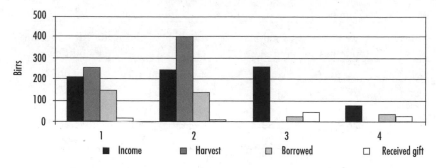

Sources of income of the ten survey households

were higher), farmers were not able to maximize the value of their production. Households that did not repay their debts promptly reported having difficulty finding people who were willing to continue to lend to them. In some cases, they were obliged to sell their high-value property as well as the grain from their harvests to cover household expenses.

There was a sharp drop in reported earned income during the last month of the survey. This was largely attributed to the lack of available wage labor in the area in the months following the harvest. Those households that had enough income or grain in the earlier months to get them through this period were able to draw on their reserves in the postharvest season. Those who did not have enough either borrowed money or sent one or more members to Sudan in search of work. It also seemed, from my informal interviews with the households, that the level of interhousehold borrowing increased, although this was not significantly reflected in the questionnaire data: such small loans were not considered to be repayable, but they were also not considered "gifts."

The slight rise in gift-giving reported during months 3 and 4 (Tiri and Lekatit—January and February) in figure 2 was attributed in large part to the holiday seasons for both Christians and Muslims. Christians celebrate Christmas (Lidet or Genna) and Epiphany (Timkat) during the month of Tiri. The month preceding the Lenten fasting season (Lekatit) was traditionally a time in which many Christian weddings were held, since people had more grain than at any other (nonfasting) time of the year.[9] Guests were obliged to bring gifts of grain or cash. For Muslims, the month of Ramadan (which fell during Lekatit that year) was a period of increased gift giving although complete fasting was observed between sunrise and sunset. In addition, all households contributed food and/or cash to the

Many returnees sell a portion of their sorghum harvest to supplement their income. Here, sorghum sold to a large trading company awaits transport to market centers.

community celebration of the anniversary of the Tigray People's Liberation Front on Lekatit 11.

Sale of Assets

Several of the households sold their assets in order to pay back loans or cover their basic expenses. Three households (HH 1, 8, 10) sold high-value property (two tape recorders valued at 350 to 500 birr [U.S.$70–100] each, a sewing machine for 2,000 birr, and a large kerosene lantern for 150 birr, respectively) to pay back their loans to the microcredit program run by the Democratic Association of Tigray Women (of 550 birr each). Another household (HH 4) also sold a tape recorder to get enough money to support itself while the husband went to Sudan to look for work.

As common as sale of assets was, the sale of grain and other farm products was more commonly practiced by the households to cover basic living expenses. Table 3 shows the size of the household harvests and the amount sold by each household in the first three months following the harvest. One household (HH 5) whose harvest was 10 quintals had sold 6.25 quintals by the end of Lekatit, and another (HH 8) with a harvest of 11 quintals sold 6.75 quintals.[10] Going into the driest part of the year, there was very little food left in these households to tide them over until the start of the rainy season, when wild plants became available. The next sorghum harvest would not be for another seven months; these households would

Table 4. Levels of harvest and grain sales (sorghum)

Household number	Grain from harvest	Grain sold, Hidar–Lekatit (Nov.–Mar.)	Stored in the house at end of Megabit (mid-April)
1	5.0	1.25	0.5
2*	0.0	—	0.5
3	9.0	1.00	5.0
4	7.0	1.25	3.25
5	10.0	6.25	3.0
6	4.0	1.00	0.3
7*	0.5	—	0.1
8	11.0	6.75	2.0
9	19.5	1.75	8.0
10	8.0	1.00	2.5

* These households bought sorghum from the market (on cash or credit) or were given food by neighbors because they had no significant harvest.

exhaust their food stocks two to three months before the harvest was ready. They would need to find wage labor or nonfarm income to get through the year.

As shown in table 4, every household that had a harvest of more than one quintal sold grain to meet its expenses. Those interviewed said they thought that ideally their harvest should yield twice as much as their basic food requirements for the year (which they estimated at 2.5 quintals per person), slightly more than that estimated by highland farmers in the Holt/Lawrence study previously referred to [1993]) so that they could sell enough grain to cover their cash requirements, thereby becoming self-sufficient by working on their own farms. This harvest would have made all other forms of income generation unnecessary. Such large harvests, however, were probably not realistic given existing land tenure arrangements, grain prices, and investment costs in the area. In most households there would always be a need to seek wage labor or to supplement income with nonfarm work. Six of the households surveyed reported that one or more of their members had worked as daily laborers on the nearby commercial farms; those who had supplementary income did not engage in such labor. Nevertheless, people said that they put their efforts first into their own fields and later into wage labor and other forms of economic diversification.

Throughout the four-month period, households were slipping into greater indebtedness. However, they were able to maintain at least some measure of control over their increasing destitution. In the months following the harvest, they limited the degree to which they borrowed, severely limited their spending, and resorted to eating less nutritious foods. These changes in household resource management strategies helped to carry them over into the next agricultural and farm labor season when there would be renewed opportunities for income generation.

Community Credit: A Hard-to-Find Commodity

Limited access to credit and limited conditions for successful investment were among the biggest constraints to economic security in Ada Bai. Farmers who were unable to invest adequately in their farms and businesses could not gain reliable and sufficient returns on the small investments that they made. Lack of access to credit was, in turn, both a direct and indirect result of limited emplacement within the new social landscape. Credit sources could be divided into two groups: those from inside and those from outside the community.

Credit within the community was extremely limited because nearly all households were heavily involved in "getting to know the place." Those who might otherwise have enough assets to be able to lend to their neighbors and relatives were preoccupied with their own investment in new houses, businesses, and land, and thus did not have adequate reserves to be able to extend credit.

Limited credit was sometimes available from traders and other businesspeople to those who knew them well. A few professional moneylenders offered loans at high rates of interest. The interest rate (*harratsa*) was 10 percent, but many people also borrowed by pledging to give part of their crop (sesame or sorghum) to the lenders at harvest time. In this way, lenders were able to buy grain at extremely low prices immediately after the harvest and make large profits by selling it several months later. Most borrowing from moneylenders was done secretly since they were not authorized by the government to charge interest.

Local people turned to the town's shopkeepers for credit on purchased merchandise and cash loans more than they relied on professional moneylenders. In most cases, the shopkeepers did not charge interest. People selected shopkeepers whom they knew well, usually those who had come from the same part of Tigray and lived in the same neighborhood in Ada Bai. The traders lent money as a personal service, to the extent that they sometimes even brought economic hardship on themselves.

Patterns of loan repayment to private individuals and shopkeepers within the community followed an "ability to pay" trend. Debtors repaid loans when they had enough money to spare. They were under no financial obligation to repay promptly, though some did so in order to maintain friendly relations with the lender or to ensure that they would be able to borrow from the same person in the future. Shopkeepers rarely insisted on immediate repayment, especially if they knew the debtor well and saw that he or she was experiencing financial difficulty. One shopkeeper who recorded all of the money that was owed to him told me that in the three-month period from Tahsas to Lekatit (mid December to mid March), he extended credit and cash worth 4,115 birr (approximately U.S.$800). Of that, only 1,757 birr had been repaid within that period. Another shopkeeper said that between the months of Meskerem and Lekatit (mid September to mid March 1994) he had loaned 4,326 birr; only 1,968 birr had been repaid at the end of the period. He described the situation in this way:

> I feel upset that I lend too much. Some people owe me from two years ago. But some people can't pay and I can't ask them to pay. We were together for eight years [in Sudan]. If they have some problem, I am not going to force them to pay . . . This year [1994] is better than last year. Most people are repaying their loans. Last year hardly anyone paid me back. I went to their houses and I found nothing [of value to be sold or exchanged in order to repay the debts]. So I canceled all the debts and started over.

Indeed, the most successful traders were expected to lend money and if they did not people were reluctant to frequent their business as much as others who did extend credit. Although it is not clear that the loss of customers purchasing on credit resulted in lower profits, shopkeepers said that they did not want to lose even this business, perhaps because they anticipated that over time the purchasing power of these customers would increase and they would eventually become paying customers.

Loans from Outside the Community

Shopkeepers who had to absorb the losses often looked to larger lenders to keep their businesses going. In 1994, there were at least five external sources of credit.

First, limited loans were made available to farmers by the regional government, with the baito acting as disbursement and collection agent.

These loans were intended for seeds and tractor plowing, though there was no mechanism for monitoring or controlling what people actually spent the money on. Many farmers said they used the money to make their own farming arrangements (such as renting farmland and hiring traction animals). Farmers whose land was unusable (because it was overgrown or too far away to be effectively cultivable) said they rented land or entered into sharecropping arrangements. Such arrangements did not, in the first year, result in a large enough profit to enable them to repay their loans to the government. The loan program was not renewed in 1995 because of the low rate of repayment, and farmers had to find other sources of credit to cover farming expenses.

Second, in 1994, the Hiwot Agricultural Company, the largest land-holder in the area, offered tractor disk plowing on a rental basis, the fee to be paid at harvest time with a 2 percent interest charge. Most farmers did not use this service, choosing instead to rely on animal traction available within the community.

Third, as mentioned above, the local women's association (through the regional Democratic Association of Tigray Women) extended loans of five hundred birr at 10 percent interest to approximately 140 Ada Bai women.

Ambachew and his brother try out their new donkey plow in the house plot garden.

DATW representatives in Mekele told me in October 1994 that women in other parts of Tigray had a very high rate of repayment (80 percent repaid their loans on time), which allowed for the money to be loaned out again as a revolving fund. In Ada Bai, however, local women's association representatives said that the rate of repayment was very low (although no final repayment figure was available). Women I spoke to who had not repaid their loans said that either their investments (in livestock, land, or goods for resale) had not produced a high enough return, their husbands had gone to find work and they needed to keep the money until they returned, or they had been expecting repatriation assistance from the government or international organizations with which they could repay the loans. One of the local women's association representatives responsible for collecting the loan payments said, "If you look in their houses you see nothing. They have no hope of paying [the debt] back." Because of the low rate of repayment, the DATW loan scheme was suspended in Ada Bai for 1995.

Fourth, while local people obtained small-scale credit from traders and shopkeepers, these local businesspeople had to look outside the community for credit for themselves. Several took out loans from the Guna Private Share Company, a company whose shareholders were high-ranking TPLF members. Guna's profits were reinvested in rehabilitation and development initiatives for Tigray Region. Ada Bai businesspeople had trouble repaying these loans, even though the baito often intervened to pressure borrowers to repay their loans.

Finally, in 1995, the Commercial Bank of Ethiopia, the government-run bank that had a branch in Humera, began to offer loans to businesspeople. Selection criteria for loans included the provision that the borrower must not have any other outstanding debts and must have sufficient collateral. Borrowers from Hiwot, Guna, or the Commercial Bank of Ethiopia felt extreme pressure to repay their loans because the lending institutions were outside the community. The usual intracommunity custom of forgiving late or missed payments was not extended when credit came from outside the community. A person who failed to make timely payments could be arrested and would have strained relations with Ada Bai's political leadership.

Many Ada Bai residents who might have benefited from loans from sources outside the community did not seek them because they lacked information about how to go about getting them. I assisted Aregawi, one of the most successful shopkeepers in the village, to get a loan from the

Commercial Bank of Ethiopia. He had not realized that he was eligible for such credit and felt too intimidated to go to the bank manager on his own without an introduction from me. Aregawi borrowed too much money, and then suffered losses to his business as it became more difficult to move contraband goods (mostly umbrellas, shoes, and clothing) purchased in Asmara across the border between Ethiopia and Eritrea. Thus, he was not able to meet his monthly payments. On a return visit in 1997, I discovered that he had been borrowing money from one of the parastatal companies as well, and when he had also defaulted on those loans, he had been arrested.

The failure of the community to generate its own sources of credit, coupled with its members' inability to repay larger outside loans, highlighted Ada Bai residents' economic vulnerability and slow rate of economic integration into the local social and economic landscape. Lacking social relationships with Humera's larger traders and unable to extract maximum benefit from their physical environment to develop a collateral base that would make them eligible for credit, the community found itself somewhat isolated from surrounding communities. As income levels rose through practice and increasingly competent utilization of the environment, people were able to develop not only the collateral but also the social networks that they needed to be able to borrow funds from outside the community. The irony, of course, was that by this time the need for credit was not as great.

Informal Borrowing and Mutual Assistance Associations

In their study of repatriation to Cambodia, Marita Eastmond and Joakim Öjendal argue that:

> Economic activity depends in part on access to key resources such as land, labour, working capital and skills. However, the skills required for devising livelihood strategies are as much social as technical . . . In any rural community of farmers, livelihood strategies are shaped by authority structures, established roles and positions, culturally defined rights, and obligations. (1999, 49)

Similarly, in Ada Bai the success with which a household was able to provide for its basic needs and to integrate with the community of return was determined by its relations to other households in the community and its ability to call on the resources of others (in food, cash, or labor). These strategies were all functions of the process of social emplacement, whereby links with others in the community and in the surrounding area were forged based on a shared experience of inhabiting this new place. Such strategies helped to form the basis of a rudimentary form of class stratification within the community.[11]

In parts of highland Ethiopia (in both Amhara and Tigrayan societies), mutual assistance networks and associations have helped to create a safety net for peasant households. One formal association, known as *iddir* (እዳር), provided assistance to member households in which there had been a death. Other members of the iddir would help prepare the body for burial, cover the costs of the funeral, provide food during the seven-day wake known as *hazen* (ሐዘን),[12] and contribute money for food, clothing, and other needs to the family of the deceased. People in Ada Bai said that prior to migrating, iddir had been common only in the towns of Tigray, and that most of the people in Ada Bai, having come from rural areas, had no experience of being part of one. Thus, I did not find any evidence of iddir in the settlement.

Iqub (እቁብ) were savings associations whereby members contributed money to a central treasury and distributed the funds in full each month or each week to a different member, whose name was drawn at random. No member was allowed to receive the treasury twice until all members had received it one time. Haile was a businessman who had been a member of an iqub in Ada Bai until lack of money forced some of the members to default on their payments, forcing the collapse of the association. He said that the iqub had had twenty-two members, both men and women, who gave ten birr per week. He recalled that in Sudan it had been much easier to keep the iqub going: "We had [iqub] a lot in Sudan. It was easy to get money in Sudan so it was good. We collected 60,000 [Sudanese] pounds each week." There were reportedly only two iqub functioning while I was in Ada Bai among those traders who had enough money to participate. They helped to bind together those who might otherwise have been competitors, creating a kind of marketplace community. The drop in income experienced by nearly all of the returnees after leaving the refugee camp and moving to Ada Bai forced a change in the social organization of the community for those who were no longer able to take part in savings associations. Ties between traders were not as strong, and some lamented the fact that there were few occasions in which businesspeople worked together anymore.

Maheber (ማህበር), the most common form of mutual assistance association in Ada Bai, was an association of neighbors that gathered on a particular saint's day to feast together, each month at a different neighbor's house.[13] most maheber were composed of women only, though a few men-only maheber existed as well; maheber never had both male and female members. The hostess would invite a priest to come to her house to bless the food and drink that she intended to serve to her guests. The priest would entreat the saint being honored to answer the prayers of the group assembled. Many maheber that had been active in Sudan were disbanded upon return to Ethiopia because, former members said, they did not have enough food or money to contribute to the feast.

Tirhas, a young woman whose mother also lived in Ada Bai (but in a different neighborhood than her daughter's family), told me that she had belonged to a maheber in Sudan:

> At Wad Kowli [refugee camp] my mother belonged to a maheber for Mariam. She made me a member of that one. We continued in Safawa. We have it here still. We are twelve [women]. In a year each [member] takes one month [to host the feast]. At Ada Bai, if we have nothing [i.e., no food] we drink coffee. If there is one injera only, we eat that. Mine [her turn to host] is coming in Hamli [August]. If it was in Safawa I would have to prepare a lot of things, but here I don't. The priest always comes. We prepare the food with our own money.

Members of a maheber tended to be neighbors who had come from the same awraja in highland Tigray or who had shared important experiences together. They were usually organized on a much more informal basis than those in the highlands, however, and the obligations to provide mutual assistance that had bound members to each other were in some cases not as strong as they had been in the highlands or in Sudan because people had fewer resources to share.

Although this kind of association did not involve exchange of money, it helped to define a woman's closest kin and friends, the first people she would turn to if she needed help. Although the maheber was not usually directly intended to distribute funds, people often turned to other members for credit or assistance in times of hardship. In the absence of a formally recognized iddir, members of one's maheber would assist at a funeral. For these reasons, most of the women who belonged to a single maheber were of a similar economic status. Therefore, no one member was able to rely on the association more than the others.

As the overall food security of the village improved, particularly at harvest time or following the distribution of grain rations, many of the maheber that had been disbanded in Sudan were reconstituted. A few new maheber were also created. In fact, food aid wheat was considered perfect for making *himbasha* (ሒምባሻ), the leavened bread most preferred for serving at social gatherings, but aid wheat was not suitable for making injera (unless mixed with sorghum). Thus when a household received food aid, hosting a small celebration in honor of a saint was seen as a good way of fulfilling one's social and religious obligations. Keshie Gebre Selassie,[14] who was one of my principal teachers in the history and customs of the Orthodox Church, told me,

> First there was a promise made by God that "Anyone who believes in [a saint], for example, Giorgis [St. George], must prepare a maheber [feast to be attended by maheber members] and I will listen to them." If a person has nothing but water, he should bring guests and have [the water] blessed. It is enough. It is written like this in the book [the Bible and associated texts of the Orthodox Church], but most people do not do it . . . If a thirsty person wants water, you can give it to them in the name of the saint . . . In Sudan there were many maheber because people were richer . . . This Mikael [the Sunday that just passed] I went to fifteen mahebers. There were that many because there was grain [distributed by the government that week]. But last month I did not go to any . . . If a person does not have a maheber he feels very bad. People want to cry [i.e., to pray to a saint] but no one will hear them . . . He may borrow from others if he cannot afford a maheber, but now there is [usually] not enough even to borrow.

Returnees saw food aid distributions as an opportunity to fulfill their social obligations, which they felt had been neglected for too long. Many people gave away their grain rations to the church or to those who were extremely poor following a general distribution, since it was considered as important to fulfill these obligations to the community as to preserve the household's own food reserves. Failure to do so, people feared, might induce God to bring famine, fire, or epidemic to the village. Except in cases where households were desperate for food, grain rations made little, if any, impact on improving households' nutritional status because they were usually given away or sold.

In saying that people often gave food away, I do not mean to imply that they did not need food aid. One reason they gave it away may also have been that it took so long for the food to arrive in Ada Bai that, by the time it was distributed, the most acute food needs had subsided. In 1994, wheat arrived six months after the need had been determined and assistance requested. Those who were desperate had either left the village to find support elsewhere or in a few cases had died before relief arrived. The vegetable oil that was intended to be part of the general food ration arrived another six months after that. The cruel irony of Ada Bai returnees having to wait an entire year for oil to arrive from the United States when the area was known for its production of sesame (a valuable oilseed) was not lost on the residents of Ada Bai. The validity of Amartya Sen's argument (1981) that famine is caused more by entitlement failure than by food availability shortage was graphically demonstrated in this case.

A final type of interhousehold exchange system was the *tsebel* (ፀበል), a celebration held by the same household once a month, once a year, or on selected saint's days as the household could afford. Selection of the saint's day to celebrate was often passed from one generation to another. Abraha, whose household celebrated St. Mikael's day, told me:

> My father and his father before him had a special belief in Mikael [patron saint of healing], so every year in [the month of] Hidar [April], I celebrate St. Mikael's day. I teach my [two young] daughters to do that, too, so when they are grown I am sure they will have tsebel in their home for Mikael.

"Even though they didn't know your father and your grandfather?" I asked him.

> Right. It is part of our family heritage and for that reason it is important to carry on the tradition. In other ways I will tell them about their relatives, about my brothers, my parents, my grandparents. As they get older I will tell them about where we came from.

The tsebel was usually held by more wealthy households who could afford to host the event themselves. Like the mehaber, however, it was a gathering of friends and relatives who were closest to the host. Participants understood themselves to be the hosts' closest associates and knew that they would be expected to assist that household in times of trouble (and in most cases the guest had the same expectation of the host).

Informal Household Cooperation

Those who borrowed were not necessarily the households who had the most collateral. Very often it was the poorest households who borrowed the most. This was particularly true in the case of intracommunity borrowing. By far the most common form of interhousehold exchange in the community came from small gifts or loans of food, money, kerosene, and charcoal, and services such as labor. Gifts were the household resources that were most difficult to track in the household survey that we conducted. Most small gifts were never mentioned, particularly if they consisted of food consumed while visiting another household. In the case of money, the recipient would refer to the transaction as a loan rather than as a gift, even if neither donor nor recipient expected the money to be repaid. Usually such "loans" were so small that those who give them rarely expected repayment. To ask for repayment of a loan of one birr or two injera would have been considered incredibly rude. Requests for small amounts of money from one's relatives or immediate neighbors likewise could not be politely refused. Although respondents to the survey tended to report most cash that they "borrowed" from their neighbors, the rate of borrowing of food items was likely much higher. For instance, Mebrat, the woman who headed Household 7, regularly borrowed salt and *berbere* (spice) from neighbors during Tiri (January) but did not report the full amounts she borrowed. Mebrat was so poor that these items with injera formed the staple of her household's diet; she could not afford beans. She told me after the completion of the survey that she did not consider them to have been significant enough to record daily because she borrowed in such small amounts and had no intention of repaying in kind the people who had given them to her. Indeed, even if she had wanted to repay her neighbors' generosity, she did not have the resources to do so. Neither did she consider these items to be gifts. As small as they were, however, they probably prevented her children from becoming seriously malnourished. It would have been almost impossible to track such small interhousehold exchanges with complete accuracy.

Labor Migration

In their efforts to meet their households' basic needs, returnees preferred to stay within their own new community. Income and assets derived from working one's own land were preferable to that earned working on someone else's land or through wage labor, particularly if such labor required the worker to leave his or her house. However, Ada Bai's strategic location close to the borders with both Sudan and Eritrea provided opportunities for working on commercial farms in Sudan and for trading items purchased in both neighboring countries. When they did supplement their income from these sources, however, the proportion of household income attributed to such work was considerable. For most, the most desirable wage labor option was to work on the commercial farms in the immediate vicinity. In October and November, men and women who were not busy with their own fields worked for wages in the large sesame and sorghum plantations that surrounded the town. They were joined by high-landers from Tigray and Gondar, as well as a large number of Sudanese, many of whom were refugees from the war in southern Sudan and were trying to raise enough money to go to Addis Ababa to apply for political asylum from UNHCR and the government of Ethiopia. From December to April, many Ada Bai men returned to Sudan to work harvesting the irri-gated sorghum and cotton fields. Workers tended to be young unmarried men who lived with their parents or newly married men whose wives could stay either with their own or with the men's parents.[15]

Of the ten households participating in the survey, only one sent a man to work in Sudan during the survey period. Despite the general profile I have painted of "spare hands and mouths" being the primary type of men who went to work in Sudan (based on interviews with households not participating in the survey), this man left his wife and children behind. He said that he did not want to leave to find work, but that he had no other choice. He kept delaying his departure hoping to find some work closer to home, but finally left in January. By the end of the survey period (mid-March 1995) he had not returned, though he had sent money and a message to his wife and children (he arrived several months later).

I interviewed several other Ada Bai men who had gone to Sudan in the last harvest season. The following is excerpted from my field notes:

Berhe, eighteen years old, reported going with six of his friends to the Gedaref area to work in Tahsas. They received a contract to cut and collect sorghum. For twenty days' work, they earned 230,000 Sudanese pounds between them.[16] When they finished this work, they were unable to find another contract because there were so many other laborers. They thus worked in one place for three days for seven hundred pounds per day [approximately nine birr a day], and at another for five days at six hundred pounds per day [approximately eight birr a day]. Before returning home, Berhe said that he bought new clothes for himself and fourteen plastic jerry cans to sell in Ethiopia. At the border he was taxed by the Sudanese police two hundred pounds per jerry can, but he said that if he could sell them for twenty-two birr each, he would still make a profit. After exchanging the money on the currency market in Humera, he said that he had fifty-two birr to bring home to his family [not including the proceeds from the jerry cans].

Girmay, aged thirty, went to Sudan in Tiri [January]. He also traveled with six other people to the Gedaref area. Because of his past experience working in the fields, he found work feeding a combine harvester [considered a skilled job]. Workers on the combines were paid eighty pounds for every two quintals of sorghum fed into the machine. Girmay said, "I did the same work in previous years in the Sudan. This year was very good because the pay rate was high even though the foreign exchange rate was low. I bought clothes for my family and brought the rest of the money home . . . I got about three hundred birr in the end."

For a household with more than enough able-bodied people, sending a son to work in Sudan provided an important income supplement and could help the household to settle its debts. A worker who left the household for two or more months also helped to relieve the burden on the family by eliminating the need to feed him. The contribution of this worker was, however, not great enough for it to be the sole source of income for the household. The unfortunate farmer who relied on such income for more than supplementation would have to stay away for much longer, as can be seen in the example of the man whose household participated in the survey.

Despite the fact that men were the primary participants in labor migration, some women in the village also benefited from the presence of guest workers in the area: those who were engaged in the restaurant, beer-selling, hotel, and prostitution businesses (and these were usually not mutually exclusive) experienced a dramatic increase in business during the harvest season. Likewise, when men left town to work in Sudan and the guest workers returned to the highlands, the women complained that business slowed down dramatically.

As time went on, returnee households were able to ameliorate their situation through improved harvests, new alliances with kin and friends in other towns that allowed for exchange of resources, and wage labor in the Humera area, and to a lesser extent in Sudan. People attributed their more stable conditions to the fact that they "knew the place better" and thus were better able to take advantage of the opportunities it provided. Wage laborers were engaged in another layer of emplacement that extended far beyond the boundaries of the settlement. For these men, safe, usable spaces extended across the international border and into places that they had previously been emplaced while living as refugees.

The achievement of greater household food security closely followed progress in the process of emplacement. The more intimately people came to understand their environment and learned how to exploit it for economic benefit, the more viable the place became as a site on which to build a future. For a community that had faced life-threatening poverty, the ability of a place to provide for their basic needs was an essential aspect of the home-making process. A place that did not provide this security was clearly unsuitable. The fact that Ada Bai offered greater economic security as people came to realize its productive potential was a major reason that people decided to stay on.

5

"We Have Each Lost a Child": Birth, Death, and Life-Cycle Rituals

My neighbor Tibbletz had given birth to two children and buried them before they were five years old. Both had died in the refugee camps and Tibbletz was desperately afraid to lose another. At the same time, she and her husband, Ambachew, were eager to try again to have children. Their lives in Ada Bai had become more settled than they had been in Sudan, and they felt that they were secure enough economically to raise a child. Tibbletz finally became pregnant nine months after coming to Ada Bai. She was reluctant at first to let anyone know in case it was a false alarm or she miscarried.

Once her womb started to swell, however, her pregnancy became clear to all. Tibbletz began to make vigorous efforts to protect herself and her unborn child from harm. She asked me to bring her *tsurura* (ጽሩራ)—three small golden amulets in the shape of crosses—to braid into her hair along her hairline; these amulets symbolized the Holy Trinity and were thought to ward off spirits that might threaten her pregnancy. Ambachew brought her the most nutritious food he could afford—meat, fruits, beans—and when she refused to eat before he did or to eat with him, he left larger portions on the plate for her to finish, saying that he was satisfied by the small amount he had eaten. He, too, was afraid of losing another child.

When the baby was born, they named him Kiros. They found it difficult to explain the meaning of the name but said that, like the name Gidey (which means "my turn"), parents gave it to children when they had lost others previously. "It is a message to God," they said, "that is to say, 'You have already taken yours from me, now leave this child for me.'" The names could be given to either a boy or girl and were meant to confuse evil spirits as to the sex of the child. When Kiros was very young, they often dressed him in a girl's dress, saying that this might further confuse the spirits and prevent them from taking him from them. Finally, they shaved his head (and covered it with butter or sesame oil to protect him from scabies, lice, and cradle cap) but left a small button of hair on his forehead (some parents left the hair at the nape of the child's neck)—just in case, they said, if "God decides that He must take the child, He will be able to pull him up to Heaven by taking hold of the child's hair."

Birth and death in Ada Bai were closely linked in symbolic and ritual terms. Childbirth, a dangerous ordeal in the best of circumstances in most of Africa, was much more so in Ada Bai because of the generally poor health of mothers and the low level of health care available. In addition, people in Ada Bai believed that a woman in labor was highly susceptible to spirit possession, which could cause disease or death. Children, too, were considered extremely fragile beings, and a variety of rituals existed to protect the newborn from the clutches of death. Despite these perceived dangers, a woman's self-definition was largely derived from her role as a wife and through her reproductive power; she therefore attempted to have as many children as possible, even if she had already lost several. The failure of a woman to bear children was considered her fault, rather than her husband's, and was considered justifiable grounds for her husband to divorce her.

In this chapter I examine birth and death simultaneously, to show the conceptual and emotional proximity each held to the other in Ada Bai. Beliefs, ideas, and rituals surrounding birth and death, the individual physical body's entrance to and exit from the community, served to emplace the individual, both physically and spiritually, within the larger collective. Such emplacement was largely carried out through the medium of the body: bodies forged a connection between the individual, community, and place. Place was encoded in rituals and everyday practice so as to inscribe the landscape into the fabric of socialized meaning that gave the person both individual and group identity.

Impoverishment set the stage for the construction of personal and communal senses of identity. Rituals and beliefs were conditioned by the reality of poverty, by the particular implications for life that it implied, and by the legacy it brought to each child who was born under its clutches. Through these rituals of protection and healing, the individual was marked for membership in communities both in Ada Bai and in the afterlife. The individual's relationship to the community into which he or she was born, and the role of that relationship in defining the individual, were extremely important. Actual or potential disruption of the link between the individual and the community through displacement was a significant source of anxiety.

The proximity of birth and death is quite common in extremely poor societies, and, as Nancy Scheper-Hughes points out, it was common in what are now industrialized societies as recently as the beginning of the twentieth century. In a section of *Death Without Weeping* subtitled "The Discovery of Child Mortality," she reminds the reader:

> Throughout much of human history, as in a good deal of the developing world today, women have had to give birth and nurture infants under environmental and social conditions inimical to child survival as well as hostile to their own well-being. Consequently, a high rate of infant and child mortality has been a fairly standard feature of human reproduction ... The dialectic between birth and death, survival and loss, remains a powerful one in the lives of most people living on the peripheries of the modern industrialized world ... In these contexts, disease epidemics, food shortages, contaminated water and inadequate medical care interact with patterns of high fertility and sometimes prejudicial forms of infant care to consign millions of children to an early grave. (1993, 273)

The fact that so many children die soon after they are born, and the susceptibility of children to diseases that can claim their lives, begins to explain why avoidance of death in a place such as Ada Bai is a deliberate and overriding concern for parents.

During the first years in Ada Bai, household incomes were so low that most children and adults did not receive adequate nutritious food. The chronic malnutrition reduced everyone to a state of heightened vulnerability, and there was a palpable fear, though rarely spoken of, that at any moment a person could lose his or her fight to keep death at bay. If one uses de Waal's (1989) definition of famine as hunger or dearth rather than as "mass starvation unto death"—as he argues the term has come to be used in the English tradition thanks to analyses derived from the works of Malthus (1958 [1798]) and Sen (1981)—then it is not too extreme to say that the population was chronically famine-stricken.

The Dangers of Childbirth: Clinics and Spirits

When they went smoothly, births were a time of celebration and close bonding between women. Most births tended to take place at night, perhaps because of the cooler temperatures or the generally more relaxed atmosphere. Infant deliveries were attended by women only: the woman's husband would wait anxiously outside the house in case he was needed to bring water or to fetch help. A bright fire of kindling wood was lit and coffee and snacks (injera, himbasha, or roasted corn, sorghum, or barley— *kolo* [ቆሎ]) would be offered to those who were present by a female relative or friend of the woman in labor. Most women knew the basic procedures for delivering a baby that was positioned properly, and did not call a midwife unless complications arose or at the very end of the delivery when there was a danger that the placenta might be ruptured or retained. There were fifteen midwives in the village, most of whom were active in the Democratic Association of Tigray Women. They had been selected to receive training from the government, often in recognition of their roles as leaders in the community. Even though most women preferred to have their close relatives and friends help them in child delivery, the midwives also worked nearly every night because there were so many births. Medhin, a well-known midwife who was active in the women's association, told me that she delivered two or three babies most nights. I would often visit her in the mornings as I passed by her house; more often than not she had just arrived from a delivery. She said that she did not demand payment because she felt that to charge a fee to such extremely poor women who were in a time of great need would be inappropriate. She said that she would have appreciated it if those who could afford to gave her some payment for her services, and lamented that hardly anyone ever offered to pay her for helping them.

Complications during childbirth were common in Ada Bai, as they were throughout Ethiopia. In 1998, maternal and infant mortality rates in Ethiopia were 1,400 per 100,000 and 110 per 10,000, respectively.[1] The chances of a woman dying in childbirth were one in nine.[2] Ada Bai was no exception: many women died during childbirth, and infant and child mortality (under one year and under five years, respectively) rates were also high. The clinic in Ada Bai only kept records of deaths that occurred in the clinic itself. Most deaths occurred in the family's house, and a few at Humera Hospital, and were therefore never recorded by Ada Bai health staff. I did convince the village priests to start recording all deaths in a registry book that I had provided them with, noting the person's name, sex, age, date of death, and cause of death if known. Over a four-month period in 1994 (March–June), forty-three deaths were recorded in Ada Bai, twenty-eight of which were children under the age of five (according to the village sheik, no Muslim deaths were reported during that time). Although exact population figures were not available, a rough estimate of Ada Bai's population, 8,000, would give a monthly child mortality rate of between 6.25 and 12.5/10,000.

Many women were chronically anemic and were unable to recover from the loss of blood during labor. They were said to have died "because they had no blood."[3] Another common problem was infection caused by the use of unsterilized instruments, including rusty or dirty razor blades used to cut the umbilical cord, and the dirty hands of the traditional birth attendant. Other women had retained or ruptured placentas that could not be removed by the midwife or the clinic staff. The Ada Bai clinic staff lacked the equipment and training to deal with complicated deliveries, and the Humera Hospital staff, although slightly better trained, lacked such basic supplies as blood transfusion equipment and adequate stocks of oxytocin (used to induce labor). Lacking a surgical ward and trained surgeons, the hospital was unable to carry out Caesarean section operations. Twice I drove women in labor who needed blood transfusions and surgery to the Eritrean town of Tesseney, 100 km from Humera. I would load the car with health assistants and insist that they wear their white lab coats so that we could get past the immigration checkpoint, since none of us had visas to enter Eritrea. One of the women lived; the other died.

For nearly every biomedical explanation for a woman's death in childbirth, there was a counterclaim of sorcery. I was often surprised to hear people discussing their interpretations of deaths that had occurred in the previous months, some of which I had witnessed, as clear cases of sorcery. Evil Eye, or *buda*, was the most common spirit to be blamed for a death, yet if the circumstances of the death did not fit known explanations of how *buda* worked (and the variance between plausible explanations of behavior attributable to the spirit was extremely wide), then the culprit could be any one of several other types of spirits or spells cast by sorcerers (*tenkweley*, ተንቋላይ).[4]

In Ada Bai, the most serious threat to pregnant women was thought to reside in the clinic itself. It was widely suspected that the guard at the Ada Bai clinic was a carrier of the Evil Eye, a *tebib*. As proof, they cited his misshapen forearm and hand—those who carried evil spirits were said to often be disfigured. In addition, people claimed that many of those who became possessed, when exorcised, spoke in his voice when they revealed the name of the spirit that possessed them. He was said to have come from a notorious family of tebibs. I was sternly scolded for allowing his brother, who was visiting Ada Bai, to help carry my bags when our taxi to Humera had broken down two kilometers from the town. People warned me that I had placed myself in danger by associating with him.

The guard, Abraham, was thought to be responsible for the deaths of as many as four or five women in childbirth each month. People complained that they were powerless to do anything to get rid of the guard, since belief in spirits had been prohibited by the TPLF. Most people treated him respectfully to his face. They said they were afraid that if they quarreled with the man, he would cause them to become possessed. However, they kept their children far away from him, never permitting him to touch them. Children who were too young to speak were said to be particularly vulnerable to possession.

Women lived in fear of having to go to the clinic at night to deliver their babies, yet I was asked to bring women to the clinic during the night as often as five times a week. Relatives would insist on leaving the woman in the car until we had woken the guard up (his bedroom doubled as one of the two examination rooms), roused the health assistant from his sleep, and prepared the delivery/examination room, which minimized the chances of the guard having any contact with the woman.

The story of Medhin is typical of many other episodes I witnessed. Medhin's husband, an assistant priest (*haleka*, ህለቃ) who expected to be accepted as a full priest in the Ethiopian Orthodox Church in the coming months, blamed Abraham for a miscarriage that his wife had had while six months pregnant. After having been examined at the clinic in the middle of the night, she was referred to the Humera Hospital, and I drove as fast as possible while still trying to avoid the potholes and bumps in the road that might cause her discomfort or increase the likelihood that she would bleed internally. When we were just outside of Humera, she began to wail and yelp in a voice dramatically different from any I had ever heard her use. Immediately her husband asked me to take her to the traditional healer instead of the hospital. I knew she was suffering from heavy internal bleeding, and suspected that a delay might cost her her life. I therefore had to choose quickly whether to accede to the man's wishes or try to get her to the hospital. I proposed that once we had her admitted to the hospital, he and I could go and get the medicine (a drink made from a mixture of plants and herbs that had been consecrated) and bring it to the hospital. He agreed; the woman received both types of treatment and recovered. She and her husband attributed her miscarriage to spirit possession that had originated with the clinic guard, and her recovery to the traditional medicine that she received.

Finally, after many months of private mumbling and complaint, the issue of the guard was raised at a public meeting. The majority in attendance demanded that Abraham be relieved of his duties at the clinic and sent away from Ada Bai. A minority pointed out that because of his disability there was no other work that he could do, but stronger voices prevailed, and Abraham left Ada Bai to return to his home in Tigray.

Gender Inequality in Death

The death of a woman was considered more tragic than the death of a man, for the woman was the bedrock of the household. Among her many tasks, the wife prepared meals, cared for children, herded small domestic animals that remained close to the house, and fetched water (Rahmato 1991, 166). A man whose wife had died in childbirth was to be pitied, and his quick remarriage was encouraged so that someone would take care of him and his children.

Child deaths that occurred during or immediately after delivery were said to be caused by spirits or because God had not wanted the child to live. "How could it be anything else?" people asked me, rhetorically, when I discussed the causes of infant death. "The child had not had a chance to live yet." At such a young age, children were not thought capable of deciding to die, or of losing his or her will to live. Children were not thought to have their own soul until after they were born, and usually not until after they were baptized. Other recognized causes of child death included malaria, fevers of various kinds, pneumonia, tuberculosis, and spirit possession. Hunger alone was not understood by people in Ada Bai to cause the death of a child.

This explanation of child death may be contrasted with Scheper-Hughes's analysis (1993), in which children of the Brazilian altiplano were understood to choose to die. In both cases, the parents consider the fate of the child to be out of their control, but rather than choosing not to live, Ada Bai parents consider it to be God or an evil spirit that takes the life of their child.

As the incident of Abraham the clinic guard illustrates, while suspicions of spirit possession could easily set one neighbor against another, nowhere was the fear and protectiveness more pronounced than over a child. Indeed, many of the rituals that filled a child's first days were concerned with protecting the child and mother from supernatural harm (also found in Papua New Guinea, see Lepowsky 1993, 86).

The Power of Mariam in Childbirth Rituals and as a Feminine Spirit

Saint Mariam, or Mary, is the matron saint of motherhood throughout the Christian world. In Ethiopian Orthodox Christianity, Mariam protects both mother and child throughout pregnancy, childbirth, and motherhood. A priest explained to me the story of Mariam as he knew it. He said that Mariam was a descendent of Adam and Hewan (Eve), who had been promised a child by God. The child, Yesus Kristos (Jesus Christ), is known to Ethiopians as Medhane Alem or Savior of the World. The priest told me:

> All these things happened in Egypt. At that time Herodotus [King of Egypt] heard that a child was born who would become King of the World. He ordered all [male] children to be killed. Mariam escaped. On her way to Jerusalem she was praying to be saved by those in her path. If people insulted her or wanted to kill her or take her child, she prayed to God to take them away and he did. So she was a good prophet.
>
> While she was fleeing she stayed under a big tree to hide from the soldiers. They arrived to kill her, and she prayed to have shelter in which to hide. A big tree appeared. She and her son walked inside it when it opened and when the soldiers came they looked all around the tree but couldn't find them.
>
> After that Herodotus died with the help of God and she was fine. She stayed for a long time with blind people. She could cure them, bring dead bodies back to life, or cure a disease.

For the priest, as for others who knew this or a variation of this story, deeds attributed to Mariam were proof of her power. Women were not the only ones for whom Mariam was important; men also looked to her for protection. Mariam was therefore one of the most popular saints, the subject of tributes and prayers. It was also common to name a child out of respect to Mariam: Lettemariam or Gebremariam (both meaning Servant of Mariam), Hailemariam (Power of Mariam), Woldemariam (Son of Mariam), though naming a child simply Mariam was not usual.

When a woman delivered a baby in her house in Ada Bai, it was common to find older women who had already borne many children lying prostrate on the ground at the door to the house, praying to Mariam to protect both mother and child. Seven days after the birth of the child, a small gathering (*geleb*, ገለብ) was held inside the house to give thanks to Mariam for the safe delivery. Women from the immediate neighborhood, as well as female relatives who lived farther away, came first to collect the new mother's clothes that had been soiled in childbirth to be washed in the river, and then returned to see the new baby, to eat (usually a basic but nutritious meal of beans and injera, *ga'at*, ገዓት, a thick porridge made from wheat or barley, or himbasha) and drink coffee with the new mother. The father helped to serve the food from outside the house, but did not usually enter the dwelling. As each woman took a piece of injera or himbasha, she would kiss the edge of the plate and press her forehead to it, in the same way that a priest's handheld cross was kissed to receive God's blessing whenever one encountered a priest in the village.

In domestic space feminized by the geleb celebration, songs were sung to Mariam; typically these were one line verses sung repeatedly as the women clapped and danced forwards and backwards, forming a circle around the inside of the house as the new mother looked on from the bed, where she lay with her newborn baby. Typical verses included:

Mariam mebrihit tselmat.
ማርያም መብርሂት ፀልሞት
Mariam has delivered you from darkness to light.

Mariam wahabit, Wahabit Mariam.
ማርያም ወሐቢት ። ወሐቢት ማርያም
If she loves you, Mariam will give you a gift [the child].

Deke Mariam halifin gidi
Seti Semhal qoina mengedi.
ደቂ ማርያም ሀሊፍን ጊዲ
ሰቲ ስምሀል ኮይና መንገዲ
Mariam's maids [the women who have washed the new mother's clothes] have passed by [here].
I know because I have seen the lovely green grass [used for ceremonies] on the road [blown onto the road by Mariam who loves the women attendants].

Because of the special significance that Mariam had for women, in addition to the geleb many women hosted a small celebration in their homes, made a special offering at the church on one of Mariam's feast days (which fell twice a month), or made pilgrimages at least once a year to the nearest church named for Mariam. Men and women from all over Ethiopia who could afford to travel to Axum, where Ethiopian Orthodox Christians believe that the Ark of the Covenant is kept, made pilgrimages to the Mariam church there at least once in their lifetime on the most important Mariam feast days (particularly in January, when Mariam was said to have died). None of the residents of Ada Bai could afford such a journey, so instead they traveled to the church at Rawayan (the smallest of the returnee settlements), which was named for Mariam. On one such feast day, I drove a carload of women to the church at Rawayan. One of the women traveling with me insisted that she had been instructed by Mariam in a dream to bring offerings for her to the church.

Circumcision

Between five and seven days after the birth of a son, the child was circumcised by a traditional healer. Circumcision (*megaraz*, ምግራዝ) was considered necessary; it was widely feared that an uncircumcised boy would not be able to penetrate his virgin bride on the first night of their marriage. A child who had been circumcised by the seventh day after his birth was thought not to be likely to bear a scar from the operation, whereas if the boy was older when the procedure was performed then it was believed that certain additional precautions would have to be taken to absolve him of sin and to ensure that he was not scarred. One old man who had performed circumcisions and other healing practices for more than forty years told me that if the boy was older than seven days,

> You must kill a chicken and prepare sewa and injera before the circumcision takes place. You must drop the foreskin into the blood of the chicken. You must mix the foreskin with the blood and garlic and bury it. Then you must eat the chicken. There is a belief that if you throw away the skin without burying it, it can be taken [and eaten] by an animal and the wound will never heal.

If the boy was younger than seven days, the chicken sacrifice was not necessary. The circumciser told me that a small seed known as *shinfa*, taken from wild greens, should be mixed with garlic and buried together with the foreskin so that animals will not smell it and dig it up.[5] The healer then mixed part of the garlic and shinfa with water, splashed the combination on the ground and over relatives of the child who were on hand to witness the procedure (an act that was thought to protect the baby), and then washed his hands with it.

This procedure, still followed in many highland villages, has been adapted in the towns. The healer told me: "In the town we use procaine penicillin injections instead of white onion [garlic] to prevent infection. We also do not bury the foreskin . . . some may use termite powder [called qun'quno, ቁንቍኖ] to put on the cut area [i.e., the penis]. That is often done here."

Parents paid as much as ten birr to healers to circumcise their sons. Once I was asked to bring an infant, whose birth I had witnessed in the family home, to the clinic because he had developed an abscess on his penis as a result of having been circumcised that day with a dirty razor blade. After giving the infant an injection of penicillin, the health assistant told me that he had never been requested to circumcise even one child in the year that he had been in Ada Bai, even though the clinic offered the procedure for free. It was evident that parents considered the ritual surrounding the circumcision ceremony to be an essential part of the procedure.

Although prohibited by law, girl children are still circumcised or infibulated in some parts of Tigray. I found it very difficult to gather information concerning female infibulation, since the practice is prohibited by law and most people were unwilling to admit that they continued to practice it. One woman healer told me that she used to perform the operation, but that she was "afraid" to do it now. Others said that although they did not practice female infibulation themselves, they knew that it was done in the far east and far west of Tigray, and that those who practiced it believed that failure to infibulate a daughter meant that the parents did not value the child. They said that the operation was conducted on girls between the ages of one and three. I saw no evidence of the procedure being followed in Ada Bai, though it may have been done in secret on a limited basis.

Explanations of circumcisions for both boys and girls cite social conformity as a justification. Although it was not customary for either of the circumcision rituals to be celebrated by a feast or other gathering, the procedures were considered necessary to ensure that the child was able to participate fully in society through marriage and childbirth.[6]

Christening: Entry into the Christian Community

The Christena (ክርስትና) or baptism was one of the most important rituals involving a newborn child in Ada Bai, as it is throughout Christian communities in Ethiopia. The Christena is an important example of the intrinsic role of the body in imbuing space with meaning. Christening typically took place forty days after the birth of a boy and eighty days after that of a girl, though the family sometimes postponed the ceremony slightly to ensure that it took place on a Sunday or to wait until a fasting period had ended. The Christena marked the child's entry into the church and acceptance into God's family. At the Christena, the priest selected a name for the child, which was usually only used by priests throughout the child's life at church ceremonies such as his or her own wedding or funeral. The name would also be used if the child entered the service of the church as a priest, monk, or nun.

The Christena also signified the mother's emergence from the liminal state of profanity that she had occupied since giving birth. After the child was christened, the mother was allowed to enter the churchyard again; she could also resume sexual relations with her husband. During the liminal period that began two months before the birth of the child and ended with the Christena, the mother and father were not supposed to have sexual relations. The priest told me that this was a measure to ensure that the woman did not become pregnant too quickly after the birth of the child, though most women I spoke to said they believed they could not become pregnant while they were lactating. They did, however, take seriously the injunction against sexual activity for two months after the birth.

One of the most important benefits to a baptized child, Ada Bai parents said, was that when the child died, he or she would be entitled to be buried in a sanctified church cemetery together with others who were baptized, rather than in a separate grave for newborns and infidels (i.e., those without souls). In their mortality records, the priests often did not list the name or even the sex of a child that had not been baptized, which suggests that they did not consider the death of an unbaptized child to be significant. Priests were divided over whether an unbaptized baby could be expected to go to heaven. Some said that at such a young age a child is innocent and thus its place in heaven was assured. Others said that they did not see how anyone who had not been baptized as a Christian could ascend to heaven. I observed the implications of this difference of opinion several times. In the most dramatic example, priests were divided over whether Tsehai, the woman I referred to earlier whom I had brought to Tesseney, Eritrea, but had died while in labor, could be buried in the Orthodox cemetery (as opposed to a cemetery for unbaptized people) since the unbaptized (and also dead) child was still inside her womb. After bitter debate, she was buried in an Orthodox Christian cemetery that had been established exclusively for members of the Tigrayan community who had died in Tesseney. Even in death, the location and status of the interred body continued to generate meaning for relatives who remained and to ensure that the individual's membership in the community was perpetuated into the afterlife.

Several reasons were offered for the difference in the timings of the christenings for boys and girls. One priest said that the christening was not supposed to take place until the mother had stopped postnatal bleeding, and there was a widespread belief that with the birth of a boy the mother bled for 33–40 days whereas after giving birth to a daughter she would bleed for 66–80 days. I discussed this explanation with Tibbletz, who scoffed, saying, "How would [the priest] know how long a woman bleeds? He is a man." The priest also advised me that it had taken God forty days to create Adam, and that only when Adam was complete did He take a rib from his side to create Hewan, which took another forty days. Thus the girl's baptism should take place after eighty days.

When a child was seriously ill and was expected to die before the Christena, the priest told me, he was obliged to advise the family to christen the child early, so that it could be buried as a Christian. Failure to advise the family in this way, he said, could bring God's punishment to both the family and the priest.

In addition to being the baby's rite of entrance into Christian fellowship, the Christena also signified his or her entrance into the community. During the church service, the child would be accompanied by relatives and friends. One or more godparents were selected to present the child to the priest, who then dipped him or her naked into a basin of cold water and uttered a blessing. A thin string of yarn was tied around the child's neck as a souvenir of the event to mark the child as one who has been baptized. After the church service, the family returned to their house and began a day of feasting, in which the entire neighborhood was invited to participate. Depending on the wealth of the family and the timing of the christening, which was almost always held on a Sunday, a goat, sheep, or ox was slaughtered (wealthier families often chose to wait until the fasting season was over in order to have a larger feast with meat, while poorer families were somewhat relieved if the event fell within a fasting period, since then they were obliged only to provide injera and a sauce made from beans to their guests). Sewa was served in large quantities (often an entire *berrimill*, a 220-liter oil drum, was filled), and the festivities went on into the evening with music and dancing. In this way, the child was welcomed into the community and his or her socialization process, in which the entire community was involved, began.

Mapping the Body into the Community through Healing

In addition to the emplacement of the child on the physical landscape through the opening of spaces for meaningful interaction throughout and beyond his or her life, the process also worked in reverse, whereby the place was inscribed on the body of the child. This occurred most visibly in the sphere of traditional health care. Cuts and burns were administered to all children to protect them from spirits and other threats to health. Many illnesses were thought to reside in the blood.[7] Parents often brought their young children to healers who, using more or less clean razorblades, slit their eyebrows or sliced their temples to prevent or cure eye infections, headaches, or fevers. They also commonly sliced children's foreheads in the shape of a cross, "to mark the child as belonging to God." These wounds produced permanent scars. These highly visible markings also helped to identify the person as being Tigrayan. In Addis Ababa and other parts of Ethiopia, Tigrayans are easily recognizable to each other and to non-Tigrayans by the "number elevens" (parallel lines inscribed on their temples) and other markings on their faces.[8]

Individuals receive cuts and burns throughout their lives for various illnesses. People in Ada Bai said that there were two illnesses that were not known in other parts of Tigray, and for which biomedical doctors were said to have no cure. They were known as *waz* (ወዝ) and *shofer* (ሾፈር), and were most often thought to be caused by spirit possession or other supernatural intervention. Although the illnesses were thought to be similar to one another, the clinical symptoms of waz resembled that of leishmaniasis (also known as kala azar), a disease transmitted by the bite of certain types of sand flies, with symptoms that include enlargement of the spleen, high fever, chills, fatigue, loss of appetite, and diarrhea.[9] The symptoms of shofer were said to resemble hepatitis. With shofer the iris of the person's eye was said to turn white, while the area under the eye turned green. The urine of the person with shofer was said to look like hot tea or blood and the body to become full of bile, causing the fingers to turn green.

Treatment of waz included incision of forty-four marks on the patient's body, in groups of two or three, with a cross cut into the head. People told me that waz was caused by the blood "turning bad," and swore that when the cuts were made into the flesh of the person, the blood that came from the wounds was black. Shofer was treated with sixteen burns, administered with a needle or piece of metal heated in a fire, to the wrists, forearms, elbows, upper arms, and top of the head (in the shape of a cross).

Many of the biomedical doctors in Humera expressed their belief in the efficacy of traditional medicine to treat waz and shofer. They could not give me precise equivalent diagnoses for these illnesses in biomedical terms. One doctor even told me that he had administered the cuts to a young child when all other forms of treatment had failed, at the request of the child's mother. He did not know whether the cure had worked.

The reasoning behind cauterization and incision was explained to me in the following terms: when a person is burned, he or she inhales and exhales sharply, forcing the spirit that has taken up residence within the body to be expelled. Although I found the notion of curing with burns and cuts strange and difficult to understand, I did not find it disturbing until I witnessed the treatment being applied to infants and very young children. Tibbletz and Ambachew's son, Kiros, had several cuts and burns administered during his first year of life. When he was four months old,

Tibbletz brought him to a traditional healer to have the Frenulum snipped. She said that this is a common procedure done to children out of the belief that, if it is not, the child might become unable to swallow the mother's breast milk. On the same day, he had had the cross in his forehead recut to protect him from buda. Tibbletz told me that she had been concerned that he was not eating well, and wanted to make sure that he had not been attacked by a tebib. A few days later, the child had a high fever and was vomiting. I brought him to the clinic and he began a course of daily injections of procaine penicillin. That evening, Ambachew, his father, came to my house looking extremely distraught and asked me to come and see the boy. The following is an excerpt from my notes of that day:

I got there and found a house full of people—Berhan was making coffee; Lettemariam [his paternal aunt] was holding Kiros, who had finally fallen asleep. Aboy Gebreselassie[10] had come—whether he knew that Kiros was sick or not I don't know. Medhin was also there with her tiny baby—so tiny I can't believe she's alive, and now marked with burns all over her body from attempts to treat her with habesha medehanit. Medhin herself still has her TB cough and it is likely that her baby has it too . . .

Tibbletz was sitting there listlessly, exhausted by the day. Kiros . . . wasn't feverish, so I suspected that the worst had passed. Whatever it was that his body had wanted to expel from his stomach seemed to have gone.

Meanwhile attention turned to Aboy Gebreselassie, who had found Tibbletz's old umbrella, ripped and broken, hanging under the [straw shade outside the house]. He started examining it closely, I thought because he was under the impression that it was the umbrella he had [recently] given to Tibbletz. Then Tibbletz got up to go to the field [which was used as an open-air latrine]. I thought she wanted to get away on her own. Aboy Gebreselassie put one of the rods of the umbrella into the fire. I was still under the impression that he was trying to fix the umbrella. Then the scene suddenly became horribly clear to me when Lettemariam pulled up Kiros's shirt and Aboy Gebreselassie applied the burning rod to his stomach in two places. I started screaming at them to stop, as did Kiros. The others laughed uncomfortably and Ambachew tried to explain to me that this was "medehanit nay buda" [medicine for Evil Eye]. I retorted that I thought his sickness was only of the stomach, not from buda, but I realized that they thought I was crazy or just plain wrong. I also realized that that was why Tibbletz had left—so she wouldn't have to watch her baby being tortured, even if it was meant for his own good. [After the procedure was finished, she returned to the house, looking disturbed.]

Kiros stopped crying relatively quickly, and drank a lot of breast milk, which seemed to stay down. But then Tibbletz [tied] him [onto] her back and walked around with him, his stomach rubbing against her back and no doubt hurting him.

She said she wanted to bring the baby to Humera tomorrow to look for more habesha medehanit, but I convinced her to wait a bit until the course of injections he is taking has finished. She agreed.

Later I met [the health assistant] and told him what had happened. He agreed to see Kiros again—he said that maybe he had been given too much medicine or was even allergic to the medication. I told Tibbletz I'd go with her in the morning and she seemed glad. She said to me, "You are the only one who can get me in [to the clinic]. If I go alone or with someone else they say, 'This baby is too small to worry about,' and they refuse to see me."

Although many people found it difficult to obtain access to biomedical health care in Ada Bai, it was not clear to me that they preferred one type of health care over another. Rather, people took advantage of every option they had: ailments were typically treated simultaneously by both biomedicine and traditional methods. Thus, when a patient was successfully healed, it was difficult to determine which type of medicine had been responsible for the recovery. When Kiros later recovered, his father told me that the traditional medicine had been very powerful and had cured the boy; he did not think the procaine penicillin had had anything to do with the cure. Knowing that I had been disturbed by the painful impact of the traditional medicine, he tried to explain why they had done what they had: "We are doing this because we are scared. We are scared of losing him."

Observing such operations brought me into direct conflict with my anthropological training. In such situations I found it nearly impossible to remain an observer, to impassively report on the customs and habits of the people with whom I lived. At the same time, I knew that any attempt to get people to stop burning and cutting their children would be fruitless. In some cases, I was convinced that the traditional remedies were harmful and could even cause death. For instance, it was common for people to treat a snake bite by cutting open the bite area and sucking or squeezing the wound to draw the venom out. The snake venom, however, acted as an anticoagulant and prevented the blood from clotting. Their efforts could reduce the amount of time that a person could survive without the anti-venom medicine, which was only available in Humera (where it was kept in cold storage). I pleaded with people not to cut the bite area open, without effect. I believe that lives were lost as a result of this continued practice (it also could have encouraged the spread of HIV from snake bite victim to those administering the cuts).

The most I could do was to try to make biomedicine available to them as an additional option. However, my inability to keep my own cultural bias about which type of treatment was most effective out of my dealings with people plagued me throughout my stay in Ada Bai, and there were likely some instances in which I disregarded local beliefs and practices and encouraged people to use biomedical solutions whether or not it was clearly more efficacious.

Now That the War Is Over, It Is Important to Have More Children

Large families were common in Ada Bai. The question of how many children it was desirable to have was heavily influenced by people's experience of child loss. Most older people that I spoke with (that is, adults over the age of thirty-five) told me that half of their children had died prematurely as a result of sickness, famine, or injury during the war. These losses had instilled heavy grief in the parents, which resulted in a desire for more children to replace those who had died. At the same time, there was a practical approach to having children: it was necessary to have at least one or two children survive to adulthood so that the parents could be cared for in their old age. Children moved into a new house and compound when they married—in Tigray, the couple moved to an area close to the husband's family, while in Ada Bai there was no hard and fast rule about residence. When a parent was widowed, he or she was likely to go to live with an adult son or daughter if there were no other children remaining in the house.

Another woman told me that the ideal number of children to have was four. She said that she based this calculation on the notion that a woman should have a child every four years, from age sixteen to thirty-two. Such spacing would help to preserve the health of the mother. She acknowledged, however, that such spacing was rarely enforceable.

It is likely that the end of the war encouraged couples to have more children. People said that before they had gone to Sudan they had been afraid to have children for fear that the Derg might take the child from them. In addition, men and women were separated through displacement and enlistment in the armed forces, which prevented them from having children. In the climate of peace and relative security, there was more reason to resume childbearing. These observations are anecdotal, however; to my knowledge, no research on changes in birth rates have been conducted in Tigray since the end of the civil war.

Very few couples used any form of contraception besides abstinence (devout Christians abstain from sexual relations during fasting seasons). Women often tried to prolong the length of time they breast-fed their newborns because they understood that this could help prevent pregnancy. However, it was very common for women to become pregnant while their youngest child (aged between one and two years) was still breast-feeding. The loss of breast milk caused by the start of a new pregnancy deprived this child of its most important source of nutrition (see Palloni and Tienda 1986 and Defo and Palloni 1995). Wealthier families supplemented the child's diet with goat or cow's milk, or even powdered milk (which was extremely expensive), but most families were too poor to be able to afford additional milk or food for the child. Several times, I visited homes where a baby had just been born to find the next oldest child, who was younger than two years, exhibiting severe signs of malnutrition. In many cases these children died, often despite desperate but too late attempts to save them through therapeutic feeding in the hospital. By the time medical treatment was sought, opportunistic infections had already claimed the child and made recovery impossible. George Foster, citing Burgess and Dean (1962), argues that in some African societies the cause of malnutrition in the child whose access to breast milk has been disrupted by the birth of a new child is "insufficient quantities of love and affection" (1965, 299). From this Burgess and Dean conclude that "there does not seem to be an easy acceptance of the idea that there can be enough love for all." Parents in Ada Bai never said that there was a shortage of love. At the same time, the mother would stop breast-feeding the toddler in favor of the newborn. The toddler's inability to thrive on whatever food was available to him was explained as the result of either disease, spirit possession, or God's will.[11]

For people in Ada Bai, bearing children was a way of making a new start in this peacetime era, of helping to erase the losses they had suffered during the war and refugee experience. Despite their poverty, few people considered having many children to be a liability. Women wanted children whether they were married or not, whether the father played a role in their upbringing or not. Once, while sitting with a group of women, most of whom were single, I was asked why I didn't take a Tigrayan husband. I joked that it did not seem that men were very reliable in Ada Bai, and that having a relationship with them did not seem like a good idea. "They stay for one month, and then they leave," I said. Belaynesh, a gorgeous woman who openly shared her husband and house with another woman with whom he had fathered two children while she had been away visiting her family (despite the fact that multiple wives were prohibited by Christian law), gave a short laugh. "A month? They stay for a week." I asked her whether she thought it was okay to have a man stay for such a short time, and she said, "Yes, because you will have a child." And how is it to have a child on your own? I asked her. "It's fine," she replied. Shortly after that, she took her daughter and returned to her family in the highlands of Tigray. The other wife soon left the man as well, and when I returned in 1997 I found him fetching his own water and complaining that he had no wife at all anymore. Most people felt that he had gotten what he deserved and joked about his predicament. When I visited in 2002, however, the man had died; most people believed that he had had AIDS.

The Woman Who Gave Birth to a Cloth

So great was one woman's desire to have children that she faked a pregnancy. Tsehai came to my house one evening in tears, saying that she was pregnant and was bleeding, and asked me to take her to the hospital. She was afraid to go to the Ada Bai clinic because she did not want anyone to know who the father was, though she was quick to tell me that he was a prominent political leader in the community. I agreed, and the next day I brought her to the hospital. The bleeding subsided, and I thought that she had miscarried. A few weeks later, however, she assured me that she was still pregnant, but that the bleeding had not stopped completely. We returned to the hospital, and I left her to be examined. Later, I met the medical director of the hospital and mentioned to him that I was concerned about Tsehai—would the child be safe if the bleeding continued, I asked him. Did he think that she should be referred to Tesseney Hospital close to the date of delivery in case she needed a blood transfusion?

The doctor hesitated, clearly wondering whether to breach the principle of patient confidentiality by discussing her case with me. Finally he said, "I have done two pregnancy tests. Tsehai is not pregnant." He explained that he had seen such a case only once before; he explained it by saying that the woman wanted a child so badly that she had convinced herself that she was pregnant, and that her uterus had in fact swollen as if she were pregnant. He said that in the earlier case, the swelling had reached a certain level, but once the woman had accepted the fact that she was not pregnant, it had gone down.

In this case, Tsehai was clearly unwilling to accept that she was not pregnant. She told me that the test must have been wrong, and scolded me because I had planned to be away on the day that she planned to deliver. I told her that I would prepare my research assistant to help get her to the hospital if she needed help, and then asked him to check on her on and around the appointed day.

When I returned to Ada Bai, my assistant told me that he had dropped in on her on the day that she had predicted she would deliver her baby. He found her in her bed, and she told him that she had delivered the previous night, but that the baby had been stillborn, its umbilical cord wound tightly around its neck. He asked her who had attended the birth, and she told him that her neighbors from Tembien had helped her. Later we heard that when those neighbors had visited her, she had told them that her neighbors from Axum had helped her. Upon my return to Ada Bai, she came and described the delivery to me in detail, virtually blaming me for the death of the fetus, saying that if I had been present then she was sure that it would have lived.

Tsehai seemed so sure of her story that I found myself almost believing her, until I concluded that the story was clearly implausible. A song immediately started to circulate through the village poking fun at the poor woman:

> *Cernai mengisti b'quila*
> *Cherki Welida Towila.*
> ሰርናይ መንግስቲ በቀላ
> ጨርቁ ወሊዱ ተዉላ
> Because she ate the government grain [i.e., food aid],
> Towila [her nickname, meaning The Tall One] gave birth to a cloth.

This situation mystified me for a long time, and I still cannot claim to fully understand all that prompted Tsehai to stage this pregnancy. She may have had a serious medical problem that she was afraid of, and chose pregnancy as the most acceptable diagnosis for her swelling and bleeding. My interpretation of her attempts to hide the fact that she was not pregnant, however, was that this woman, who had first been married at age nine, had her first child at age twelve, had been abandoned by three husbands, had already buried two children, and was supporting herself through prostitution, wanted to reestablish her reputation as a respectable and desirable woman by proving her (probably real) romantic union with the most important political figure in the community. This liaison would help legitimize her standing as an honorable woman within the community, and giving birth to his child would prove the affair. (Another woman who had borne a child with another political figure enjoyed considerable caché when the child bore such a striking resemblance to the father that her paternity was unmistakable.)

The Pathology of Infant Mortality

Although infant mortality was a common occurrence in Ada Bai, it was not treated as an inevitability. As the episodes recounted previously indicate, parents tried any treatment they could gain access to in order to cure their sick children. This included tying on amulets filled either with dried plants thought to have curing power, ash blessed by a priest, or a prayer written for the child. In trying to understand parents' attitudes toward their sick and dying children, I spent a lot of time talking to parents, particularly mothers, about their understanding of child illnesses.

Despite the fact that most children approaching death grew increasingly malnourished, most mothers said that sickness and hunger were separate maladies. They believed that once the sickness was dispelled from the body or cured, then the child's appetite would return. This belief was probably bolstered by the fact that when they brought the child to the clinic, they were usually given antibiotics (most often antiparasite medication) and oral rehydration salts, with no food component—since the

Amulets like the one worn by the girl on the right were commonly thought to ward off evil spirits that could make a child ill or even kill her.

clinic did not have food stocks to distribute even to patients who suffered from malnutrition—and sent home. The mother went away with the idea that the problem was a medical one rather than a lack of food. Many times I visited houses where children were clearly suffering from marasmus (a type of protein-energy malnutrition that results in severe wasting). The children, usually two or three years old, stood hollow eyed, the skin stretched taut across their small bones, in a cruelly ironic way giving them the look of wizened old men and women. The skin around their buttocks sagged, and their spindly legs bowed out in a manner that made it difficult to see how they could even stand. In the early stages of wasting, the children were irritable and cried a lot; in the advanced stages they just lay silent and listless, unable even to whisk the flies from their faces. Mothers of such children usually told me that the child refused to eat, and that was why he or she was so thin. They said they knew the child was ill, but they expected that its appetite would return once the illness had been cured. Only on one occasion did I see a woman force-feed a child. Before she had given birth to Kiros, Tibbletz was asked to nurse her two-year-old nephew, who was severely malnourished. His own mother did not want to care for him since the boy's father, Ambachew's brother, had left her. For a few days Tibbletz forced him to eat, holding his nose while she poured porridge down his throat. "How can I watch him die when I have already buried my own children?" Tibbletz asked me, exasperated, while her husband and brother-in-law were away from the house. She did not expect a response. "This is not fair," she complained. After a few days, when the child's health did not improve, she succeeded in convincing the child's mother to take him back. Caring for another dying child who was not even her own, when she had no children of her own, was too painful for her. The boy died several weeks later.

The apparent resignation with which most mothers treated their children's deaths left me mystified. True enough, they would try any known method to prevent sickness and spirit possession from claiming their child. Once the child became very sick, however, most parents seemed to accept that their child would die. In this respect, mothers in Ada Bai were similar to the poor Brazilian women that Scheper-Hughes (1993) writes about. Death was accepted as an inevitability, something beyond their control.

I asked Mebrat, who had a four-year-old daughter and a newborn son (from different marriages), about the role that individual choice played in determining the fate of the child. "Do parents believe that a child knows it is going to die?" I asked her. The following are my notes from that conversation:

Some say yes. A sick child who turns his head away from people or covers his head to hide from others in the room is thought to know that he is going to die. Some also say that a child who is extremely beautiful or fat, or who acts with exceeding kindness, is going to die.

Was this last case a matter of the child knowing it is going to die, or choosing to die?

No, it is a matter of God deciding to take a child. Since he or she does not have much time left in the world, God makes them extremely beautiful and generous so that the parents will always remember that child with special fondness. They will say "that was my biggest, healthiest, most beautiful child."

Still pushing, I wanted to know where the fatalism originates from.

Mebrat said that sometimes a child may not want to live [here is the high level of individual choice at a young age]. But more often [the decision] comes from God. "Most people believe that God makes a plan for each person when they are born, saying how long the person will live, what the quality of their life will be, etc.

[As an example, Mebrat told me] If I go to Adigrat and die from the cold weather there, my mother might say, "Oh, I should not have let her go to Adigrat. If she had not gone, she would be alive now." She can say that, but of course it would mean nothing, because God has his plan and if I am meant to die, I die.

Another time, my neighbor Assefash told me about the death of her three-year-old daughter. In 1983, Assefash had been living in Shire (western Tigray). One day, as she walked home carrying her daughter on her back, her daughter said to her, "Mother, soon I will go far away and leave you and Berhane [her oldest son] alone. Please let me down so I can go to play with the children who are far away." Shortly after that, the girl died suddenly. She concluded that sometimes children know when they are going to die.

Death Rituals: A Proper Exit from the Community

The fear of death that seized every parent was born not only from the frequency with which death visited each household but from the poverty and intense loss that had been experienced by nearly everyone during the war and famine. In that sense, it is unlikely that returnees' basic experiences of death were much different from those experienced in the highlands.

Expression of grief in the face of death was dramatic and uncontrolled; it was unlike other forms of suffering and tragedy, which were treated with stoicism. In the first hours after a loved one had died, people would wail hysterically, throw themselves on the ground, and rip their own clothing. They permitted themselves (and were permitted by the community) to express their usually well-guarded emotions of grief and sadness. Often the pain of having lost other family or friends resurfaced: people could be heard crying out the names of others who had died months or years before. It was in these moments that the full depth of sorrow that people carried within them was unleashed.

As in birth, the passage of the individual from the earthly life to that of the afterlife was highly ritualized. If possible, just before dying a last rite known as Nuzazey (ኑዛዜ) was administered. At this time, the person might communicate his wishes for inheritance of his assets, if he had any. If the death had occurred outside the home, the body was returned to the house, where older relatives and neighbors performed the ritual known as mugnaz (ምግናዝ), washing it with sanctified water and preparing it for burial. This ritual was performed by an older or elderly person of the same sex as the deceased; if there were no women around, a man could prepare the body of a woman, but women were forbidden from attending to the body of a man, unless of a male child. All body openings were sealed: eyes were closed; cotton was placed in ears and nostrils; a sash was used to bind the mouth shut; and feet, hands, and thumbs were bound together, straight.[12] The washed body was dressed in a new, clean shroud (*jedid*, ጀዲድ), usually made of white cloth. Priests came to the house and prayed over the body after it had been prepared (this part of the ritual was known as *metshaf nezazey*, መጽሐፍ ነዛዜ). Then the body was placed on a wooden bed, to be carried by pallbearers to the church. Relatives, neighbors, and friends gathered outside the house waiting for the body's emergence and the procession to the church. Women wore their white shawls around their torsos and under their arms in a toga-style (rather than the usual practice of wearing them over their shoulders), turning them upside down so that the colored banner that lined the edge came up to their faces, a sort of inversion of the everyday use of the garment. Men and women generally walked separately, men first and women behind them. In the churchyard, another blessing was made by as many priests as were able to attend, each wearing a brilliant white turban and a brightly colored, gold-threaded robe and matching parasol. Finally, the procession would file down to the cemetery, with men gathering around the grave with the priests, who would bless the body a final time before committing it to the earth (*hamed debe*, ሐመድ ድብ). Women would sit on the hillside a hundred or more meters away, sobbing quietly. One priest explained why women stayed away from the burial site:

> All women are kind. If [a woman] sees a dead body she may see it in her dreams and she might die. There are a lot of women who have become unconscious from seeing a dead body. Some women can be cured easily, but most become mad and can die. Our women are not educated . . . If a fighter woman [i.e., woman soldier] sees a dead body, she might carry him on her back. But if one of our women sees one, she might become sick. Maybe if we are educated . . . we will learn.

Women themselves showed no fear of seeing a dead body, and indeed they could observe the burial from their vantage point on the hillside. However, they agreed that it was not proper etiquette to mingle with the men at the graveside. The separation of the sexes may also have had to do with the belief that in the presence of God, such as in the church, men and women were to be segregated into separate spaces.

The cemetery was also considered an extremely dangerous place. It was said that when a person died as a result of spirit possession or attack, the spirit would wait until the body had been buried and then would go to the cemetery at night, dig up the body, and turn it into a goat or a donkey. The tebib who had passed the buda on to the person who had died would not eat until after the person's burial, and it was thus possible to identify the culprit. Although few people followed up in determining who had caused the death, everyone seemed to know stories of relatives hiding near the cemetery and catching the tebib exhuming the body. Because of the belief that evil or dangerous spirits may visit the graves of the newly deceased, children were not allowed to walk or play anywhere near the cemetery, and adults also stayed out of the area for fear that they might be wrongly accused of carrying the spirit.

Following burial of the body, the funeral procession returned to the house of the deceased's family, and began a mourning vigil, known as hazen (ሐዘን), that would last seven days and nights. The hazen of a child was often shorter than that of an adult, since the child did not have as many social connections. A child's hazen might last only three or four days. During that time, the family of the deceased and guests were served food (usually simple fasting food) and coffee by neighbors. Throughout the mourning period, the bereaved would not be left alone even for a moment during the seven days. They would be accompanied even to the latrine, to prevent them from becoming overwhelmed by the loss and breaking down crying. The family would sleep outside the house under a tent or plastic sheet, as would many of the guests. People would come and go, and the crowd would gradually dwindle in size. The mood of the funeral would gradually lighten, and to pass the time people would tell jokes and play card games, sometimes even betting for money—as long as there was no priest there to admonish them, as gambling was considered un-Christian— with the proceeds going to finance the hazen. Most of the bereaved relatives of the deceased, who had spent the entire seven days mourning, were eager to return to their daily responsibilities by the end of the seventh day. The most painful part of the mourning period had passed.[13]

Commemoration ceremonies, known as Teskar (ተስካር), were held on the fortieth and eightieth days following the death, and on the one-year anniversary of the death if the family had enough money. The Teskar was held to ensure that the spirit of the person would be admitted to heaven. These events were typically smaller in scale, and would last only one day. Some people reported that the Teskar were more modest affairs now than they had been in the past because the TPLF had instructed them not to spend so much money on elaborate festivities.

Crying was only permitted by priests during three moments of the funeral ceremony: when the death first occurred, when the body left the house to be carried to the church, and when the body entered the grave. Priests admonished people for crying at other times, saying that there was no reason to cry because the person would be cared for by God and admitted to heaven. Despite this injunction, and even in the face of priests who scolded them for crying, people cried freely throughout the funeral process. They often became hysterical, ripping their own clothes, tearing their hair from their heads, scratching their faces, and throwing themselves onto the ground. Often they shed tears even if they had not known the deceased well. As noted earlier, they cried not only for the individual whose death was being marked at that moment but for the deaths of all of those they had lost: mothers, fathers, children, sisters, brothers, and other relatives and friends. People could be commonly heard calling the name of the person or persons whose death they were mourning, even if that person had died years before. The deaths of children were usually mourned as intensely as those of adults during the first days, even though the total duration of the mourning period was shorter.[14]

Despite the injunction against crying at all but three moments of the funeral ritual, this was the only social space in which tears and sorrow were accepted not only by priests but by members of the community. Crying at any other time was considered a sign of sickness, spirit possession, or insanity. However, because funerals typically lasted for seven days and nights, the bereaved were able to cope with their sorrow in ways that I came to consider to be in many ways more effective than my own Anglo-Saxon experience of funerals that lasted only an hour or two. Once, upon receiving news of the death of a relative, I too attended a funeral and found myself mourning not only the child who had died but also my own relative.

The presence of a dead person and the funeral ritual were considered fertile ground to attract evil spirits. As a result, women who were pregnant or who had an unchristened newborn were warned by some priests not to attend funerals lest the Evil Eye attack them or their child. Another common belief was that if someone in your house was sick and a funeral procession passed by, you should close your door to prevent a spirit from coming and taking (killing) that person. Because of their vulnerability to spirit possession, children were taken away from the road while the procession was passing.

Deaths were treated the same no matter what the cause was, with one exception: smallpox. Although smallpox had been eradicated in Ethiopia during the 1970s (the last country in the world to become smallpox free), people said that when a person had died from smallpox, there would be no funeral, no crying, and no mourning, "for fear that the same would happen to you." The fact that, twenty years later, people continued to discuss the fear that smallpox instilled in them is a testament to the destructive power it held over the society.

When One Resting Place Is Not as Good as Another

All of the priests with whom I discussed funerary rituals agreed that a person who was baptized as an Orthodox Christian must be buried in a consecrated cemetery, but that it did not matter whether the person was buried in the village where he or she had been born or had lived at the time of death.[15] Nearly everyone I discussed this matter with, however, said that despite the assurance that it was not necessary to be buried in one's birthplace, they would prefer to return to their areas of origin to die so that they could be buried with others from the same community.

Many elderly people told me that, if they had been able to, they would have liked to have returned to their homes in Tigray to die. One man explained the difference between dying in Ada Bai and in his home area of Tembien, near the town of Abi Adi. "Death in your country, in your birthplace, is the best and most dignified way to die," he told me. Why? I asked him. "I know that every [piece of] ground is the same [he said, echoing the official doctrine concerning burial], but if you die in your birthplace all your family, relatives, and friends can participate at that time in the funeral and everyone knows who you are." The role of the funeral in celebrating the life of the person, with respect to his family, his community, and his dead ancestors, was considered extremely important by elderly residents of Ada Bai, who lamented that their lives would not receive a fitting closure if they died in Ada Bai. Another man told me that sometimes people were teased while they were refugees for not knowing where their father was buried, as if that signified that one did not have, in his words, any "roots."

Funerals in the highlands tied people not only to their immediate community but also to the wider network of villages in the surrounding area in a more profound sense than did funerals in Ada Bai. Following a highland death, an announcement (*awyat*, አወያት) would go out to the surrounding villages or tabias to call people to the funeral (Tessema 1956, 15). An elderly man in Ada Bai recalled that in the highlands people who were not able to attend a person's funeral because they lived too far away were given the opportunity to pay their respects on market day in a ceremony known as *Agobar* (አጎባር).[16] The family of the deceased would carry an Ethiopian flag and would decorate a horse with a brightly colored banner draped over its saddle so that all would know where to go to greet the family. In that way, one could fulfill one's commitment to the wider community through paying respects to the dead and to his or her relatives. Agobar was not practiced at Ada Bai, since the market was only a local one and people did not come there from other villages. People had not been settled for long enough in Ada Bai or the surrounding settlements to develop wide associative networks. If a relative of an Ada Bai resident was reported to have died elsewhere, however, a shorter version of the hazen was held at the relative's house so that neighbors could pay their respects to the family.

Concerns about death and being far from one's birthplace were a source of considerable anxiety for elderly residents of Ada Bai. Those who had spent most of their lives living in the highlands, as respected members of a community and church parish or mosque, felt uncomfortable with the idea of being buried in a place with others whom they did not know well and who were not from the same place. A man in his eighties told me:

I look at my birthplace as my "eye." [That is, just as my eye can tell me whether things are bad or good, my birthplace shows me the same.] I am thinking about it all the time and want to go back . . . Your birthplace is the place where you grew up and played with your friends, even where you quarreled. Whether it is bad or good the area itself never disappears from my eye. Even now. Everyone's birthplace is very nice if it is the same to others as it is to me. Here in Ada Bai we are saying that this is Tigray so it is our place [bota, ቦታ]. But it has a very great difference with my birth area and I will never see it as the same. I [think of] my birthplace all the time. Even as the sun rises and sun sets, and the moon rises, they are different [here] . . . Everyone [who has not left their birthplace] can see with his own eyes even if is bad or good. [People don't know the suffering that I know because they have not left their birthplace.] So I like my country [birthplace]. I am very sad being far away from my area [of origin]. The people that repatriated in 1979 from Sudan, they got farm-land, oxen . . . By now everything is okay for them. But for us still we are suffering and have a hard time. Here everything seems very bad to me and every day I am very sad. I have no helper, no land, everyone is in a problem too and I don't have any kind of chance to go home. I am old enough. I am nearly ready to die.

This desire to be close to one's birthplace (*addi*, ኣዲ, or *hager seb*, ሀገር ሰበ) was directly related to the extent to which the person felt tied to the community in which he or she lived. Younger Ada Bayans, who had come of age in the returnee settlement, were more concerned with participating in the community that they had helped to form in Ada Bai. They felt that their prospects for economic survival were better in the returnee settlement, and that in time Ada Bai would be as compelling a home as the highlands had been for their parents. Parents who would have liked to return to their highland homes to die in many cases agreed to stay with their families in the lowlands, sacrificing a proper closure to their lives in the interests of being able to better feed their families.

Even among those for whom Ada Bai had become more homelike, it was important that those who died were buried in the village rather than in Humera or elsewhere. I got involved in a heated debate with one mother who wanted to bring her eleven-year-old daughter, who had advanced tuberculosis and appeared to be in a coma, home to die. Initially, she had told me that the girl was already dead, so I was quite surprised to arrive at the hospital to find that the girl was actually alive, though it was not clear if she was conscious. I asked the girl to indicate if she could hear us speaking, and I thought that she raised her eyebrows in acknowledgment. I pleaded with the mother to keep the girl in the hospital in case there was any chance at all that she might recover. The mother argued strongly with me that there was no point in waiting, that she would certainly die, and that if she was not brought back to Ada Bai now, she would have to be buried in Humera because she did not have the money to pay for a taxi to transport the body. Here my training in cultural relativism and my feelings as a person about what was ethically the right thing to do came into sharp conflict. I could not bring myself to agree to take the girl back to Ada Bai. A few days later, she did die, and I contributed money to bring her back to Ada Bai, where she was buried.

This incident left me feeling guilty for having refused the mother her wish, and led me to wonder whether I had made a mistake in not helping her to bring the girl home before she died. I also wondered whether Tigrayans considered a person who was in a coma or unconscious to have already died, since I had heard that the bodies of some people who had died from spirit possession had remained warm after death. I asked many of my neighbors what they would have done in such a situation. Opinions varied. Most people said that if the girl was still breathing, she should be considered to be alive, and should remain in the hospital. Some people said "*mereyt mereyt iyu* [ground is ground; it is all the same]" and that it did not matter where she was buried. Others said that no matter where she died, she should be buried in the village where she had lived. Being buried "alone" as they put it, meaning among strangers who were not from the same community, was to be avoided at all costs.

Institutional Indifference to Illness and Death

In her study of life in the Brazilian altiplano, Scheper-Hughes describes the seemingly matter-of-fact and almost uncaring way in which mothers resign themselves to the deaths of their children, as a trait which is similar in kind, though admittedly perhaps not in scale, to the general insensitivity shown by the Brazilian government toward its poorest citizens (1993, 276). Although mothers in Ada Bai appeared uncaring only when they had become resigned to the child's death, the institutional indifference of the health care workers in both Ada Bai and Humera was strikingly similar to the Brazilian case and to other cases throughout the developing world where health care workers are not paid enough even to ensure quality medical care let alone a sympathetic bedside manner.

My relations with most of the health care workers in Humera, and to a lesser extent Ada Bai, were double edged. On one hand, I sought to cultivate their respect and friendship so that when I needed them to assist with one of the referral patients I brought them, they would be cooperative. On the other hand, I was continually fighting with them to view their patients not merely as bodies or cases but as individual people. The struggle was a losing one, since they had enormous caseloads—I calculated that the health assistant in Ada Bai was able to spend an average of three to six minutes with each patient, and many patients had to be turned away if they did not arrive at the clinic early enough to receive an appointment number, which were limited to sixty a day. Those who were able to get numbers sat outside in the hot sun until their number was called. In Humera, the hospital staff were reluctant to work after hours unless they were on call, even if the life of the patient was threatened. Many doctors worked in their own private clinics at night and often referred people to those clinics or (reportedly intentionally) gave them wrong or incomplete treatments at the hospital so that they could charge them for care at the private clinics.[17] Those who could not afford the private clinics often went without any care. I once had to disrupt a service at the local Protestant church to summon a doctor—who was on call but who had left the hospital to attend the prayer meeting—to assist a woman who had gone into shock while in labor. After I berated the doctor for not telling anyone where he would be, the doctor assured me that he would pray over the woman all night to make up for his transgression. (He later attributed her recovery to his prayers rather than to his medical skills.)

On one occasion early in my fieldwork I brought a man with advanced tuberculosis to the hospital and returned three days later with his wife to see him. He was not in his bed. The hospital staff told us that he had been released, and suggested that we might find him at the outpatient clinic, on the other side of town. We went there, but there was no record of his having been either treated or discharged at the outpatient clinic. We returned to the hospital, and one of the health assistants quietly suggested to me that he might have died. I asked him why he had not informed the man's wife and told us where the body was. He said that he "did not want to make her cry." Even then, he refused to tell the woman that her husband had died, and I was forced to do so using what were then my halting Tigrinya language skills. The health assistant said that the body had probably been taken to one of the cemeteries in town (when no kin were present to take the body from the hospital morgue, the bodies were buried on a rotating basis in one of the town's several cemeteries, with no funeral). Since the man had died on a Tuesday, it was likely that he had been buried in St. Mikael's Cemetery. We located the gravedigger, who acknowledged that he had indeed buried the body, and he led us to a grave, marked by a pile of stones, which he claimed was the man's but which looked like all of the others. The wife, clearly distraught by the way her husband had been disposed of, stood by the grave weeping and praying before I led her back to the car to take her home.

Poor medical care was exacerbated by a lack of space or equipment to treat people. I discovered that several people who had gone to the Ada Bai clinic who needed intravenous treatment had been given the IV bag attached to the patient's arm and sent home. Not knowing what to do with the bags, the family had left them on the floor under the patient's bed or in the bed, the needle still in place in his or her arm. Empty bags were discarded in the open air, where children had easy access to them. Upon being asked to bring a man to the hospital and finding his IV bag lying under his bed, I angrily confronted the health assistant about the matter. He protested that he did not have space in the clinic to treat all of the people who needed care, and had thought that sending them home with the IV was better than not treating them at all. This error in judgment was later corrected when I reported the matter to the district health officer, who threatened to remove the health assistant from his job if he continued such neglectful practices.

The indifference shown by the health care professionals toward their patients, and the difficulty that people had in obtaining access to biomedical care, certainly did little to foster faith in *tseada medehanit* (ፀአዳ መደሃኒት, white people's medicine, or biomedicine). In the absence of a caring form of medical treatment, traditional medicine (*habesha medehanit*) was much more appealing, and the community itself bore much of the responsibility for caring for its ill and dying members.

In rituals of birth and death, the importance of place and community was central. The person's significance was never only individual, but was also always defined in relation to the larger collective identity of the village or the homeland. Older people, through their experience of displacement, were conscious of their ties to community and family in ways that they did not seem to have been cognizant of before.

Preservation of rituals learned in the highlands, passed down through the generations, helped to maintain a sense of cultural continuity through the experiences of displacement and return. They also helped a group of people, from different parts of Tigray, with different histories, to become a community once more. They were, in effect, the building blocks of that new community.

6

Ada Bai's Place in the Wider World

One evening while drinking coffee at Tibbletz and Ambachew's house, Ambachew said to me, "I think that Meles Zenawi must have malaria." I asked him why he thought this was true. "Because," he said, "he is sleeping." Though joking, Ambachew was referring to an important theme that emerged during my stay in Ada Bai: people felt that political leaders were unaware of, or unresponsive to, the plight of the returnees and the challenges of integration they faced every day.

So far, I have primarily focused on the means by which Ada Bai returnees constructed their lives at the most local level, and on the rules governing individual lives, households, interhousehold relations, and community formation. My focus has been on the internal dynamics of the community—the means by which internal resources were used to map a community onto a landscape. My discussion of emplacement processes would be incomplete, however, without an examination of the ways community formation was influenced by, and at the same time exerted influence on, forces outside the geographic confines of the community.

The experience of emplacement was circumscribed by actors occupying spaces with varying degrees of distance from Ada Bai. Despite their external locations, they influenced emplacement processes and helped define the parameters within which community creativity and improvisation functioned. These parameters helped to define the possible and impossible, and to establish a foundation for future action.

Returnees coming to Ada Bai faced not only the challenge of emplacing themselves within their geographic surroundings and building a new community but also of negotiating their position within the wider political and economic contexts of Tigray as a region and Ethiopia as a whole. They were no longer subversives and supporters of a guerrilla movement fighting for the overthrow of a dictatorial regime. They were victors, their leaders having taken control of the two palaces in Addis Ababa (one for the president, the other for the prime minister) from which central control emanates. Yet the role that these new holders of state power would play in local lives (just as their role vis-à-vis the other Ethiopian regions, neighboring states in the Horn of Africa, and farther abroad) had yet to take shape.

Returnees celebrated the fact that the TPLF/EPRDF military victory enabled them to return to Ethiopia. Yet they returned with questions about the new arrangement of power and their place within it, and with the expectation that the new government and the international aid community would assist them in their quest to reestablish themselves. They soon were forced to come to terms with the fact that the government and aid agencies had other ideas about their obligations to the returnees, and that facilitating postreturn integration was not high on their list of priorities.

The State in the Third World

In examining the role of the state and political actors outside Ada Bai in internal village dynamics, it is necessary to look closely at the workings of the state. Joel Migdal notes that: "Today, for those of us in the West, the state has been part of our natural landscape. Its presence, its authority, its place behind so many rules that fashion the minutiae of our lives, have all been so pervasive that it is difficult for us to imagine the situation being otherwise" (1988, 15). The image of the state as "neutral arbiter above the conflicts and interests of society . . . [which] conceals the workings of relations of rule and forms of discipline in day to day life" (Alonso 1994, 318; see also Nagengast 1994) is one born from analysis at the level of the political capital, from looking at the nominal holders of power rather than at those over whom that power is supposedly exerted. This image also assumes that state power is exercised and felt in the same way in all parts of the country.

Recently in anthropology the role of the nation-state has been brought into question, in recognition of the increasingly important role of transnational information, population, and commodity flows that bring with them changing relationships to power (Appadurai 1996). While Arjun Appadurai hails this shift as instrumental in bringing about the sort of deterritorialization that ultimately erodes the notion of the nation-state, Ong has pointed out that "the very suggestiveness of Appadurai's formulation begs the question of whether imagination as a social practice can be so independent of national, transnational, and political-economic structures that enable, channel, and control the flows of people, things, and ideas" (1999, 11). Ong's question may be particularly applicable to forced migrants, whose displacement and return are made possible or necessary by the movements of the state. What happens at the political and economic margins of the nation-state may take on a dynamic of its own, but at least in the case of the Ada Bai returnees, the political realities of living in postwar Ethiopia set the context for defining, at least in part, possibility and potential with respect to cultural creativity. Ada Bai returnees can be better understood as "unprivileged" migrants rather than the sort of "privileged" migrants that Appadurai seems to be referring to when he celebrates action independent of the nation-state (Stefansson 2003). Although transnational flows and globalization's influences on culture have had some effect on changing the relationship between state and locality in the present case, there are limits to this theoretical application that are well demonstrated by the ethnographic evidence.

In Ethiopia, the control of the state—by which I mean the central government—over peasants, particularly those living at the geographic peripheries of the country, has always been tenuous. Tribute was traditionally paid locally to agents of the state, but the relationship as seen by the peasant was between him or herself and the priest, parish, local lord, or local feudal king rather than to the emperor and later to the peasant association or *kebele* rather than to the central Derg bureaucracy. Unlike virtually every other border area in Ethiopia, however, where ethnic groups have grown accustomed to years of marginalization and neglect, Ethiopians living along the Tigray/Sudan/Eritrea border had a close relationship with the EPRDF by virtue of their ethnic ties and their involvement at the grassroots level in supporting, harboring, and supplying personnel for the TPLF during the war.[1] In the refugee camps, close ties with the TPLF had been maintained through public education campaigns, recruitment of refugees into the TPLF army, and through the assistance provided by the Relief Society of Tigray. Despite these close relationships, return to Ethiopia involved a reexploration by the TPLF and the former refugees of their relationship with each other and a tentative questioning by the returnees of the meaning(s) of citizenship, including the privileges and obligations that came with it, because they no longer opposed those who controlled the central government, yet were also no longer as politically valuable to the TPLF as they had been as refugees.

Repatriation signified a move away from the kind of managed care that characterizes many refugee situations (though arguably not most, as a sizable percentage of the world's refugees are never assisted or even recognized). Ada Bayans were moving to a place where there were no international NGOs and where the only national NGO present seemed eager

Relief Society of Tigray (REST) officials distribute food to recent repatriates in a settlement near Ada Bai.

to withdraw as quickly as possible because it considered the returnees to have been "spoiled" in the camps and to have unrealistic expectations of the kind of assistance they should be receiving. In this sense, repatriation involved a move from tightly managed care to a space that was, for its residents, disappointingly unmanaged.

In this chapter, I look first at the ways that different agents of the state and international organizations viewed and were viewed by the Ada Bai returnees. These actors wielded the power to decide where returnees would be settled and what their legal rights to resources would be. However, they were not able to completely determine returnees' experiences, since those returning to Ethiopia had their own ideas and expectations about the rights that should be available to them. I then examine how Ada Bai residents perceived the state and other holders of power, including government agents, aid agency personnel, and religious leaders, as shapers of their experience.

Decentralization of Power in the Postconflict Era

State control was not exercised from the center to the periphery directly. The EPRDF introduced a strategy of decentralization that gave the regions wide powers of autonomy.[2] Regional administrations were much more involved in establishing legal and other juridical conditions for their people than they had ever been before. These conditions were, in turn, translated into local codes and communicated to the populace through a narrowing spiral of political power by the zones, woredas, and baitos.

At the same time, nonstate actors and systems were also active in establishing the postwar social order. Religious institutions enjoyed a resurgence of influence. Private entrepreneurs, who controlled much of the labor market in the area, also wielded a great deal of influence over the organization of local economic and social relations.[3] Law and order, therefore, was a negotiated and malleable concept that resembled a "mélange" of different institutions, in which the state was but one of a variety of actors wielding control:

> The image of a mélange conveys two facets . . . First, the groups exercising social control in a society may be heterogeneous both in their form (for example, a small family and a sprawling tribal organization) and in the rules they apply (for example, based on personal loyalty and founded on profit maximization). Second, the distribution of social control in society may be among numerous, fairly autonomous groups rather than concentrated largely in the state. (Migdal, 28)

In Ada Bai, power emanated not only from the state bureaucracy but also from religious leaders, commercial farm operators who controlled access to employment, and—through their absence—the international organizations that had played such an important role in Sudan, not only in determining the kind and amount of resources the refugees needed but also in imposing their own version of order on them.

From Highest to Lowest Priority

When the EPRDF came to power, one of its highest priorities was to repatriate the estimated 160,000 citizens (in addition to Tigrayans, Amhara and Oromo refugees were also repatriated to their respective regions) from the refugee camps in Sudan (TGE 1992). Bringing refugees home was meant to be a convincing demonstration to the Ethiopian population, to the Diaspora—made up of several hundred thousand people who had escaped or left Ethiopia during the Derg years and were now living scattered throughout the globe—and to foreign observers that the factors that had forced people to flee Ethiopia in 1984–85 had been eliminated. Such thinking mirrored approaches by international humanitarian assistance agencies toward refugee repatriation, summarized in Chris Dolan's algebraic reasoning: "if $x + y = z$ then $x = z - y$, so in international refugee law, if *Individual citizen + War = Refugee*, then *Refugee - War = Individual citizen*" (1999, 93). Conversely, failure of the Ethiopian refugees to return from exile could have led to speculation by the international community about whether the differences between the EPRDF and the Derg were as significant as the former claimed.

At the same time, the extension of the regional boundary of Tigray to incorporate much of the former Begemder awraja (including Wolkait) made it politically expedient for the Tigrayan refugees to be returned to that area. Resettling fifteen thousand Tigrayans in the area served to sway the ethnic balance between Amharas and Tigrayans, making the area incontrovertibly ethnically Tigrayan.[4] By allocating some of the land used by the former state farm to returnee households, the government believed it could reintegrate the former refugees without placing additional strain on the highland communities (whose landholdings were already so small that most could not produce enough food to meet their households' needs for the year).[5] In addition, settling people in the lowland areas around Humera would provide a pool of workers for the large commercial farms that were being reopened by private investors or share companies. The largest of these was the Hiwot Agricultural Corporation, a private share company owned by TPLF loyalists whose profits went to social development projects within Tigray.

The government of Ethiopia expected that with the area's fertile farmland and wage labor opportunities, the returnees could become self-sufficient. However, little or no economic analysis had been done on the cost of living or the components of self-sufficiency that returnees would need to accumulate on their own. The government had attempted to reach an agreement with the United Nations High Commissioner for Refugees, which was eager to promote repatriation so that it could close the camps in Sudan, to provide "reintegration packages" to the returnees. When no agreement had been signed by the beginning of June 1993, the government became concerned that people would not be able to plant crops in time if they did not return to Ethiopia that month. The government therefore repatriated people on its own, giving them only nine months' food rations, a few household utensils, and no cash grant. This low level of assistance undermined returnees' trust in the government as having their best interests at heart and eroded the community's support for it. Had more resources been available, returnees' reintegration experiences would have been easier.

The Shift to Civilian Rule and Ideas about Individual-State Relations

For the first few months following the repatriation in June 1993, political and administrative leadership in Ada Bai was held by a TPLF political cadre known as Wedi Shambel.[6] In his mid thirties, he was something of a war hero. He had been injured while fighting in the war and traveled by donkey for one week through western Tigray to Sudan where a team of MSF-France surgeons amputated his leg at the thigh. He had continued his service to the TPLF, working as an administrator in the refugee camps. His sacrifice and bravery earned him the respect of people in Ada Bai, though most people were also easily intimidated by his gruff manner and unswerving dedication to "the Struggle" above all else. It was Wedi Shambel who decided that I would be welcome in Ada Bai, but also that my house plot would be next to his house. He explained that this arrangement was for my "safety," though it was clear to me that he also intended to keep an eye on me as I worked.

After repatriating with the refugees from Safawa, Wedi Shambel's mandate was to establish and organize the settlement at Ada Bai. His duties included overseeing the allocation of house plots and businesses and arranging for the hand-over of power to elected civilians. He also was to prepare the people to participate in the first national elections of the Transitional Government of Ethiopia, and to help present the new draft constitution to the people for discussion and ratification. These discussions, held in January 1994, provide important insight into returnees' ideas about such seemingly abstract concepts as land ownership and use, citizenship, and the defining principles of culture.

The mere fact that the Transitional Government of Ethiopia was able to organize these meetings in every locale throughout the country was an impressive display of its considerable organizational and logistical skills. Every village received a copy of the draft constitution. Each article in the document was presented to the assembled group as a choice of two or more options, which were to be discussed and voted on by the public.

Woreda officials had been trained on how to present the choices to the people—with procedures for explaining each item in a balanced manner that did not convey partiality on the part of the facilitator. Participants in the meeting, who included at least one adult—usually two, including the woman—from each household, voted on each article.

The entire process lasted for two eight-hour days. Men and women sat on opposite sides under a purpose-built shade made from wood and straw to discuss the constitution. Despite the scorching heat, the cries of young

Officials explain the possible provisions of the proposed constitution to Ada Bai residents at a public meeting.

children, and the shortage of drinking water (women periodically passed around pitchers of water to the crowd), attention was fixed on the pressing matters of defining citizenship, government structure, a national language, the rights of ethnic groups, and the judicial process. Questions for discussion ranged from the general—should government have complete authority, some authority, or less authority—to the specific—which human rights should be mentioned in the constitution. Debate was lively, but, with nearly every vote, the crowd voted together. Perhaps not surprisingly, their decisions matched those of the ultimate document adopted in Addis Ababa.[7]

Debate was particularly lively on two issues that resounded with the people of Ada Bai. The first was land ownership. Most of those who had lived as refugees in Sudan had lost their access to land. Farming was seen as the principal means of recovering one's productive assets, so people were sensitive to the need to prevent such losses in the future. Participants at the meeting were asked to choose between two positions:

1. If land is not owned by all people, it can bring problems between government, people, and nationalities (as some will have land and others will not), so it should be owned by the government.
2. If land is not sold or passed [inherited], it becomes less valuable, so it should be sold/owned privately. Also, citizens should have a right to own any kind of production (e.g., farmland, business property, etc.).

Lengthy debate took place about the benefits and disadvantages of private versus state ownership of land. One old man stood up and said, "Land should not be sold or [its ownership] changed because people who are poor cannot afford to buy it." Another said, "If we sell [land], slowly slowly [i.e., through multiple sales] it will go to a rich person. If I grow [crops] on it, I am producing some food. I may think I am gaining by selling it [the land], but in the end I have gained nothing." Others nodded and murmured their agreement.

A woman expressed her conviction that the same precautions should be taken to safeguard houses in urban areas. A person should not, she said, have to live in danger of losing his or her house. Others agreed, but a man brought up the idea that an individual should be able to sell a property that is a place of business: "If someone builds a big place like a hotel, he has a right to sell the house but not the land," he said. "This is what we were taught." The facilitator, a TPLF-trained official from the woreda council, quickly stepped in, saying, "I want to hear what you believe now, not what you were taught."

Both men were referring to the TPLF political education programs that had been carried out both in Tigray prior to the evacuation to Sudan and in the camps while the war was going on. These campaigns were an essential part of the TPLF's ideological strategy. Ada Bai residents recalled that the most important subject of these education campaigns pertained to land ownership and the importance of equitable access to land for all. TPLF propaganda did not advocate private ownership, but did insist that farmers should have control over their agricultural production—unlike the Derg, which required that farmers sell their products at unfair prices.[8] The

TPLF worked to garner and maintain support for the ideals of the movement throughout the war, and was extremely successful in molding peasant consciousness. Thus, many people found it nearly impossible to develop an individual perspective on the issue because the propaganda had become so deeply entrenched in their consciousnesses.

The testimonies of Ada Bai returnees were apparently not much different from those of highland Tigrayans who had either remained on their farms or had returned from the refugee camps in Sudan earlier. As J. Young notes:

> Without exception the peasants I interviewed in 1993 voiced their strong opposition to . . . proposals (of a free market in land). Their view was that in the absence of off-farm work, a free land market would only benefit a small minority, while poor peasants would be forced into the towns and a life of destitution. As a result, conditions would replicate, as more than one peasant noted, the feudalism of the past. The TPLF leadership also subscribed to this view, although they maintained their desire to move towards a free market in land as and when economic conditions in the province [i.e., region] allow. (1997, 198–99)

J. Young's research found a similar level of consistency between early attitudes toward access to land and the political ideology of the party concerning land ownership. He quotes the "Draft Economic Policy of the Transitional Government," as it appeared in the EPRDF News Bulletin of September 30, 1991:

> They [the peasants] would be compelled to sell their land to a few wealthy individuals, leaving themselves landless and without any means of livelihood. This process would surely lead the peasants back to a situation similar to that of the feudal era, where a few landlords owned and controlled most of the land. (1997, 246 n. 5)

It is perhaps a testament to the success of the TPLF propaganda and education campaigns that scholars and aid workers who have worked in Tigray since the end of the war have found it difficult to determine whether people's statements about political issues were what they really believed or reflected what they had been taught during the war by the TPLF—or whether there was really any difference between these two perspectives. Supporters of the TPLF, including many foreigners who assisted the movement in the cross-border operation during the war, say that the TPLF's political ideology is an expression of the will of the peasantry, and thus that there is no difference in the ideological stance between individual and movement. Other—some might say more cynical—observers say that the political conditioning of the peasantry and the hold that the TPLF exerts over its people are forms of coercion that silence any dissenting opinions. After two years in Tigray, it was difficult for me to side completely with either of these views. While I do not completely agree that every position of the TPLF was a product of grassroots ideology, I do think that, particularly in the first years after the end of the war, people honestly believed that most of what the TPLF stood for was, at least in its revolutionary ideological mode, worthy of support, even if the ideas were introduced to them by the movement itself. As time went on, individual viewpoints began to be more firmly expressed. Indeed, in 2002, these issues were at the heart of a split within the TPLF leadership that resulted in the expulsion of the president of Tigray Region and several of his associates from the party.

Who Is an Ethiopian?

Another issue from the constitutional meetings that sparked a great deal of debate involved citizenship. People were asked to consider the following propositions and give their reactions to them:

1. If a person is born from two Ethiopians, no matter where he/she is born, he is to be considered an Ethiopian citizen.
2. If a person is born [anywhere] from one Ethiopian and one foreigner, he/she should be entitled to Ethiopian citizenship if he accepts the language and culture.
3. If a person is born in Ethiopia but is a foreigner [i.e., with both parents being non-Ethiopians], he may be an Ethiopian citizen.

The issue touched a sensitive nerve for those who had delivered children in Sudan or had themselves been born there, and even more so for people who had conceived children with a Sudanese man or woman (though these were extremely few). The question was whether the *place of birth* should be the determining criteria for Ethiopian citizenship, or whether other factors, such as language, culture, or heredity were more important. Women spoke up emotionally on the subject. One woman said, "If a child is born to an Ethiopian woman and a *ferenjee* [foreigner] and he comes and says he wants to be with his mother, he should be allowed [i.e., he should be given Ethiopian citizenship]. Another man agreed with her: "If the child's mother is Ethiopian, surely the child must be as well." This interested me, since in other contexts, this being a patrilineal society, the child's identity is derived from the father. A second man said, "A baby is not born knowing what country he is in. [When we repatriated] he was not left in Sudan because he has a Sudanese parent; he was brought here [by his parent(s)] with the rest of us."

In this context, the birthplace of the individual was not thought to be important in determining the child's citizenship. Participants spoke of language as the basis of culture, the primary defining element that bound people to a region, and insisted that anyone who spoke Tigrinya and had at least one Tigrayan parent should be considered an Ethiopian citizen and have the right to petition for Ethiopian citizenship no matter where they had been born.

This redefinition of the importance of the birthplace to identity was markedly different from ideas about rootedness that older adults had, as I discussed in chapter 5. Displacement had forced people to adapt the meaning that they associated with the birthplace—from the affective ties of loyalty that had been maintained in previous generations to a more flexible, practical association among members of the younger generations, who had been born or had given birth in exile.

Rights and Obligations of Peasants Vis-à-Vis the State

The views expressed by Ada Bai residents at the constitutional meetings reflected their ideal of how they thought a government *ought* to act with regard to property, and of what citizenship *should* be based on rather than their experience of how they themselves had experienced government and citizenship. At that early stage, government and citizenship were still largely abstract concepts.

A few months later, in June 1994, the TGE held its first nationwide elections. The TPLF fielded candidates for parliamentary office, and a few independent candidates also vied for office, though no one expected them to win.[9] Again, the TPLF's organizational structure was brought into play. Everyone over the age of 18 was issued a voter identification card. Training meetings were held among the *gudgeles* (household groups) to instruct people in the logistics of voting. A special polling station was built in the center of the settlement, with straw "booths" covered with shawls to ensure secret voting.

On voting day, people came to the polling station early to wait for their turn to vote. People I interviewed that day said that they were excited about being able to vote. One man told me, "This election is the end of our struggle . . . we have had enough of a struggle. We should not be fight-

Women line up to participate in their first election, June 1994.

ing all our life." A woman dressed in her finest traditional Ethiopian dress (worn only on special occasions) also used the imagery of the struggle to explain the importance of the election. She said, "We have struggled for this election to be possible . . . Some people went out into the forest and some struggled in face to face (combat). Some stayed home and helped in any way we could. We have all struggled."

Most people had never voted before. Because the vast majority of the population was illiterate, voting involved placing one's thumbprint on the symbol (e.g., dove, ox, lantern, ox plow, sickle) that represented their candidate. They did not know which candidate was which, though they knew that the TPLF candidate was represented by the dove. People were reacting not to the campaign of one candidate against another but to the symbolism of an election held under peaceful and free conditions. Many spoke of the importance of being able to elect a government that was of the people, rather than having one imposed upon them. The day had a festive air to it, as people discussed their expectations of the future government and their relief that the war was finally over. In this context, the election was one of the punctuating moments of their homecoming.

Although state-society relations are constantly changing in any society, in this case, the relations were undergoing a period of particularly intense

Votes are cast in "ballot bags" at the polling station.

and rapid transformation. After years of imagining what life would be like back in Ethiopia while in exile, these visions could now be tested. The following year in Ada Bai tested them further; practice in everyday life helped to further shape people's conceptions of the type of relationship, level of services, and involvement in their daily lives that they could expect from the government. For most, this involved lowering their expectations and resignation to the fact that they would have to help themselves, that no one was going to continue to help them as they had for the previous ten years. This realization was sobering and caused a great deal of confusion and discontent.

One of the first experiences that gave Ada Bai returnees the feeling that they had not been treated fairly by the new government of Ethiopia was their reception upon repatriation. Having been repatriated from Sudan by the government in the absence of an agreement between UNHCR and the TGE, they had received only minimal reintegration support and no cash grant at all to help establish themselves in Ada Bai. Most people had had to sell the food rations they had been given in order to purchase house-building materials, tools, and other necessities of life in Ethiopia. They soon found that basic household items in Humera were extremely expensive due to their remote location. The price of kerosene used to light lanterns, for instance, was five times the rate in the rest of Ethiopia.

In 1994, an agreement was worked out between the TGE and UNHCR to repatriate an additional 2,400 refugees from the Umrakoba camp in Sudan to Rawayan, the smallest of the three returnee settlements that had been established in 1993. Rawayan was only seven kilometers from Humera, at the intersection of the main road to Gondar (and on to Addis Ababa) and the road to Sudan. The 1994 returnees received 1,500 birr per head of household, nine months' food ration, plastic sheeting, and a box of household utensils. I visited Rawayan several times during the repatriation exercise, and interviewed many households as soon as they arrived as well as a few months after repatriation. They seemed generally better off than Ada Bai returnees. The following year, several thousand more were returned to Rawayan, Mai Kadra, and a new site called Abderafi (located south of the other three sites in an inhospitable area along the Sudan border). These returnees were given 750 birr per adult (as the TGE and UNHCR said that many people the previous year had split their households, divorcing in order to get one cash grant for each adult in the household), household utensils, and plowing assistance for the first year.

To facilitate the repatriation of refugees beginning in 1994, UNHCR opened a branch office in Humera. The mandate of the branch office staff included monitoring conditions in Ada Bai, Rawayan, and Mai Kadra, the areas where those who had repatriated in 1993 lived. My second year of research was partially funded by UNHCR, in exchange for information that I gave to the branch office and the Regional Liaison Office in Addis Ababa. Despite the information I provided to decision makers within UNHCR that the refugees were not thriving in their new environment, additional individualized assistance was not forthcoming. Instead, UNHCR arranged with the regional government and its line bureaus to fund the construction of a clinic, a school, and a public water supply for each of the settlements. This would be the last assistance that UNHCR would provide to the settlements, and the government line departments would be responsible for staffing and maintaining the facilities.

From the perspective of the returnees, each successive wave of returnees received a more generous package. The discrepancy in treatment was a result of the TGE, UNHCR, and the Relief Society of Tigray having signed separate agreements with each other for each "repatriation season" that were based more on available resources from donors than on what a household needed to reach self-sufficiency. Those who had repatriated earlier resented the fact that those who came later received more generous assistance. It made no sense to the first returnees to Ethiopia since the end of the war that they had received no cash, while their cousins who had stayed in the camps one more year received all of the benefits of refugee assistance, including what seemed to be a whopping 1,500 birr. A few people attempted to return to Sudan to re-repatriate in order to qualify for the repatriation package, or invited their newly repatriated relatives to come live with them and thus share their cash grants. The Ada Bai baito issued a declaration that anyone caught trying to take advantage of the new repatriation scheme would lose their rights to land.

In meetings with UNHCR in Addis Ababa, I suggested that the agency should consider providing grants retroactively to returnees who had repatriated earlier without receiving any money. These people, I argued, were still suffering from lack of purchasing power and were not able to pull themselves out of destitution. With 1,500 birr they could buy an ox or several goats and sheep, a sewing machine, or other property that could help them earn more money. Some officials suggested to me that retroactive grants were not feasible, but that development activities might be initiated to assist returnees who had been in Ethiopia for more than one year. These activities were never instituted.

Ada Bai returnees tried to take matters into their own hands. They nominated three representatives to take their case to the government. A villagewide collection raised funds for the trio to travel up through the echelons of government as far as necessary. The group traveled first to Endaselassie, the zonal capital, and then to Mekele, the regional capital, to present their grievances. They met with the regional administration and officials of REST. An official with REST who met me several weeks later expressed amused disbelief that the people of Ada Bai had come so far looking for assistance. He had met them, but did not agree to their demands, explaining that the agreement had been made in the capital. The representatives of Ada Bai had left empty-handed. Finally, they went to Addis Ababa. The UNHCR office told them that because they were repatriated in the absence of an agreement with the TGE, they were not eligible for assistance from UNHCR. They then went to the prime minister's office, where they were turned away without being given an audience. They left a letter containing their grievances for the prime minister, and returned to Ada Bai dispirited and empty-handed.

Before the delegation began their trip, people in Ada Bai had been excited at the prospect of sending their representatives to the political leaders to ask for help. They were optimistic that their case would be heard and that the situation would be settled in their favor, since their political leaders had been responsive to their needs and concerns during the war years. When the three representatives returned, however, bitter disappointment ensued, and people began to speak for the first time about being disillusioned by the new government.

In November 1994, two representatives from the regional administrative council, the head of the Bureau of Labor and Social Affairs (a woman who had been a TPLF officer during the war) and the head of the Disaster Prevention and Preparedness Bureau, came to Humera to visit the returnee settlements and meet with the people to discuss their grievances. When they came to Ada Bai, they found a somewhat hostile reception at a public gathering.

"Is there enough health service?" one man asked rhetorically, "The graveyard is full. In Safawa things were better." Another man said, "On the radio we hear that we are drinking clean water [referring to news reports about the returnees], but you are only trying to hide your faults [i.e., with this misinformation] . . . What is the use of a generator that sits idle? How many people must die? How many must pass [out of here]?"

Others spoke about how helpful the TPLF had been to them during the war, noting that they had understood the problems of the peasantry and had assisted people to leave their homes safely during 1984–85. They accused the leadership of having turned their back on the returnees. One man said, "We came [to Ada Bai] and found nothing. We were just dropped here."

I attended these meetings, but when the tone of the discussions started to sour, I was sent a message by one of the regional officials telling me that I should leave. I was later told that a public meeting was not open to "outsiders" who did not belong to the village. "If the president of the United States spoke to a public meeting in America, don't you think that I would be asked to leave?" the official later asked me, expressing disbelief when I said that the meeting would be open to all.

Following the visit of the regional officials, the baito and woreda met for several days in Ada Bai and Humera to discuss ways of placating the people. The local clergy were asked to help discuss the problems with the people, to convince them that the government had not turned its back on them. This was a rare example of how the political leadership sought to co-opt the religious leaders to help them in persuading people of the validity of the government's political agenda. Yet the government had nothing to offer the people to satisfy their demands. There was no cash and no food. Efforts were made to speed up completion of the school and clinic that UNHCR had promised to build for each of the three settlements. Although these projects were meant to provide assistance at the community level, their completion also helped people to feel that their individual needs had not been forgotten.

The experience gave the returnees the impression that while their collective identity as refugees living in Sudan had been politically valuable to the leadership of the TPLF during the war, as returnees in postwar Ethiopia they had lost this value, and thus were without an important form of bargaining leverage. The rehabilitation and development needs of the region were enormous, and available resources were meager. They were considered to be peasants just like everyone else living throughout Tigray in rural poor communities, and were expected to be able to help themselves, not to seek handouts from either the government or relief agencies.

As disappointing as these scenes were to people in Ada Bai, however, the experiences did help them to find their own political voice. In articulating their grievances to the political leadership, they expressed their conviction that the relationship between the people and the state was one of a system of rights and obligations that had to be upheld on both sides. Listening to people complain about what they did not have—as compared to what they had had in Sudan—I realized that most people believed that it had been the TPLF, rather than UNHCR or the many international NGOs working in the camp, that had been instrumental in assisting them when they were refugees. Even if they knew that UNHCR or the NGOs had delivered the relief items, much of the credit for having received help had been given to the TPLF. Back in Ethiopia, the failure of these same international and national organizations to provide assistance was seen as a failure on the part of the political leaders to mobilize the assistance on their behalf.

All political leaders were not seen the same way, I learned. Abera, a farmer and father of two young children living in Ada Bai, gave me his impressions of the public meeting with the regional representatives as we drove home in my car from Humera one evening. He said that he did not think that the fault lay with the leaders in Addis Ababa, for "they do not know our problems: that is their fault [i.e., how can one be expected to do something about a situation he knows nothing about?]." But, he said, the regional representatives know the problems well, and that made them more culpable and responsible to do something to help the people of Ada Bai.

Over time, as people emerged from their wartime consciousness as a society under siege and became accustomed to living in peace, some gained the courage to stand up for what they thought were their rights, to express dissatisfaction with the government and its treatment of them.

Tough Love? From Dependency to Self-Help

Many government and aid agency officials I spoke to in Humera and Mekele said the Ada Bai returnees had been spoiled by their years in Sudan where all of their needs had been met. This argument might seem strange to those who are accustomed to seeing African refugees throughout the world portrayed in the media as the most destitute, hungry, and desperate of a country of poor people (Malkki 1996). In contrast to this image, these officials said that the people who had repatriated from Sudan had been dependent on generous aid and needed to be weaned from humanitarian assistance. As refugees they had been given free access to medical care and medicines, provided a monthly ration of food, and had even received periodic distributions of soap, special foods such as dates (a popular donation from Islamic countries during the Ramadan fasting season), and secondhand clothing. The refugee camps had become marketplaces for goods brought from Ethiopia and Eritrea, and for bartering relief supplies in exchange for goods from the Sudanese cities of Gedaref, Kassala, Showak, and Khartoum. In addition, the availability of wage labor on the commercial sesame, sorghum, and cotton plantations had given them access to cash. Proponents of the dependency argument said that the refugees had become so accustomed to handouts from the Sudanese government, UNHCR, and the NGOs that they were bound to be dis-appointed when they returned to Ethiopia, where such aid was not forth-coming. The remedy for their disillusionment, officials believed, was to educate them about the importance of self-help, to reorient them to the TPLF's *struggle for development*, which had supplanted the *struggle for military victory*.

The TGE's Proposal for the Repatriation and Rehabilitation of Refugees from Sudan, prepared in 1992, included "food-for-work" and "food-for-recovery" (this term is never defined) schemes:

> Such schemes will help in overcoming dependency syndromes for the returnees will be expected to engage themselves in activities like building tukuls, constructing feeder roads etc. while receiving food assistance. In addition they will give the returnees the opportunity to make use of their acquired skills during their years of exile. (TGE 1992, 5)

Other assistance to be provided as rehabilitation assistance was expected to include "minimum recovery input . . . in the form of plough oxen, ploughs, hand tools, seeds, house building materials, utensils, etc." (TGE 1992, 5).

The struggle for development involved individual and collective efforts to improve the economic well-being of the people of Tigray, through production-maximization and resource conservation techniques. Self-help was stressed, and free relief was frowned on for anyone who was able-bodied and could work. The TGE sought to make reintegration assistance compatible with development assistance, so as to avoid making it a "disincentive to self-help" (Cuny 1994, 89–93). The proposal for reintegration states:

> The primary objective of the repatriation process is to facilitate the reintegration of the returnees into their respective areas of origin and reinstate their livelihoods through provision of rehabilitation and development assistance. Such an undertaking requires a multi-disciplinary integrated approach which not only takes into consideration the immediate needs of the returnees but also encompasses the all-round long-term and development requirements. Indeed if the aim is to ensure effective integration of the returnees into the socio-economic environment of their regions, provision of relief, rehabilitation and development assistance should not be considered as distinct packages but as intertwined components of a whole on-going development process. (TGE 1992, 10–11)

The TGE's concern with perpetuating dependency on relief assistance turned out to be unnecessary, since the refugees were repatriated in the absence of an agreement with UNHCR. Without such an agreement, there was hardly any money to finance the rehabilitation of returnees, and they never saw most of the components of the package described in the proposal for reintegration.

Barbara Harrell-Bond describes the "dependency syndrome" attributed to refugees as "a blanket term used for all the undesirable social behaviour found in the settlements" (1986, 283).[10] Dependency is also associated with manipulation by refugees who seek to maximize the amount of assistance they receive (Maren 1997, 69); laziness and loss of the ability of a community to govern itself (Harrell-Bond, 359–60; Deng and Minear 1992, 72–73); and continued exercise of power by external interests over people who have no option but to accept such domination (Deng and Minear, 73; Maren, 69).

It is true that the refugees had become accustomed to international assistance (a large number had even been employed by the UN and NGOs as guards, storekeepers, and health workers). In the years after the initial food emergency, they began to take for granted the availability of health care and education in the camps; their understanding of what an acceptable standard of living entailed was elevated. On the other hand, they were prevented from owning land and growing their own food anywhere but in their own kitchen gardens inside the house compound. Many of the ways that they had sought to earn a living had been illegal. Those who had an interest in continuing food assistance included the officials of the Sudanese government, the UN, international NGOs working in the camps, and even the TPLF. Some had an interest in preserving their jobs and their organization's presence in the camps. Others had more corrupt interests: refugees reported being sold ration cards from camp officials seeking personal gain. Finally, the TPLF—with its close relationship to the peasantry even as they were living in the camps—had a vested practical interest in making sure that the refugees had enough food so that they could preserve their own base of support. Refugees were not encouraged to settle among their Sudanese hosts (Rogge 1985; Kibreab 1996a, 243), which—together with the uncertainty surrounding the outcome of the war—made it difficult for them to pursue long-term economic strategies and plans from year to year.

Reliance on external actors to provide life-sustaining support affected the entire social fabric of the camp community. Gaim Kibreab, working with Eritrean refugees in Sudan, notes:

> The community is unable to enforce rules on its individual members
> when the economic tie which binds the member to the collectivity has
> been weakened or has disappeared completely. The individual refugee is

dependent for his and his family's sustenance more on his efforts, on COR [the Sudanese office of the Commissioner for Refugees] and on the refugee support systems than on the collectivity . . . when mere survival becomes a priority and when local communities lose control over the allocation of the basis of survival, social institutions also lose their legitimacy. (1996a, 207)

Reconstructing these social institutions in the months and years following return was central to the process of emplacement.

Another way of considering dependency, as the quote from Kibreab implies, is to see it as a case of people who merely made the best of the resources available to them. Were they to blame for having accepted aid? Clearly not, since they had no choice in the matter. Should they, on repatriating to Ethiopia, have been expected to lower their standards of living such that it became acceptable to lose a wife or a child to what they had come to consider in Sudan to be preventable illnesses? Should they have resigned themselves to the fact that their children could not go to school or that the water they drank was contaminated? These questions were more difficult for returnees to answer. In other contexts, when a poor farmer or peasant's source of income is disrupted—such as the loss of wage labor opportunities that James C. Scott (1985, 150–51) associates with the industrialization of rice production in Malaysia, or even the suspension of food-for-work opportunities in Ethiopia during the late 1990s—peasants are pitied. There seems to be no reasonable justification for condemning returnees who find it difficult to adapt to suddenly being severed from the source of the resources they have become accustomed to over the course of ten years.

In the refugee camps, people wove the new influences to which they were exposed—both from abroad as well as from the Sudanese cultures that lived near them—to imagine new lives for themselves. In using the opportunities and limitations of their environment to fashion their lives, refugees in Sudan were no different from people anywhere, who constantly adjust and adapt their visions of themselves and their position in the social world in response to their environments. Those who argued that the refugees had become dependent lamented the fact that they had not abandoned the practices and strategies they had developed while living as refugees upon returning to Ethiopia. Yet from the returnees' perspectives such a change would have been, particularly in the first months before re-emplacement in Ada Bai had taken hold, ludicrous.

This re-emplacement involved negotiation and reimagining of people's relationships to the international assistance community, the government (at all levels), and the political party—where there was a perceived difference between the party and the government. As I demonstrate below, the lines of distinction between these latter two were often blurred.

The "New Code of Good Citizenship"

In chapter 3, I introduced the notion of a "new code of good citizenship" whereby people position themselves in relation to the local political leaders in order to obtain access to resources such as land. I take this issue up again here, to explore relations between people and the government at the most local level. Ultimately, these relations extended to individuals' and the community's relations with the government at higher levels as well.

Vying for land was necessary because there was insufficient land for every household in Ada Bai. Most of the available land was either not cleared (and therefore had twenty years' bush growth that would have to be removed before the land could be planted) or was far from the village. At the outset, it was difficult to define a notion of who was "deserving" of land because the community and its leaders had not yet evolved a well-defined code of "proper" behavior or of legitimate membership in the community. Avenues to prestige and power were not yet well-established (Lepowsky 1990). Many of the lines of social stratification, determined by internal community dynamics, had not yet been developed, and those that had applied before the experience of exile no longer did so outside of the communities of origin. In the absence of an established definition of who deserved land, returnees started to think imaginatively about how they could distinguish themselves as members in good standing of the returnee community, such that they would not be overlooked when land was distributed.

The simplest way of doing this, in the eyes of the people, was to align oneself with the political leadership. Community members noticed right away who *had* gotten land: members of the baito and militia,[11] priests, veterans, and families of soldiers who had fought for the TPLF during the war. Political and community leaders tended to be men between the ages of thirty and forty rather than the village elders. This was partly because those who provided community service were otherwise unpaid, and allocation of land was seen as a way of rewarding them for having volunteered their labor. The suspicion of favoritism, even if such practices were defensible, led to a degree of ill-feeling, but it also encouraged people to evaluate how they could position themselves so that they too might be seen to be deserving of a land "reward" for services rendered.

Discussion of "rules" became something of a battlefield. People complained when they felt there was too much favoritism. Unsubstantiated rumors were commonly spread that members of the baito were keeping the best land for themselves and their families, that they were stealing aid resources from the warehouse that were meant for distribution, and that if you crossed one member of the baito the wrong way, you would never get land. One priest was disliked by some people for disagreeing with several other priests[12] over the role of the church and the clergy within the community. He was accused of keeping for himself the contributions that people had given him toward construction of the new church. These rumors, most of which appeared to be unfounded, communicated to the leaders the strong message that they were being held accountable to the community. For the most part, forms of currying favor would have to follow acceptable lines of conduct that the majority of the community tacitly or overtly agreed to, or else the person who had broken the code would be ostracized and criticized by the community. If the baito, clergy, or any other source of institutional power abused their privileged positions egregiously, community members were not afraid to complain publicly.

By July 1995, when I left Ada Bai, the third round of land allocation was in progress. By then distinct rules had evolved by which people sought to obtain access to land. Although political loyalty was still the main defining feature of those who were allocated land, the way that loyalty was expressed had taken on additional meaning. People would, for instance, participate in communal work projects such as laying the pipeline for the water distribution system and participating in environmental sanitation campaigns (collecting and burning garbage) or conservation projects in the knowledge that, if they did not, they would be fined and, they imagined, probably would not receive land.

Most of the methods improvised by people to obtain access to land were directed toward the local politicians. Community participation and volunteerism were rewarded. One lucky fellow was even given land in recognition of the service he had performed to the community for being the resident anthropologist's research assistant! However, the lines between people's understanding of their relationships with local power brokers and their relationships with other layers of the political superstructure became blurred. The example of the 1995 elections illustrates my point.

Voting for Candidates and Land

In 1995, another round of national elections was held to elect members of the regional assembly and central Council of Representatives. Although I had been an official UN observer during the 1994 elections, this time international observers were not allowed to monitor the event, as I had been informed by a somewhat embarrassed baito official. I dutifully stayed away from the polling station, though my house was only fifty meters from the site, and spent most of the day working on my field notes.

Toward the end of the day, however, members of the Ada Bai Women's Association came to me to ask if I would drive some of the sick people who wanted to vote to the polling station. I agreed, delivering them to the election site without entering the station. The following is an extract from my notes of that day:

> At around 6 p.m. I was asked to bring a woman to the polling station who had given birth two days ago. [With the help of two members of the women's association] we somehow [also] managed to get a man sick with advanced tuberculosis into the car. At the polling station two other sick people were coming out of the booths [supported by their relatives]. One woman could not walk. She had been brought by cart on her bed [the bed loaded onto the cart] to vote.

Surprised that people would insist on going to the polls to vote even in such weakened conditions, I asked the woman who had just delivered the baby why she was voting. Did she really think that her vote was so important that she had to struggle so much to cast her ballot? "No," she said. "I am voting because if I do not I will not get any land this year." This was the first time I had heard of voting being associated with access to land.

That evening, sitting around Tibbletz and Ambachew's house drinking coffee with the neighbors, I asked how the elections had gone. Without telling them what the woman had told me earlier in the day about voting to get land, I posed a hypothetical question to Tibbletz, "If you had just given birth to a baby, and you were bedridden, would you try to vote anyway?" Ambachew, usually not one to speak for his strong-willed wife, broke in right away. "I would carry her on my back if I had to. If I didn't, we would lose our land." She nodded her agreement with him.

What was important in this incident was not whether voting actually guaranteed access to land (or rather, whether not voting deprived one of access to land). More significant, such an action was *perceived* to have this effect, and therefore the popular definition of being a good citizen, with access to resources, came to require this behavior. It should be noted that for most women, this was the first time they had voted and thus the association of land for votes was a new one for them. The behavior associated with obtaining or maintaining access to land was not voting for a particular candidate, since votes were secret and there was no way for election officials to know who people had voted for. Rather, participation in the voting procedure, which was recorded by record keepers at the polling station, was the qualifying activity.

The fact that people came to associate voting with land (some people claimed to have been warned that they would not receive land in the next distribution if they did not vote) was consistent with their increasing disillusionment with government as an entity (not merely as the government of one party or another). Over the course of a year, elections had undergone a transformation in the symbolic associations they conjured for the returnees. People were no longer celebrating the end of "the Struggle," and were somewhat sobered by the fact that politicians in the region and the capital did not seem to respond to their needs.

Peasant disillusionment was not limited to people living at the geographic periphery of the state. J. Young recorded evidence of discontent in 1993 among people who accused those in power of

> forgetting them, questioning what had been gained from years of struggle and condemning the lack of resources. The TPLF leadership's response to these complaints was to argue that they represented an individualistic perspective and that there have been important collective gains, putting development programmes in local hands, and ensuring that Tigrayan concerns are heard at the national level. TPLF leaders also stressed local initiative and urged peasants not to look to the government for solutions for all their problems. However, it is clear that having been repeatedly told that their poverty was largely due to the state being controlled by regimes unsympathetic to their plight, peasants look for support from a government led by those they consider their sons. (1997, 200)

J. Young does not agree with the peasants that the state had forgotten them. He notes strategic redeployment of leading members of the EPRDF from Addis Ababa to Tigray in 1995 as evidence of the government's mindfulness of the importance of maintaining their base of peasant support in Tigray. He says:

> These transfers make clear the commitment of the TPLF leadership to the development of Tigray, as well as the importance attached to retaining

the loyalty of the movement's peasant base in an Ethiopia where the EPRDF-led government faces considerable opposition from the intelligentsia and often scepticism by non-Tigrayan peasantries. (1997, 200)

Although this may have been the case on a regionwide basis, my experience in Ada Bai/Humera suggests that agents of the state were eager to move away from giving returnees any special treatment. There was a strong impetus from the government to encourage returnees to help themselves and not to expect a continuation of humanitarian or other specially targeted assistance.

Competing with the Church for Power

The state was not the only bearer of power over the community. Religious institutions and their agents in the community also exerted power, which was sometimes complementary and at other times competed with that of the state. Unlike the Derg, which had sought to cripple the Ethiopian Orthodox Church, the TPLF chose a more gentle path of reform. J. Young notes, "The TPLF pressed for changes within the Church and in the practices of its adherents, but it was never prepared to allow confrontation to develop over these issues" (1997, 176). Many of the monasteries in Tigray located in areas where TPLF land reform had been instituted were allowed to retain their large landholdings. Attempts to reduce the number of saint's days and religious ceremonies that people marked by feasting and refraining from work, which the political leadership saw as damaging to economic productivity and draining to household resources, were largely unsuccessful. So, too, were efforts to discourage young people from becoming clergy (J. Young 1997, 176). Most large families continued to select one son to join the church clergy.

Failure to diminish the number of feast/rest days was due to the considerable power that priests held over the public. Not only did priests warn against working on saints' days in their sermons at the church each week, they were even known to sit along the main paths waiting for errant farmers to pass by on their way to work. Negussie, one such unlucky farmer who had been caught by a priest on the feast day of Mariam, returned to the village looking disappointed. He told me, "The priest told me that if I went to my field, a big storm might come up and cause lightning to hit a house. If that happened, it would be my fault." Similarly, Muslims were not allowed to work on Fridays, and their fasting during the month of Ramadan usually kept them from working as well.

Keshie Gebreselassie told me that one of the most important functions of the church both in exile and in Ada Bai was to safeguard the culture, to ward off change. Changes in marriage practices, work practices, and even dress style were associated with loss of piety and opening oneself to sin. Priests did not believe that they held the power to excommunicate those who disobeyed them, but did believe that transgressions would be punished by God.

TPLF attempts to restrict the influence of the church were for the most part intended to preserve people's resources. Large or extravagant marriages and funerals were discouraged, to limited effect. The TPLF also practiced what it preached. In 1995, at the celebration of Lekatit 11, the twentieth anniversary of the formation of the party, people were advised that after that year, there would be large celebrations to mark the anniversary every five years only. People should not spend more than they could afford on such celebrations. When these events were held, however, the clergy played a prominent role. They would enter the meeting grounds, a natural amphitheater at the edge of the village, beating their drums, dressed in their brightly colored ceremonial robes, parasols woven with gilt thread unfurled, and take their places in a specially reserved area near the front of the crowd.

The Web of Power

Actions at the local level were framed in response to the incentives, rewards, and punishments that people perceived to be associated with their actions. Distant from the political center of both region and nation not only geographically but economically and socially, returnees in Ada Bai developed their own rules for accumulation of power and participation in the larger discourses of regional and national rebuilding. The practices that people improvised were what Finn Stepputat (1999, 213) calls "everyday forms of state formation," the myriad actions and patterns of behavior that emplace the individual and the community within the structure of power that—together with agents of the state—they are implicated in.

In this chapter, I have referred to state power not only in the legal, juridical sense that most Westerners associate with it but also in the ways that the state touched the lives of local people. The state made itself felt at all levels: in the public meetings where ideology was introduced and discussed, in the processes of voter registration and holding elections, in the presence of the military in the village, and in the engagement (or lack of engagement) with the international assistance system. State power and influence was interpreted and applied to the construction of meaning in ways that were sometimes unintended and not always subject to external control. The people of Ada Bai were always connected to the world outside the geographical limits of the village.

Access to resources dictated the terms by which Ada Bai residents sought access to power, and ultimately the terms through which they reestablished their position as citizens of the postwar region and state. Such processes, in turn, helped to secure returnees' access to the very resources over which they negotiated, thereby creating stability and greater economic security. Returnees successfully formed a symbolic code of what could be considered "acceptable" or "proper" behavior. They did this in response to directives issued from those in higher positions of authority as well as from community leaders and other influential people, through local level discussions, debates, and arguments about the form that such behavior should take. While leaders required compliance in exchange for resources, their followers demanded accountability in exchange for support.

By the time I left Ada Bai at the start of the rainy season in 1995, households were much better off than they had been during the first year after return, in food security, health, and earning potential. I noted further significant improvements in their well-being during visits in 1996, 1997, 2001, and 2002. Residents attributed their steadily improving standard of living to the fact that life was "more settled" and that they "knew the place" better than they had when they first arrived.

I was surprised in my last two visits to find that the political leaders who had been elected by the community in 1994 were still in place and that they still seemed to enjoy general popularity. This might suggest not only a level of stability but also a degree of consensual support for the emergent political order that was only starting to develop during the returnees' early years in Ada Bai. Conversely, it could have been an indication of the amount of power they had amassed through their control over land and other resources, to the extent that their political positions were secure.

Ada Bai and the Global Refugee Regime

Refugee camps are often written about as sites in which transnational and local power politics are contested (Horst 2002; Hyndman 2000), and often these political interests can follow the refugees back to their country of origin when they repatriate. Such has certainly been the case in Afghanistan, Somalia, Guatemala, and other well-publicized repatriation movements. More often, however, return signifies a de-escalation of these power politics, such that people who had "enjoyed" attention or been considered politically important during the period of exile find that return signifies the international refugee regime's desire to turn its gaze away from this particular group. Peace agreements, cessations of hostilities, and regime change are usually taken as indications to the international political and assistance community that attention can be directed elsewhere. Donor fatigue, competing claims for media attention and resources in "hot spots" in other parts of the world soon result in refugee camp closure and rushed repatriation operations.

Postrepatriation life in Ada Bai was largely unmarked by the kinds of power brokers that people had been accustomed to in the camps: the refugee camp administration, the United Nations and nongovernmental agencies, the Sudanese government, and even the TPLF and REST. Repatriation was a movement away from the kind of "managed care" (Hyndman 2000) that characterized their refugee experience. There were no international NGOs working in Ada Bai. REST, which considered the returnees to have been "spoiled" in the camps and to have unrealistic expectations of the kind of assistance they should be receiving, was eager to withdraw from the returnee settlements as quickly as possible. Thus, Ada Bai was, for its residents, disappointingly unmanaged; they felt that they had been abandoned at a time when their need for assistance was great. It took some time for people to see this lack of control by external forces in postrepatriation life as an opportunity.

Despite their long-term success in constructing their community and creating stability, I feel strongly that more should have been done to help the people of Ada Bai in the first months after their return. In my roles as ambulance driver, genealogist, and "clerk of the records" (Scheper-Hughes 1993, 29), I saw too many people die and too much suffering to feel that "reintegration" had been successful. I would like to think that the reason that more assistance was not more forthcoming was that those who were in a position to grant assistance did not understand the challenges of postrepatriation life well enough to know better. I may be wrong in this assumption. Political considerations, organizational mandate limitations, lack of interest, or callousness may have had more to do with why returnees did not get the assistance they needed in the first months after they returned to their country of origin. There is no guarantee that merely knowing what a community's needs are will ensure that they receive the assistance they require. As I discuss in the conclusion, however, anthropological analysis of the type I have carried out should have practical implications for policy makers and assistance providers in that lack of information can no longer serve as an excuse for inaction.

Conclusion: Forced Migration, Anthropology, and the Politics of International Assistance

Ada Bai residents' efforts to achieve self-sufficiency and to emplace themselves within their new environment were hampered because they were denied virtually all forms of humanitarian and development assistance. One, although certainly not the only, reason for this was that none of the potential assistance providers—the government of Ethiopia, UNHCR, local or international NGOs—knew exactly what was required to achieve successful reintegration and how long it might take to reach that stage. The humanitarian assistance community's lack of awareness was paralleled by a scarcity of academic research into the long-term process of postreturn integration. Until the late 1990s, this aspect of the refugee cycle had not been problematized by either scholars or practitioners. Repatriation was equated with homecoming and was not recognized as a challenge that could be as difficult as living in exile had been.

Anthropological concepts of emplacement and social change that question the primacy of sedentarist orientations and explore the creation of meaning, identity, and community in the context of flux and disorder can and should be used to investigate what happens to people who return. These theoretical tools, as this study of Ada Bai shows, help to reveal the complexity, and often the extreme difficulty, that former refugees face in constructing social relations, economic practices, and ritual meaning in such a way that their lives are both viable in terms of providing the essential requirements for life and valuable in helping people to feel connected to one another and to their environment. Questioning the nature of the relation between the returnee and his/her environment (whether the person's area of origin, birthplace, or an entirely new place) helps to redirect the analysis to more clearly focus on individual and collective agency as determining elements in the experience of return.

For anthropology as a discipline, bringing the study of forced migrants (at whatever stage of their migration cycle) more clearly into the realm of mainstream anthropological study helps to expand the horizons of the field by revealing the workings of processes of change at some of their most extreme stages. It is an unusual opportunity to observe the kind of emplacement that transforms a blank field, initially devoid of any meaning to a particular group of people, into a community and home. Yet the processes of emplacement that I have described here occurs in all societies under all conditions. Emplacement is a continuous process of generating meaning; extreme forms of experience are not necessarily different in type from more comfortable or commonly lived experience. Moreover, conceptual frameworks that explain the former can often help shed light on the latter, and vice versa.

In addition to the intellectual benefits that may be derived from critical examination of life after repatriation, there are important practical implications for policy makers, many of whom look to academic studies of migrant communities for guidance in directing their planning. Redirecting the study of refugees toward a more actor-centered approach allows the use of anthropological concepts that seek to elucidate the process of home-making and the specific acts of emplacement that it entails. This kind of analysis also brings into focus political and economic forces at local, regional, national, and global levels with which the group must interact. Such an approach can suggest potentially fruitful areas for postconflict rehabilitation to which development planners can provide appropriate assistance. The analysis also suggests a framework for defining and measuring self-sufficiency, with the important caveat that livelihood systems are so variable from one culture to the next that it is important to explore each case in detail. In this chapter I outline a strategy by which academic research can influence better service delivery, which in turn may lead to more humane development policies in postreturn contexts.

Bringing Anthropological Theory to the Study of Refugees

With the shift in anthropology toward global processes and movements of people, goods, and ideas across borders of all kinds, there has been a growing fascination among a relatively small number of researchers with the study of migrant communities, in particular those of forced migrants (including refugees, internally displaced persons, stateless persons, expellees, trafficked persons, and demobilized soldiers). This interest has been sparked by the belief that the experiences of these groups have a great deal to offer to a range of theoretical debates. In particular, studies of immigrants and other voluntary migrants have had a particular impact on theories of social change, identity and community formation, political economy, state–civil society relations, and more recently transnational and globalization studies. The multidisciplinary field of refugee studies, established during the early 1980s, has been guided by these concerns.[1] As Harrell-Bond and Voutira note, "One of the gains for anthropology in studying refugees is that it offers the chance to record the processes of social change, not merely as a process of transition within a cultural enclave, but in the dramatic context of uprootedness where a people's quest for survival becomes a model of social change" (1992, 9). Richard Black, a geographer, is concerned with the ways in which refugee and displacement studies relates to more general elements in processes of social change:

> There is . . . a theoretical sense in which the study of refugees is of particular interest to geographers and other social scientists, in that an understanding of socioeconomic or political processes under the specific conditions of refugee migration may provide crucial insights into the operation of these processes at a more general level. For example, in many refugee situations, individuals and communities must act to rebuild social networks, economic structures, and patterns of political expression and representation, often in adverse circumstances. The evolution of these structures may be rapid compared to that in more "stable" populations, providing the researcher with a unique opportunity to document and explain social and economic change. (1993, 9)

Despite the fact that most researchers involved in the study of involuntary migration agree that such work can make important contributions to anthropological and other social science theory, this potential remains largely unfulfilled. The voices of migration and refugee studies are hardly heard in mainstream anthropological discourse. This is partly because migration studies have tended to be associated with applied, advocacy, or development anthropology and with disaster studies (Oliver-Smith 1996; Malkki 1995b), all of which are considered marginal in the eyes of what John Davis calls

> comfortable anthropology . . . which is concerned with social organizations which we represent as working more or less normally, ticking over, with occasional spasms of adjustment—changing pains, as you might say—but in general reasonably autonomous, locally construed arrangements for living which attract the commitment and creativity of those who live in that way. (1992, 149)

Anthropological case studies of migrant groups tend to be funded by, and thus written for, development or humanitarian assistance organizations for policy formulation, needs assessments, and project monitoring and evaluation. Anthropologists have focused on chipping away at the bureaucratic inertia that tends to surround development and humanitarian assistance by providing valuable field-based data that can be easily understood and applied to improving service delivery (Waldron 1988). However, authors of this type of reporting and writing have tended not to apply their field research to theoretical analysis. The result has been a plethora of case studies with very little in the way of theory to hold them together or to relate them to academic discourse. In addition, some of the assumed unproblematic aspects of refugee experiences have not been questioned.

Rosemary Preston describes the history of migration studies as following a temporal development that closely mirrors the temporal divisions of the migration process:

> The evolution of research into involuntary war-related migration places the 1970s as the decade for the study of the parameters of flight and the 1980s as the period of study of asylum and resettlement. The 1990s, not entirely coincident with changing policy and practice, have become the time to research repatriation. However, just as a chronology of exile explains the changing emphasis of this theorising across decades, so within the study of repatriation, researchers are mapping a temporal path of analysis. From different stakeholder perspectives, studies have accounted for orientations towards and preparations for return . . . the process of return and its effects . . . and finally, post-arrival integration and reconstruction. (1999, 21)

Preston notes that while information on repatriation has heretofore had to be cobbled together from "grey literature"—aid agency reports, journalistic accounts, project evaluations, and other unpublished works—increasingly this research is being published, although largely in the format of the case study.

Critiques of Sedentarism and Implications for the Study of Return

Malkki's antisedentarist position, which questions the presumed static relation between identity and place (1995a, 1995b, 1992, 1990), has been very influential in migration and forced migration studies. The sedentarist perspective, she argues, casts displacement as a cultural rupture and thereby denies refugees and other migrants the ability to engage in home-making and place-making in new localities. Migrants, in Malkki's view, are more adaptable than they have been given credit for in academic and political discourse.

Malkki takes aim at what she sees as a "functionalist" perspective on displacement, which describes the experience of forced migrants "as an anomaly in the life of an otherwise 'whole,' stable, sedentary society" (1995b, 508). Sedentarist rhetoric uses territorializing and botanical metaphors about the inseparability of identity and culture from place or "roots" to describe refugees: they are *uprooted displaced, transplanted*; "the territorializing metaphors of identity—roots, soils, trees, seeds—are washed away in human floodtides, waves, flows, streams, and rivers" (1995a, 15–16). Their supposed natural tie to the land having been broken, refugees are considered to have lost or been stripped of their culture, subjected to a pathological condition because of the loss of their individual and/or collective identity (e.g., Daley 1991). Alternatively, anthropologists have described refugees as people who are forced to abandon their "familiar *way-of-being* in the world" because of new "sociopolitical circumstances" (Daniel and Knudsen 1995, 1), produced largely at the hands of the state. They represent a subversion of categories; their experience is made meaningful in negative terms by the very categorical order from which they are excluded, that is, as a stripping away of the rights and privileges of citizenship or as being caught between two cultures. Refugees are thus often considered to be a problem, dangerous (and in anthropological terms, polluting) to their hosts. The lived experience of this absence of structure may engender fear, uncertainty, and psychological trauma (Douglas 1966; Malkki 1992; Malkki 1995b, 508; Kearney 1995; Kibreab 1989; Stein 1981).

Theoretical viewpoints that consider displacement as deculturing also tend to cast the displaced as helpless or dependent on the assistance of external actors. Countering this disempowering narrative is a broad perspective that insists that migrants never lose their agency entirely, but must learn to adapt it to their rapidly changing circumstances. They are described as people who, while admittedly having experienced a potentially traumatic and life-altering event, do their best to maintain their culture and identity, or do adapt it to a new environment, in the face of considerable obstacles. This idea is not necessarily new: Elizabeth Colson's and Thayer Scudder's longitudinal studies of the Gwembe Tonga (Scudder 1962; Colson 1971) in what was then Northern Rhodesia (now Zambia) offer the notion that people who are displaced or resettled use their cultural backgrounds to help them adapt to a new physical and social environment. This notion has become one of the guiding principles of refugee studies. De Waal's study of famine in Darfur, Sudan (1989) outlines how people took steps to ensure their recovery from disaster through the retention of tradition and by using well-known coping mechanisms rather than by inventing entirely new forms of social and cultural practice. This approach acknowledges peoples' ability to engage in cultural creativity and improvisation while recognizing that most people do so out of necessity rather than choice. This, I believe, is how Ada Bai residents saw their own process of cultural invention.

Such studies of migration experiences may help to expand our understandings of cultural change, improvisation, and creativity, releasing them from the celebratory rhetoric they often seem to come packaged in, and giving us a more richly nuanced understanding of cultural innovation.

Toward an Anthropology of Disorder

Anthropology's reluctance to look at what is ugly, shameful, or destructive about cultural processes has been challenged by recent world events. No one would argue that the particular kinds of atrocities witnessed in the post-Cold War era are entirely new. Media coverage and increasing global connectedness have arguably made us more aware of the terrible things that people do to one another. Prior to the mid-1990s, anthropologists have considered genocide, mutilation, rape, and starvation as weapons of war to be unfathomable, literally incomprehensible and therefore outside the realm of legitimate scholarly enquiry. The availability of images, and the likelihood that those in privileged countries may be affected, even if indirectly, by wars, acts of terrorism, refugee flows, and other examples of the "inhumanity of humanity" have forced us to confront the ugly side of culture. Horrific images of atrocities carried out against civilians in the former Yugoslavia and Rwanda, among other places, helped to bring the anthropology of violence to the fore. Too slowly, anthropologists are being compelled to confront the reality that extreme forms of experience not only can be analyzed and understood but that they must be examined if there is to be any hope of avoiding them in the future. Books such as Alexander Hinton's *Annihilating Difference: The Anthropology of Genocide* (2002); Jeremy MacClancy's edited volume *Exotic No More: Anthropology on the Front Lines* (2002); Carol Greenhouse, Elizabeth Mertz, and Kay Warren's *Ethnography in Unstable Places: Everyday Lives in Contexts of Dramatic Political Change* (2002), and Carolyn Nordstrom and C. G. M. Robben's *Fieldwork under Fire: Contemporary Studies of Violence and Survival* (1995) all maintain that anthropology must bring such extreme forms of experience into the inner confines of anthropological enquiry.

John Davis's early suggestion that anthropological insistence on the inflexibility, regularity, and durability of structure is outmoded remains salient. "The image . . . is not that of the perfect hexagons of a honeycomb, but of a shantytown, patched and improvised, constructed from whatever lies to hand in a creative and often doomed attempt to keep chaos out" (Davis 1992, 159). Appadurai, who shares with Davis, Foucault (1972), and others a fascination with the unstructured, disordered, constantly fluctuating aspects of cultural life, seems to revel in the creative freedom that social actors engage in as a result of inhabiting what he calls "ethnoscapes," "ideoscapes," and "mediascapes" (1996). Yet creativity and improvisation need not always be positive experiences to be meaningful. In their struggles and confrontations with the unknown, the strange, and the threatening, migrants do not always emerge victorious. The many Ada Bai friends whose funerals I attended are a testament to the fact that people do not always "get it right" when they seek to emplace themselves, and that "coming home" can be deadly.

Implications of Repatriation Studies for Globalization Theory

The present anthropological moment, with its "recognition that people are increasingly 'moving targets'" (Breckenridge and Appadurai 1989, i; cf. Malkki 1992, 25; see also Ong 1999 and Appadurai 2003 [1996]) and the shifting of its lens of enquiry to examine peripheries, boundaries, borderlands, migrants, and processes of apparent flux and disorder (Malkki 1992, 25; R. Rosaldo 1989; Alvarez 1995; Limón 1989 and 1994) provides an opportunity to reassess the conventional belief that refugees inhabit a dangerous, decultured, liminal space, and that repatriation constitutes a return to structure and order.

My research with the people of Ada Bai suggests that descriptions of refugee/returnee experiences as positive have, at least in some cases, been overstated. Tigrayans living as refugees in Sudan did not lose their culture or become uncultured, nor did they fully assimilate by adopting the culture of their hosts. They did not embrace the changes that their circumstances obliged them to make in their cultural practices. Rather, postreturn life, and the very process of emplacement, was anxiety producing and many people did not survive it.

Refugees maximize the social, cultural, and economic opportunities available to them while in exile. They learn skills, adopt new vocations, and develop new social frameworks. These influences become components in evolving senses of individual and collective identity, vis-à-vis new world-views that are neither entirely like nor unlike the identities and worldviews that people held before fleeing their country of origin. Global culture has an increasing influence on local lives, through contact with the international assistance regime, the media, and the expanding network of friends and relatives who leave the refugee camps to resettle in third countries.

Implications for Return Migration

The process of problematizing the refugee as being without culture, history, or identity and "making strange" the country of asylum (Malkki 1995b, 509) gives privilege to the country of origin as the place to which the refugee belongs and in which he/she is best situated. Appadurai observes that anthropologists have bound people to place: "Natives are not only persons who are from certain places, and belong to those places, but they are also those who are somehow *incarcerated*, or confined, in those places" (1988, 37). Applying the analogy to refugee/returnee populations, we might say that those who have fled their native country must be returned to it in order to restore the proper "order of things."

While the need to recognize the sedentarist biases inherent in much of the language surrounding migration and return is important, critics of the perspective advocated by Malkki and Appadurai remind us that a large number of forced migrants, probably a majority, want to go home whatever the cost. Kibreab has countered Malkki's claims about the adaptability of migrants by reminding us that most refugees and exiles, while capable of engaging in home-making and emplacement in new spaces, do maintain dreams of returning to their countries and villages of origin, and that their inability to return is in many cases anxiety-provoking (Kibreab 1999). In his study of returning Bosnians (Muslims, Serbs, and Croats) to Sarajevo, Stefansson argues that people wanted to return even though they knew they would never be able to reconstruct their prewar lives (2003). These critiques help to show the variation that exists within returnee profiles. While some migrants may not see homecoming as the most desirable option, or may prefer to build new lives in new places, others may wish to return home regardless of the difficulties that such return may entail. Attitudes about return tend to defy generalization; theoretical constructs need to allow for this variation. Emplacement, which takes place in all of these spaces, helps to bring together the many paths that people may choose into a single theoretical framework.

Aid agencies and governments involved in transporting people from exile to their country of origin usually treat repatriation and homecoming as synonymous. This conceptual confinement of people to the places in which they were born may be adjusted when such return is not possible. In such cases, people who return to the country in which they (or their parents) were born, but to a specific place within that country where they have never lived, are said to "come home." To returnees, however, home has many meanings and is best understood as a place that is constantly being made and remade, no matter what the individual's relationship to that space is. For instance, in Lucia Ann McSpadden's analysis of the repatriation of Eritrean refugees from Sudan (which took place at roughly the same time that Ethiopians were returning to Ada Bai), homecoming was a "return to the national process of reconstruction in the country as a whole . . . home is thus constituted as a viable and sustainable national economic base in the homeland, rather than being tied to a particular place" (Black and Koser 1999, 7). In Marita Eastmond and Joakim Öjendal's analysis of return to Cambodia, the definition of home became extremely problematic:

> Is "home" where one was born, used to live, where one's relatives live (or lived), or anywhere one can make a decent living? While the meaning of "home" is not culturally universal and not always tied to a single place, the disruptions of war may require new and more pragmatic considerations. (1999, 54)

As flexible as the definition of home might seem to planners, the time frame for homecoming is not. Assistance providers expect the process to take only one or two years; it is squeezed into time frames to accommodate project cycles or funding calendars. The ability to create a home, I have argued, is dependent on people's abilities to invest a place with a sense of social history, with ties between individuals and households, and between the community and larger social, political, and economic entities and processes that make up Tigray and Ethiopia in the postwar context. This process may take many years, even generations.

Are We Home Yet?

Notions of home are strongly influenced by a person's age: elderly people feel more strongly the need to return to their birthplaces before they die. Younger adults and children are more willing to associate Ada Bai with home. Several adults told me that they had started their lives over so many times that the concept of "going back" to a life they had once known was so unpractical as to be unthinkable. One man told me: "We see our life as two lives, the life before [1984] and the life after. The life before was better because we were in our homes. But this is a new life and we must try to make it as complete as possible." Another said that he considered that he had lived three lives: one in the highlands, one in Sudan, and one in Ada Bai. He said that he had no desire to go back to the highlands. Since leaving he had had numerous occupations, married a second time, had several more children, and made a complete break with his family in the highlands. These men were typical of the middle-aged group that had chosen to begin a new life in Ada Bai without apparent regret or longing for their birthplace.

Such pragmatism was also found among parents of small children. They expected their children to eventually develop an identity as Ada Bayans. A woman from a town in the central highlands said that her children "know that they are from [the town of] Abi Adi by story [i.e., they have heard me talk about the place], but they do not know it so [instead] they can say 'Ada Bai is our home'." Another man said, "We are teaching our children now to be Ada Bai people. They should say they are from Ada Bai when someone asks them."

Although the idea that Ada Bai was the best or most practical home for their children played an important role in parents' sense of home, their children did not always adapt in the ways that their parents envisioned they would. On a visit to Ada Bai in June 2002 I asked several children, who had either been born in Sudan or in Ada Bai, which place they considered to be "home." A fourteen-year old girl, who had been born in Sudan, said to me, "Our home [*addi*] is Axum" [the district in the central highlands from which her parents had come]—then she turned to her mother and asked, "What is it called?" "Adiet [meaning the name of the village]," she was told. Although she had never been to Adiet before, she considered it to be her "home" because of her family's connection to the place. Other children agreed that their addi was not Ada Bai. A few children who had paid visits to the family home in the highlands since repatriating said that they preferred Ada Bai, either because the school was closer to their houses, the water was closer, or, in the words of one seven-year-old girl, because the highlands are "full of stones . . . [and] you have to walk so far [to get from the village to the house]." The responses of these children indicated a sort of bilateral construction of home, with Ada Bai occupying the role of "everyday home" and the highlands that of "family home," which I suspect was also shared by some of their parents.

Over the ten years that I have been conducting research in Ada Bai, I have had to revise my own conclusions about how long the home-making process would take. When, in 1993–95, I asked parents and grandparents how long it would take before their children and grandchildren would think of Ada Bai as home, some told me that it would take three generations. At the point when a person could say that their father and paternal grandfather were both born in Ada Bai, they told me, they would be a true Ada Bai person. Others saw the process as being more prolonged. Incest prohibitions stipulate that a man and woman cannot marry if they have had any common paternal ancestors within the past seven generations. Children are taught the names of their paternal ancestors, and when I asked children in 2002 to name these relatives, I was surprised to find that even six-year-old children could name their grandfathers five or six generations back. Parents said that when all relatives in the seven-generation lineage were Ada Bai residents, then the tie to the highland home would truly be broken.

I did not take these statements as seriously as perhaps I should have. I assumed that they were speaking more rhetorically than literally. Perhaps on a subconscious level I discounted their words because I did not think that the funders of my research, who were aid agencies involved in repatriation, would take me seriously if I were to say that the return process would take seven generations to be completed. However, through this long-term research I have come to see that when people told me the process of redefining home would take seven generations, they were in fact speaking quite literally.

As anthropologists, we need to be mindful that many aspects of the processes we study do not fit easily into relief and development practitioners' time frames. At the same time, we must avoid casting our analysis into such arcane terms that it has no practical applications. Certainly, even though conceptual and affective homecoming might take several generations, there were concrete needs that aid agencies could respond to within the first few years following repatriation that needed to be highlighted, particularly in the areas of health care, education, access to credit, and infrastructural development.

Implications for Redirecting the Study of Repatriation

Social scientists are not the only ones who have treated "putting people back into their place" as the most convenient option. Aid practitioners and governments have also identified repatriation as the most desirable "durable solution" (more preferable than third country resettlement or local integration in the country of asylum). This idea perpetuates the notion of unproblematic return, and allows more developed countries to shirk their responsibilities to provide safe haven to refugees. The year 1992 was hailed by Sadako Ogata, UN High Commissioner for Refugees, as the first year in a decade of repatriation. The international aid system has used the media to project images of successful repatriations by bringing journalists to interview returnees as they climb down from the trucks or planes that brought them from exile, but the journalists are nowhere to be found when the returnees realize that their lives following repatriation may be the hardest thing they have yet had to cope with (Jackson 1994, 130).[2]

During the early 1990s, a series of academic studies commissioned by the United Nations Research Institute for Social Development (UNRISD) identified homecoming as a problem worthy of further investigation. The two volumes that resulted from this project, however, emphasized case studies rather than theoretical or even practical implications (Allen and Morsink 1994; Allen 1996). Still, this research has helped to highlight some of the difficulties of return. Policy statements from UNHCR and speeches by the commissioner reflect a growing concern that repatriation, especially by refugees who have experienced protracted periods of exile or who are returning to a country devastated by war, may be more difficult and may require more in the way of humanitarian and development assistance than had been previously thought. By May 1997, the UN High Commissioner for Refugees was decidedly more guarded in her outlook on repatriation, though probably more realistic, than she had been in 1992 when she ushered in a decade devoted to repatriation. In a speech to the Inter-Governmental Consultations on Asylum, Refugee, and Migration Policies in Europe, North America, and Australia, she called repatriation "'the least worse option' in a 'no win situation'" (Ogata 1997).

Ten years later, UNHCR and the international community continue to promote repatriation, even arguing that people should return to areas of their country of origin that are safe if the places from which they fled are not (referred to as the "internal flight option"). However, there is also more discussion now about the need to promote "self-reliance" in refugee populations, a strategy that closely resembles efforts during the 1980s to develop self-sustaining refugee camps.

If repatriation is recognized as being more complex than a mere transporting of people from one side of an international border to another (that is, if there are more financial costs involved) then there is a challenge to UNHCR, other UN agencies, NGOs, donors, and governments of return countries to either provide more assistance to help these returnees emplace themselves in such a way that they do not fall into a cycle of spiraling destitution or else to find an alternative to repatriation. Lacking sufficient resources to perform the functions with which they are presently charged, let alone to provide additional services, these actors have (in many cases deliberately) chosen not to look closely at the medium- and long-term experiences and needs of returnees. They know that no single agency can meet the needs of all returnees. In the aid world, to understand is often to recognize, and to recognize is to take responsibility.

Slowly, agencies have started to realize that they must work together to meet the needs of people involved in postreturn integration. They have begun to explore new forms of coordination and cooperation among themselves to respond to the needs of returnees. Such collaboration is often riddled with difficulties.[3] Many opportunities for sustainable development and preventive action to prevent future refugee flows have been left unexploited as a result of the failure of interagency cooperation.

Part of the problem is that no single UN organization has the mandate to respond to the needs of returnees. UNHCR has a responsibility to provide protection (first and foremost) and assistance (secondarily) to people who face a well-founded fear of persecution. UNHCR also has a duty to ensure that refugees are returned "in safety and dignity" to their country of origin when the source of persecution is no longer present. Where UNHCR's responsibility after repatriation ends, however, is not clear. In many contexts, UNHCR has sought to enlist the assistance of other UN agencies, particularly UNDP and UNICEF, to join with them in making the transition from reintegration to development. This has been as much a practical as a conceptual adjustment. The needs of people returning from exile to a wartorn country are understood to be so great that only a combined approach by UN operational agencies can begin to address their needs. Furthermore, while UNDP might seem to be the appropriate agency to take the lead in providing reintegration assistance, it is not operational and usually works at the central level through the line ministries rather than at a decentralized level.

In the search for solutions, agencies involved in repatriating refugees and assisting returnees have turned to anthropologists and other consultant social scientists for guidance. In this role, anthropologists have a special opportunity to translate their theoretical views into practice. A decentered anthropology that questions the primacy of place and looks carefully at processes of emplacement can help guide repatriation policy and assistance so that repatriation is seen for what it usually is: a complex process that can span many years, in which assistance is needed to enable people to construct their lives to the point that they can operate on equal economic, social, and political footing with other citizens of their country of origin.

Information that anthropologists should include in their analysis, at the most basic level, should involve the principles of community formation, the means by which interpersonal relationships are formed, the basic cost of living in the reintegration area, and any opportunities for, or limits on, income-earning potential that returnees have. Recommendations may include skills training, more secure access to land or other property, provision of interest-free credit, and food-for-work schemes.

An anthropology that takes seriously its practical implications without sacrificing its theoretical backbone is needed, both for the discipline and for those it seeks to influence and assist. The difficulties that Ada Bai returnees faced in the first two years following their repatriation could have been minimized, I believe, if those who claimed responsibility for assisting them had understood which basic requirements for a viable life were lacking.

The approach to repatriation illustrated in these pages is fairly typical of repatriation operations in other countries, and is also used as a model for other kinds of resettlement. In 1998, while working for UNDP in Somaliland to help develop a strategy for reintegrating refugees, I saw the same types of assistance being given and the same assumption that most forms of assistance could be withdrawn a year after repatriation. The same approach is being used in Afghanistan, Rwanda, and other countries.

In Ethiopia, the model is being used in 2003 in the context of a government-sponsored resettlement program for food-insecure and land-poor farmers who wish to move to the lowland areas of the country where there is better land. Rather than investigating the cost of living or examining the potential for resettlers to generate assets in the first few years following resettlement, the government is insisting on a one-year assistance package including food, land, housing, limited water supply and health care, and in some places small cash grants. When I visited these areas in 2003, I found that people had joined the resettlement program thinking that all their needs would be addressed; they had thus come to their new farmland with no tools, furniture, seeds, or other assets. Most came wearing only the clothing on their backs.

If the mistakes made in Ada Bai are to be avoided in these resettlement areas or in other repatriation contexts throughout the world, anthropologists and rehabilitation/development practitioners must forge a strong partnership to produce better planning, monitoring, and evaluation. Only this will lead to repatriation and postconflict development strategies that are successful.

Epilogue: The Ethiopia-Eritrea War in Ada Bai

On May 6, 1998, war broke out between Ethiopia and Eritrea. While the fighting was precipitated by disagreements over the exact location of the border between the two countries in several places, additional disputes over the use of Assab port, trade, exchange rates between the new Eritrean currency (the nakfa) and the Ethiopian birr, and the status of nationals of one country residing in the other had caused tensions between the two countries to escalate. The fighting was concentrated along the two countries' common border, most intensely near the Tigrayan towns of Badme and the Yirga Triangle in the west, Tsorona, Zelambessa, and Alitena in the center, and Bure and Manda (both in Afar Region) in the east. It was characterized by intense but relatively short bursts of military activity, followed by periods of relative calm. Although no official casualty figures are available, it is estimated that tens of thousands of soldiers lost their lives in two years of fighting.

When the fighting broke out, the Ethiopian government took steps to evacuate people from areas within forty kilometers of the border. Approximately 315,000 Tigrayans were displaced from their home areas (and another 35,000 in Afar Region). In most parts of Tigray, people were integrated into local communities. They stayed with their relatives and friends and received food assistance because they were not able to farm their land.

Although the border between Ethiopia and Eritrea near Humera was not part of the contested area—the border in that area is clearly marked by the Tekezze River—it was feared that Humera might be attacked because of its economic value and strategic location. The town was in fact shelled several times. The Tigray regional administration evacuated Humera, and the woreda administration was moved to Ba'eker. Ba'eker was a village that had previously been a collection of about ten teahouses set up along the road to Gondar to serve truck drivers and buses. The people of Ada Bai were outside of shelling range from Eritrea, and most people stayed where they were. However, a massive military recruitment campaign was conducted throughout Ethiopia. Many men of military age (18–40) in Ada Bai enlisted in the military.

In April 2000, the Ethiopian military launched an all-out offensive on Eritrean positions, driving the Eritrean forces out of areas it considered to be Ethiopian territory, and chasing them far inside land recognized to belong to Eritrea. This led to discussions in Algiers—brokered by the Organization for African Unity, with support from the United Nations, the United States, and the European Union—and a Cessation of Hostilities Agreement was signed in December 2000. As I write this, a 4,200 person UN-led peacekeeping force known as the UN Mission for Eritrea and Ethiopia (UNMEE) is patrolling the border area, monitoring the implementation of the agreement. Ethiopia has resumed its administration of areas that were under its control before May 6, 1998, and Eritrea has redeployed its forces twenty-five kilometers away from Ethiopian positions. Ethiopia has refused to accept the findings of the Border Demarcation Commission, despite its earlier promise to accept the commission's ruling. The peace between the two countries remains extremely fragile.

I have been to Ada Bai twice since the end of the war. Residents told me that they fled for only three weeks during the war, sheltering in their dry-season watering hole. "It was terrible," Tibbletz told me. "We were living like refugees again. We decided that we did not want to have any part of that. We would rather be here in Ada Bai, even if it is not safe."

With each visit I make, Ada Bai seems more and more like an established village, and I struggle with the question of whether the people I have written about here should still be considered returnees. Ada Bai is now the second largest town in the woreda. People's household assets are increasing, as their control over their environment has increased. Still, the local economy is hampered because the border with Eritrea remains closed. Sorghum and sesame prices have collapsed because Eritrean traders can no longer buy from Ethiopia. Cross-border trade of other items has also been suspended.

Ada Bai residents are resolute in their support of the Ethiopian government, at least when they speak of the war. They complain that Eritrean militia have crossed the Tekezze River many times to steal their cattle. In 2001, I arrived the day after Ambachew had lost all five of his cattle to raiders he claimed had come from Eritrea. The household was busy trying to find a milking cow for the calf whose mother was among the stolen livestock. In Ada Bai, the conflict was not just a national struggle; it had become personal, and the outrage expressed by residents reflected their own sense of having been victimized by the enemy.

Despite the signing of the peace agreement, the conflict goes on, and it will be many years before real peace is achieved. The people of Ada Bai are resolute in their intention to remain where they are no matter what happens. Although their emplacement may continue, they are keen to bring their experience as refugees to an end.

Notes

Note on Transcriptions and Use of Tigrinya Terms

1. Words such as Ge'ez, which are written in English with a prime, are pronounced with a glottal stop at the punctuation mark.

Introduction

1. Fifteen thousand returnees are estimated to have returned to Tigray Region, Ethiopia, from Sudan in 1993, settling at three sites. Ada Bai, with a population of 7,500, was the largest of the settlements. The other settlements, Mai Kadra and Rawayan, had only a few thousand people each initially, but grew in later years as more Tigrayans repatriated from Sudan and as others from the highlands joined them looking for better farmland and wage labor opportunities.

2. All personal names have been changed, with the exception of national political figures.

3. They were joined in Sudan by more than four hundred thousand Eritreans who had fled the fighting further north, having suffered through similar conditions.

4. I also worked for UNDP Somalia in 1998 on developing a reintegration strategy for returning Somali refugees from eastern Ethiopia.

5. In 1995 a new hospital was opened in Humera, with 150 beds and improved staffing and equipment.

Chapter 1. Narratives of Displacement

1. Spear (1990) argues that the political aspects of the famine may have been exaggerated by the political, anti-Derg positions of some of these authors and by their concern that the ethnic interests of the refugees be represented. Regardless of the role of ethnic politics in the perpetration of the famine, it seems clear from testimony that I gathered in Ada Bai that this famine was largely caused by deliberate attempts by the Derg to prevent people from using the risk-minimization strategies that they had developed and on which they relied during times of drought.

2. Derg (ደርግ) is an Amharic word meaning "committee." The Tigrinya equivalent, used to refer to the government at that time, is Dergie (ደርጊ).

3. Also known as the Tigray Nationalist Union (TNU).

4. An awraja (አውራጃ) is roughly equivalent to a subregion or province. During the imperial era, Tigray was divided into Tembien, Raya, Inderta, Agame, Adwa, Axum, Shire/Endaselassie, and Wolkait awrajas. Awrajas were further divided into woredas

(ወረዳ), similar to counties, and finally into *tabias* (ጣቢያ), comparable to parishes. When the TPLF/EPRDF gained control of Ethiopia, the map of Tigray was redrawn to include Wolkait awraja (including Kafta Humera woreda), which had previously been administered by Gondar Region. Awrajas were officially dissolved by the Transitional Government of Ethiopia, being consolidated into zones (in Tigray Southern, Central, Eastern, Mekele, and Western), but most returnees still identify themselves as belonging to a particular awraja.

5. Hager Selam tabia lies in Tembien awraja in central Tigray.

6. The speaker refers to 1969 in the Ethiopian, or Julian, Calendar. This calendar is seven years behind the Gregorian Calendar, which is followed by most of the rest of the world, and thus refers to 1976 G.C.

7. A *dajazmatch* (ደጃዝማች) was a local feudal lord during the imperial era.

8. Endaselassie ("Place of the Trinity") is also referred to as Shire. It was the capital of the Western Zone in Tigray Region until 2002, when Humera was made a separate zone.

9. Eritrea gained its independence with the overthrow of the Derg in 1991 and officially became recognized as a separate state following a referendum held in May 1993.

10. With the end of the war, REST officially became a registered nongovernmental organization (NGO). Presently the largest and most active NGO in Tigray and the largest indigenous NGO in Ethiopia, it works with a large number of international NGOs and donors.

11. Tigrinya speakers commonly refer to the government in the third person singular masculine.

12. Many towns in Tigray are named for the day of the week that the market was traditionally held (for example, Edaga Rebui means "Wednesday market"). It was thus easy for the Derg to target their attacks. Despite the adoption of a common market day during the war, the places have kept their pre-war names.

13. In 2003, the government initiated another resettlement program, this time to relocate 2.2 million people over a period of three to five years. While the program by 2004 was largely voluntary, inadequate planning and preparation in some areas led to high rates of morbidity and mortality.

14. The area where this road enters Tigray, known to Ethiopians and Eritreans as Badme (Bademe) or the Yirga Triangle, was disputed by Ethiopia and Eritrea at the time this book was written. Armed conflict broke out in February 1998 and continued on a sporadic but extremely ferocious level until June 2000. Ethiopia rejected the binding decision of the Boundary Demarcation Commission, which determined that Badme belonged to Eritrea, and in 2003 the two countries were threatening to resume fighting. Commonly referred to in the media as a "barren plain," the strategic, logistical, and historical significance of the dirt road that runs through it has not, to my knowledge, been recognized as a factor in the land dispute between the two countries. See epilogue.

15. Article 14 of the Protocol II Additional to the Geneva Conventions of 12 Aug. 1949, Relating to the Protection of Victims of Non-International Armed Conflicts, states, "Starvation of civilians as a means of combat is prohibited. It is therefore prohibited to attack, destroy, remove or render useless, for that purpose objects indispensable to the survival of the civilian population, such as foodstuffs, agricultural areas for the production of foodstuffs, crops, livestock, drinking water installations, and supplies and irrigation works."

16. One tin equals approximately one liter.

17. E$ is used in this case to refer to Ethiopian birr. At the official exchange rate of the time, U.S.$1 was worth two Ethiopian birr. Values indicated for ox prices therefore dropped from U.S.$150 to U.S.$30.

18. "Hamesien" is a pejorative term used to refer to pastoralists from western Eritrea, who frequently crossed the Tekezze River to seek pastureland in Tigray. Tigrayans resented the pastoralists' use of their land.

19. The tensions described here intensified following the secession of Eritrea from Ethiopia in 1993. Badme was the site of some of the fiercest fighting in the 1998–2000 Ethiopian-Eritrean war, in which each side claimed the area as its territory.

20. Approximately U.S.$5 per day at the official exchange rate. By way of comparison, wages in Humera during 1993 and 1994 remained unchanged at ten birr a day. The exchange rate, however, had changed to make the dollar value only U.S.$2.

21. Approximately U.S.$25.

22. Approximately U.S.$1.30.

23. The discourse of warfare in Tigray is largely about the "Struggle" for self-determination and the overthrow of the Derg. In this sense, the war is referred to by many peasants as "the Struggle"—*Qu'alsi* (ቃልሲ). The Struggle was associated with personal sacrifice, bravery, and communitarian support for the TPLF. After the end of the war, the Struggle came to be associated with the struggle for reconstruction and development.

24. Abi Adi, a name also derived from the Tigrinya for "Big Land," should not be confused with Ada Bai. Abi Adi is a large town in the central highlands.

25. Lekatit 11 (which corresponds to February 19 in the Gregorian calendar) is the date of the TPLF's anniversary celebration.

26. A *hidmo* (ሒድሞ) is a square house made of stone and mud, with walls that extend to form a courtyard enclosure for keeping animals safe at night. Commonly found throughout the Tigrayan highlands, it is not found in the western lowlands around Ada Bai and Humera.

27. *Kemim* (ቀመም) is a spice used in the preparation of most Ethiopian dishes. The word *kemim* is often used to refer to all of the spices (Tigrayans usually use seven) used in cooking *tsebhi* (ጽብሒ), or stew.

28. Médecins Sans Frontières, a medical charity, published a report condemning the forced resettlement program and claiming that people were being moved from areas that were not seriously affected by the drought. They were promptly expelled from the country and were not allowed back until 1991 when the EPRDF took control of the government (see Médecins Sans Frontières 1985).

29. In 1995, following national parliamentary elections that ended the transitional period, Meles Zenawi became prime minister, and Negasso Gidada, an Oromo, was selected by the House of Representatives to be president.

Chapter 2. Life in the Sudan Camps

1. The Sphere Project (whose standards are widely used by humanitarian agencies) gives a mean minimum nutritional requirement as 2,100/kcal/day per person (Sphere Project 2004).

2. A death rate of 1/10,000/day is considered an emergency.

3. The best description I have found of the behavior of the Evil Eye spirit in Ethiopia is given in Allan Young's Ph.D. dissertation (A. Young 1970). In Ada Bai, I read passages of this text to a traditional healer, who confirmed that the descriptions agreed with his own experience. Bishaw (1988) and Boddy (1989) also state that the Evil Eye is commonly cited by people as a cause of generalized illness.

4. See Boddy 1994 and 1989. Although the speaker in the above quote mentioned being afflicted by *zar* (female) spirits of the sort that Boddy describes, people said that these spirits were not as common in Ada Bai as the Evil Eye.

5. *Serit* was also the term used to refer to land distribution implemented by the TPLF during the war in areas under its control.

6. Hutchinson (1990) asserts that although marriage in African societies has commonly been considered to be stable, in fact divorce rates have been increasing among many groups, as a result of social dislocation and changes in property rules for men (as with the Nuer) or women (as in the case I discuss here).

7. Unlike in the highlands, where Bauer says that households of newly married children continue to share cattle with their parents and siblings who remain in the parental house, in Ada Bai people do not share resources as much, though they may help each other with projects that require a significant work input (see Bauer 1985 [1977], 120).

8. The camps were ostensibly closed because the refugees no longer faced a "well-founded fear of persecution" that would justify their continued protection as refugees (cf. 1951 Convention and 1967 Protocol on the Status of Refugees). In fact, donors faced crises in the Great Lakes region of Africa and other parts of the world, and therefore cut their funding for care and maintenance programs in Sudan. The process of closing the camps was slow, however, and was only completed in 2002.

Chapter 3. A Patchwork of Emplacements

1. Since the song is sung by children, it is not surprising that Tigray is not included in the comparison, since most young children were either born in Sudan or left Tigray when they were so young that they have little or no memory of it.

2. I do not subscribe to Casey's argument (1996) that space cannot exist prior to, or outside of, human experience, for such a position seems based on a notion of sedentary culture that does not move into new spaces.

3. Axum is also the heart of Tigrayan nationalism. The TPLF emblem depicts the largest of the remaining obelisks from the Axumite Empire (c. 200 B.C.–1000 A.D.) together with a machine gun, a spade, and a sheaf of wheat. Orthodox Christians believe that the original Ark of the Covenant was brought to Ethiopia and is being kept at the Church of St. Mariam in Axum (see Hancock 1992; Levine 1974). The legendary history of the Ark is given in the ancient manuscript known as the *Kebra Nagast*, or *Glory of Kings* (Brooks, trans., 1996).

4. *Hade* (ሓደ) means the number one in Tigrinya.

5. *Hidmo* and *tukul* describe the type of house (square stone or round straw, respectively), while *geza* refers to any kind of house. It is roughly equivalent to the word *home* when referring to the physical structure one lives in.

6. In the years following the end of the war, the TPLF sought to replace cadre administrators throughout Tigray with locally elected officials.

7. It was common for people who had just met me and had never heard the name "Laura" to call me Nora, thinking that my parents had given me this fitting name to reflect the fact that my skin was roughly the same color as the limestone!

8. *Hamle* (ሓምለ) usually refers to greens, such as spinach, eaten either raw or cooked in sauces. In this case, however, hamle was used to refer to anything that grows in a household garden: greens, tomatoes, spices, and even cotton.

9. Households that fetched water for their animals found that there was a limit to the numbers of heads they could keep. The water intake of the animals was also quite high compared to the highlands due to the heat of the lowlands.

10. In April–May 1994, the newly installed borehole pump stopped working for six weeks. This placed an enormous burden on households, who would send members to spend the night next to the wells waiting for them to fill up enough to collect sufficient water. The water quality was extremely poor and the rate of intestinal diseases and parasitic infections increased dramatically during this time. I had to abandon most of my field research activities to fetch clean water from Humera for me and my neighbors until the pump was fixed.

11. *Injera* (እንጀራ) is a pancake-like sourdough bread. In the highlands it is usually made from *teff* (ተፍ) a grain said to have originated in Ethiopia. In the lowlands, including Ada Bai, injera is made from sorghum, or *meshela* (መሽላ), as it is more plentiful.

12. I have examined children's emplacement in detail in Hammond 2003.

13. The association of blood with impurity is one of the most common symbolic representations in the world. See Douglas 1964; Hutchinson 1998, 171; Hutchinson 1992, 496.

14. Taken from recordings by the author of songs sung by a youth group in public celebrations to mark the twentieth anniversary of the TPLF, February 1995.

15. Snakes also occasionally came into the village, as I discovered late one night when, awakened by a man whose wife was having childbirth complications, I reached in the dark for my shoes on the sandy floor of my house and was met with the hissing sounds (and, when I turned on my flashlight, the bared fangs) of a highly poisonous snake (called *ifut*, እፉት, in Tigrinya) whose rest I had disturbed.

16. Although the Wolkait were clearly discriminated against in and around Humera, it is not clear whether they would be considered a separate ethnic group from either Amharas or Tigrayans, or if not, which of the two groups they would be included with. They spoke a dialect that was a fairly even mix of Amharic and Tigrinya, which made it difficult for other Tigrayans and Amharas who spoke only one of the languages to understand them. The physical differences between them and more light-skinned, narrow-featured highlanders were not considered significant in classifying them, since Amharas and Tigrayans did not fit one particular physical type either. Language and ancestry are the principal identifying markers of ethnic affiliation throughout most of Ethiopia. It is likely that Wolkait were ostracized merely because they were thought not to have any of the characteristics highlanders considered to be beautiful (including light skin, thin nose and lips, and long, soft hair).

17. See "Temporary Policy on Investment for Agriculture and Natural Resource Management," Lekatit 1986 (February 1993), Ministry of Agriculture, Mekele.

18. I discuss the use of social position to obtain access to land further in chapter 6.

19. This story is corroborated by the fact that for many years Ethiopia and Sudan have been involved in negotiations over the precise location of the common border; demarcation is obscured by Ethiopians living on Sudanese territory and Sudanese living on Ethiopian territory.

Chapter 4. The Household Food Economy

1. The Ethiopian Catholic Church, with its Tigray base in Adigrat, developed during the sixteenth century with the arrival of Portuguese missionaries. Most of the population in this area is Catholic. The church is now fully indigenous and has an Ethiopian bishop. The people of northeastern Agame are ethnically Irob and speak a dialect of Saho rather than Tigrinya. From May 1998 to mid 2000 the area was occupied by the Eritrean army as a result of a border dispute. Most of the population of two woredas in northeastern Tigray was displaced southwards.

2. *Kiremti* (ክረምቲ) is the long rainy season, which usually lasts from mid June to late September.

3. Women took fuelwood and men grazed their animals in the same areas as the Eritreans living further north. This sparked frequent fights between Ethiopian and Eritrean villagers. While I was in Alitena, I received reports of five Ethiopian men having been killed with axes by Eritreans. It was these conflicts that in May 1998 escalated into open warfare between the two countries. Although civilian casualties as a result of the conflict were reportedly light, it is estimated that as many as one hundred thousand Ethiopian and Eritrean soldiers may have been killed in two years of fighting.

4. This work was based on Bauer's Ph.D. dissertation; see Bauer 1973.

5. The figure of 10.2 quintals is the average of responses from Tigray Region and North Wollo and South Wollo zones of Amhara Region. The self-estimate by Tigray farmers of their needs was only 8.5 quintals. The authors attribute this to "force of circumstance rather than . . . choice" (29). People were so accustomed to scarcity that they regularly underestimated their needs.

6. At 1994 prices, U.S.$1 = five Ethiopian birr.

7. Some aid practitioners and local government officials in the highlands argue that food aid or another form of assistance (cash, employment, and so forth) should be given to this category of the poor so that they will not have to sell their plow oxen, since the poorest of the poor also depend on being able to borrow or hire these animals. Erosion of these assets will have an adverse impact not only on these middle strata but also on the poorest as they lose their ability to maintain their productivity.

8. Based on an average price of one hundred birr per quintal. Sesame is not included in the calculations, as only two of the households planted sesame, and both harvested it prior to the start of the survey.

9. The Ethiopian Orthodox Church has seven fasting periods throughout the year, the longest of which is the two months (65 days) prior to the Easter (Fasika) holiday. During this time, no meat or dairy products are to be consumed. All other foods may be eaten, although many of the more devout do not eat anything in the morning until after the noontime prayers. Throughout the year, Wednesdays and Fridays are also considered to be fasting days.

10. Based on cash received for sale of grain and an average price of 100 birr per quintal.

11. Bauer (1985 [1977] and 1976) argues that social stratification played an important role in imperial-era Tigray and conditioned relations between individuals and households. This appears to have been less significant in Ada Bai. Income differentials were not as wide between the households. People continued to use respectful salutations and titles to address members of the clergy, the elderly, and those who had at least some secondary school education. Titles such as "Gashey," meaning lord, which were still used in other parts of Ethiopia, were less common in Tigray. This was probably due to the propaganda work of the TPLF, which emphasized social equality, as well as the fact that most people in Ada Bai had lost everything and were thus on a similar economic footing with their neighbors.

12. See chapter 5 for a description of funerary rituals.

13. The Ethiopian Orthodox calendar devotes one day a month to each of the major saints and biblical characters: (e.g., Gabriel, Giorgis, Tekle Haimanot [patron saint of Ethiopia], Mikael [patron saint of healing], Mariam, Medhane Alem [Jesus Christ], Selassie [the Trinity], Aregawi [an Ethiopian saint], and Balie Egziabher [God]). Most of the saints have one or two days a year that are celebrated with pilgrimages to churches bearing the name of the saint.

14. Keshie (ቀሲ), which means priest, was also used as a title and form of address to show respect to priests.

15. During my visits to Ada Bai in 1996 and 1997, however, this practice had been suspended because of tense relations between Ethiopia and Sudan. Men claimed that it had become too dangerous to cross the border and said that they feared that the Sudanese border police would shoot anyone they suspected of crossing the border without proper identification and permission. There were rumors that this had happened in at least one instance.

16. 1,000 pounds = 13 birr = U.S.$2.60. 230,000 pounds = 2,990 birr, or 427 birr (U.S.$85.10) per person.

Chapter 5. "We Have Each Lost a Child": Birth, Death, and Life-Cycle Rituals

1. UNICEF, State of the World's Children, 2000 (statistics of infant mortality are based on 1998 estimates).

2. "Revised 1990 Estimates of Maternal Mortality: A New Approach by WHO and UNICEF" (1999).

3. Contrast this viewpoint with that of the Nuer of southern Sudan, who Hutchinson says consider "blood as the weakest point in the human constitution" (1992, 493).

4. See Chapter 1 for additional information about buda.

5. According to Hutchinson, the Nuer of southern Sudan also believe that the body is made vulnerable through the consumption of its tissues and take precautions to prevent such an occurrence (Hutchinson, personal communication).

6. In Somali society, where efforts to stop people from practicing female genital mutilation have been ongoing to only limited effect, I have heard men say that it is not they who insist on continuing the practice, but rather women who fear that their daughters will be ostracized if they are not infibulated.

7. The association of blood with illness, either as a cause of disease, the host of disease, or as a vehicle for spirit possession, is common throughout the Horn of Africa. See Hutchinson 1992, 493; Boddy 1989, 249; A. Young 1970, 73–76).

8. In recent years, these markings have been a curse to Tigrayans outside the region, since people from the region are associated with the EPRDF government and are often treated with hostility by members of other ethnic groups in Ethiopia who feel disenfranchised by the new regime.

9. Visceral leishmaniasis has been identified as being endemic to the Humera area since the early part of the twentieth century (see Hailu and Frommel 1993, 375–85). In 1997, Médecins Sans Frontières-Holland began a leishmaniasis prevention and treatment program in Humera. Most forms of treatment for the disease have low rates of effectiveness (Max Planck Institute 2000).

10. Aboy ("father,") is a title usually appended to the name of a respected elder within the community.

11. Although the importance of breast-feeding and adequately spaced births (more than 1.5 years between each) is generally recognized, the argument has been put forward in several studies that breast-feeding, while important to the health of a child during the first year, particularly during the first six months, must be considered a determinant of child mortality together with the spacing of births and the relative access of the child to resources necessary for its survival and growth, in that when a mother curtails breast-feeding because she is pregnant or has given birth to the next child, the older child has a greater chance of becoming malnourished and dying. (See Palloni and Tienda 1986, Defo and Palloni 1995.)

12. Tessema writes that the arms of a priest, monk, or nun who had been married are folded crosswise over the chest, while those of a virgin nun and celibate monk are "folded in such a way as to let the fingers rest on the mouth" (Tessema 1956, 13).

13. In other parts of Ethiopia, particularly towns, women wear black for as long as one year after the death of a relative. In Ada Bai people could not afford more than one dress and therefore wore only a black head scarf for several months after the death.

14. This is in contrast to Tessema's 1956 account, in which no funeral rituals were observed for children under the age of seven (16). In Tessema's account, it was also common for lamentor-poets—men or women who recite impromptu tribute poems to the deceased—to be invited to the funeral and to be rewarded for their poems by those in attendance (18). In Ada Bai this was not a common practice.

15. It was suggested to me that this was a new principle of the Orthodox Church, introduced by the TPLF to mollify the families of soldiers and refugees who had died during the war while they were far from their homes.

16. I also observed an Agobar in the highlands in 1999. For a detailed account of the ceremony, see Tessema 1956, 20–21.

17. Toward the end of my stay in Ada Bai the government passed a restriction preventing all doctors who were employed in hospitals in Ethiopia from also working in private clinics in an attempt to curb this practice.

Chapter 6. Ada Bai's Place in the Wider World

1. Other groups living in Ethiopia, such as the Somali, Afar, Nuer, Dinka, and Omotic pastoralist groups, have found freedom in their distance from state influence.

2. Practically speaking, the amount of power delegated to the regions varied from one region to another based on the capacities of the regional administrations to manage their own affairs as well as the level of political instability perceived by the central government to prevail in the regions. Tigray's regional administration is highly autonomous.

3. Other social institutions, such as ethnic groups, clans, competing political parties, and class differences, did not play a major role in the ordering of society, as they do in some other societies, including in other parts of Ethiopia. See Migdal 1988.

4. It was clear that this happened, even though no statistics on the demographic composition of Kafta Humera woreda prior to the end of the war were available.

5. These factors also played a major role (together with security considerations) in the government's decision to settle more than five thousand demobilized soldiers on unused land around Dansha, south of Humera.

6. "Wedi" (ወዲ), meaning son in Tigrinya, was used together with another term to form a nickname meant to describe the political Figure's strongest qualities—in this case, Shambel, meaning captain. Often his real name was not known to the public.

7. See 1995 Constitution of the Federal Democratic Republic of Ethiopia.

8. The 1995 Constitution of the Federal Democratic Republic of Ethiopia stipulates that all rural and urban land shall remain the property of the state (Article 40, no. 3), that all peasants have "the right to obtain land without payment and [are] protect[ed] against eviction from their possession" (Article 40, no. 4), and "have the right to receive a fair price for their products."

9. Nationally, several political parties boycotted the elections, including the Oromo Liberation Front and Ethiopian Democratic Union, which said that they had not been given fair and equal access to the electorate to campaign. In Tigray, these boycotts had no practical impact.

10. My use of the term "dependency syndrome" refers to refugees' and returnees' relationship to the international humanitarian assistance regime and not to the economic "dependency theory" that emerged during the late 1960s (see Escobar 1995; Cardoso and Faletto 1979).

11. The militia was a voluntary force made up of some of the most respected members of the community, most of whom had served with the TPLF during the war. They carried rifles and Kalashnikov machine guns more as a sign of their status as militia members than out of any real or perceived threat that would merit their use.

12. Ethiopian Orthodox churches typically have several priests. The Abune Aregawi Church at Ada Bai was the only Church in the community and was said to have fifteen priests (keshies) and fifteen vice-priests (halekas) associated with it.

Conclusion

1. The birth of the subdiscipline is generally associated with the establishment of the Refugee Studies Programme at the University of Oxford by Barbara Harrell-Bond in 1982. This program, which in 1999 became the Refugee Studies Centre, offered the first postgraduate degree in refugee studies and was instrumental in helping to develop similar centers of study and documentation in Africa, Asia, North America, and Europe (see Malkki 1995, 507).

2. In 1998 (while I was working for the UNDP in Somaliland) (Northwest Somalia) I heard a BBC radio broadcast in which repatriants were being asked as they arrived in Boroma, from Dharwanaji camp in Ethiopia, how they felt about "coming home." The returnees declared that they were glad to be returning, neglecting to add that the refugee camp was only eight km (and was visible) from Boroma, and that they had been resident in Somaliland for several years (only returning to the camp to collect food rations). Most had gone to the camp the night before to collect their "repatriation package."

3. See Hammond 1998 for a description of the failure of interagency cooperation in Somaliland.

Tigrinya and Amharic Glossary

Note: Where two terms are listed together, the first is Tigrinya and the second is Amharic. All other terms are given in Tigrinya.

abay	አባይ	Large
aboy	አቦይ	Father, also used as a term of respect for older men
addi	አዲ	Land (to which people belong)
Agobar	አጎባር	Ceremony to mark the death of a person in another village, usually held on market day
awraja	አውራጃ	Roughly equivalent to a subregion or province
awyat	አዉያት	Announcement, as of a death
baito	ባይቶ	Local governing council
beles	በለስ	Prickly pear, eaten in eastern Tigray during hungry season
berekha	በረኻ	Wilderness
berbere	በርበሬ	Spice
Beytelehem	ቤተለሐም	"Holy of Holies," innermost part of the Orthodox church where the *tabot* is kept
Beytemekdes	ቤተመክደስ	Area of Orthodox church surrounding the inner sanctum where the *tabot* is kept, open only to clergy
bota	ቦታ	Place (specific)
buda	ቡዳ	Evil Eye
chiguraf-gotet	ሺጉራፉ ግተት	Temporary use of land by arrangement with the owner
Christena	ክርስትና	Christening
dajazmatch	ደጃዝማች	Local feudal lord during the imperial era
das	ዳስ	Straw and wood open-sided shelter, used for shade
Dergie, Derg	ደርጊ, ደርግ	Committee, used to refer to the socialist government that ruled Ethiopia from 1974 to 1991
diessa	ዲስአ	System of land tenure based on residence whereby the farmland of a particular village is parceled out to all resident households
ferenjee	ፈረንጂ	Foreigner
fetih	ፋቲህ	Divorce

finjal	ፊንጁል	Small china cup from which coffee is drunk
ganin	ጋኒን	Spirit, usually female, that possesses both men and women (see *jinn*)
ga'at	ገዐት	Thick porridge made from wheat or barley
geleb	ገለብ	Ceremony held seven days after the birth of a child to give thanks to God and Mary for the birth
geza	ጌዛ	House (generic term to refer to house of any construction)
gudgele	ጉጅለ	Group of households organized for distribution of food aid or for political organizing purposes
habesha medehanit	ሐበሻ መደሃኒት	Traditional medicine
hade	ሓደ	One
hager	ሀገር	The nation from which one came or the general area in which one was born
hager seb	ሀገር ሰብ	The specific place in which a person was born
haleka	ሀለቃ	Vice-priest
hamed debe	ሓመድ ድበ	Burial
hamle	ሓምለ	Vegetable greens
harratsa	ሀረጸ	Interest paid on a loan, usually 10 percent
hazen	ሓዘን	Funerary gathering at the house of the deceased, usually lasting for seven days
hidmo	ሒድሞ	Square house made of stone and mud, with walls that extend to form a courtyard enclosure for keeping animals safe at night. Commonly found throughout the Tigrayan highlands but not in the western lowlands around Ada Bai and Humera
himbasha	ሒምበሻ	Flat, leavened bread made from wheat
iddir	እዲር	Burial association
ifut	እፉት	Small but highly poisonous snake found in Humera
injera	እንጀራ	Unleavened sourdough flat bread, usually made from *teff* in the highlands and sorghum in the lowlands, eaten with virtually every meal
iqub	እቁብ	Savings associations whereby members contribute money to a central treasury and distribute the funds in full each month or each week to a different member, whose name is drawn at random
jedid	ጀዲድ	Shroud, usually made of white cloth
jinn	ጂን	Spirit, usually female, that possesses both men and women. See *ganin*
jirba	ጀርባ	Riverbed
kebele	ከበለ	Neighborhood
kemim	ቀመም	Spice used in preparation of most Ethiopian dishes

keshie	ቀሺ	Priest. Also used as a title and form of address to show respect to priests
kiremti, kiremt	ክረምቲ, ክረምት	Long rainy season, usually lasts from mid June to late September
kolo	ቆሎ	Roasted barley or maize, eaten as a snack
magogo	መጎጎ	Traditional fuel-efficient stove
maheber	ማህበር	Mutual assistance organization
Maret	ማረት	Relief Society of Tigray
megaraz	ምግራዝ	Circumcision
mereyt	መሬት	Farmland
meshela	መሸላ	Sorghum, staple grain of the lowland diet
metshaf nezazey	መጽሓፍ ንዛዘ	Prayer spoken over a dead body after it has been washed and prepared for burial
mezakerta	መዘከርታ	Souvenir, keepsake
mugnaz	ምግናዝ	Ritual washing of corpse in preparation for burial
netsela	ነጸላ	Shawl made from white, usually homespun, cotton and often with a colorful banner woven into its edges
nora	ኖራ	Limestone used to whitewash interior house walls
Nuzazey	ኑዛዘ	Last confession
Qu'alsi	ቃልሲ	"The Struggle"—used to refer to the civil war fought between the TPLF and Derg (1974–1991)
qun'quno	ቀንቀኖ	Powder used against termites, also used in circumcision as an antiseptic
ras	ራስ	Provincial king
risti, rist	ርስቲ, ርስት	Land tenure system based on inheritance
safara tabia	ላፋራ ታቢያ	Assigned camp or settlement
serit	ሰሪት	Administration
sewa	ስዋ	Locally brewed beer, mildly alcoholic, made from sorghum
shifta	ሽፍታ	Bandit; also one who roams around
shinfa	ሽጣፊ	Seed used in circumcision ritual, buried with fore skin to prevent detection by animals
shirmuta	ሽርሙጣ	Prostitute
shofer	ሾፈር	Illness whose symptoms resemble hepatitis, said to be endemic in Humera area
tabia	ጣቢያ	Parish
tabot	ታቦት	Replica of the Ark of the Covenant, held by every Orthodox church
tebib	ጠቢብ	Spirits who carry the Evil Eye (*buda*), also sometimes used interchangeably with *buda*
teff	ተፍ	Staple grain grown in Ethiopian midlands and highlands, used to make *injera*
tenkweley	ተንቋላይ	Sorcerer
Teskar	ተስካር	Commemoration ceremony for the dead
tseada medehanit	ጸአዳ መደሃኒት	"White people's medicine," biomedicine

tsebel	ፀበል	Celebration held on selected saints' days
tsebhi	ጽብሒ	Stew or sauce served with *injera* as staple diet
tsurura	ጽሩራ	Three small golden amulets, braided into a woman's hair along her hairline; thought to ward off spirits that might threaten pregnancy
tukul	ቱኩል	One-room straw house with thatched roof, usually round or square
waz	ወዝ	Illness whose symptoms resemble that of leishmaniasis
wedi	ወዲ	Son
wi'il	ውዕል	Will, written contract between husband and wife stipulating goods to be exchanged in the event of divorce
woreda	ወረዳ	Administrative unit approximately equivalent to a county in the United States or the United Kingdom
zoba	ዞባ	Zone

Bibliography

Abbay, Alemseged. 1998. *Identity Jilted, or Reimagining Identity? The Divergent Paths of Eritrean and Tigrayan Nationalist Struggles.* Trenton, N.J.: Red Sea Press.

Akol, Joshua O. 1994. "A Crisis of Expectations: Returning to Southern Sudan in the 1970s." In *When Refugees Go Home: African Experiences,* edited by Tim Allen and Hubert Morsink, 78–95. Trenton, N.J.: Africa World Press.

Allen, Tim, ed. 1996. *In Search of Cool Ground: War, Flight, and Homecoming in Northeast Africa.* Trenton, N.J.: Africa World Press.

Allen, Tim, and Hubert Morsink, eds. 1994. *When Refugees Go Home: African Experiences.* Trenton, N.J.: UNRISD/Africa World Press.

Alonso, Ana María. 1994. "The Politics of Space, Time, and Substance: State Formation, Nationalism, and Ethnicity." *Annual Review of Anthropology* 23, 379–405.

Alvarez, Robert R., Jr. 1995. "The Mexican–U.S. Border: The Making of an Anthropology of the Borderlands." *Annual Review of Anthropology* 24, 447–70.

Appadurai, Arjun. 1996. *Modernity at Large: Cultural Dimensions of Globalization.* Minneapolis: University of Minnesota Press.

———. 1988. "Putting Hierarchy in Its Place." *Cultural Anthropology* 3, no. 1: 37–50.

Appadurai, Arjun, and Carol A. Breckenridge. 1988. "Why Public Culture?" *Public Culture Bulletin* 1, no. 1. 5–9.

Asheber, Yaregal Teshome. 1995. "Sesame Production at Humera, Ethiopia." B.A. thesis, Century University.

Basso, Keith H. 1988. "'Speaking with Names': Language and Landscape among the Western Apache." *Cultural Anthropology* 3, no. 2, 99–130.

Bauer, Franz Dan. 1985 [1977]. *Household and Society in Ethiopia.* Monograph no. 6, Occasional Papers Series, Northeast African Studies Committee. East Lansing: African Studies Center, Michigan State University.

———. 1973. "Land, Leadership, and Legitimacy among the Inderta Tigray of Ethiopia." Ph.D. diss., Rochester, N.Y.: University of Rochester.

Bender, Barbara, ed. 1995. *Landscape: Politics and Perspectives.* Oxford: Berg.

Berhe, Kahsay. 1991. "The National Movement in Tigray: Myths and Realities." Unpublished mimeo.

Bishaw, Mekonnen. 1988. "Integrating Indigenous and Cosmopolitan Medicine in Ethiopia." Ph.D. diss. Carbondale: Southern Illinois University.

Black, Richard. 1993. "Geography and Refugees: Current Issues." *Geography and Refugees: Patterns and Processes of Change,* edited by Richard Black and Vaughan Robinson. New York: Belhaven Press.

Black, Richard, and Khalid Koser, eds. 1999. *The End of the Refugee Cycle: Refugee Repatriation and Reconstruction.* Oxford: Berghahn Books.

Boddy, Janice. 1994. "Spirit Possession Revisited: Beyond Instrumentality." *Annual Review of Anthropology* 23, 407–34.

———. 1989. *Wombs and Alien Spirits: Women, Men, and the Zār Cult in Northern Sudan.* Madison: University of Wisconsin Press.

Bodenhorn, Barbara. 1995. "Gendered Spaces, Public Places: Public and Private Revisited on the North Slope of Alaska." In *Landscape: Politics and Perspectives*, edited by Barbara Bender. London: Berg.

Breckenridge, Carol, and Arjun Appadurai. 1989. "On Moving Targets." *Public Culture* 2, no. 1: i–iv.

Brooks, Miguel F., trans. 1996. *Kebra Nagast (Glory of Kings)*. Trenton, N.J.: Red Sea Press.

Bruce, John Wingate. 1976. "Land Reform Planning and Indigenous Communal Tenures: A Case Study of the Tenure 'Chiguraf-Gwoses' in Tigray, Ethiopia," D.J.S. diss. Madison: University of Wisconsin.

Bruce, John, Allan Hoben, and Dessalegn Rahmato. 1992. "After the Derg: An Assessment of Rural Land Tenure Issues in Ethiopia." Draft report presented at the Workshop on Rural Land Tenure Issues in Ethiopia, Addis Ababa: Addis Ababa University.

Burgess, Ann, and R. F. A. Dean. 1962. *Malnutrition and Food Habits: Report of an International and Interprofessional conference*. London: Tavistock.

Cardoso, Fernando Henrique, and Enzo Faletto. 1979. *Dependency and Development in Latin America*, Berkeley: University of California Press.

Casey, Edward S. 1997. *The Fate of Place: A Philosophical History*. Berkeley: University of California Press.

———. 1996. "How to Get from Space to Place in a Fairly Short Stretch of Time: Phenomenological Prolegomena." In *Senses of Place*, edited by Steven Feld and Keith H. Basso, 13–51. Santa Fe: School of American Research Press.

Centers for Disease Control. 1992 (July 24). "Famine-Affected, Refugee, and Displaced Populations: Recommendations for Public Health Issues." *Morbidity and Mortality Weekly Review* 41 (no. RR-13).

Chimni, B. S. 2000. "Globalization, Humanitarianism, and the Erosion of Refugee Protection." *Journal of Refugee Studies* 13, no. 3, 243–63.

Clapham, Christopher. 1988. *Transition and Continuity in Revolutionary Ethiopia*. Cambridge: Cambridge University Press.

Clay, Jason W., and Bonnie K. Holcomb. 1986. *Politics and the Ethiopian Famine, 1984–1985*. Trenton, N.J.: Red Sea Press.

Clay, Jason W., Sandra Steingraber, and Peter Niggli. 1988. *The Spoils of Famine: Ethiopian Famine Policy and Peasant Agriculture*. Cultural Survival Report 25. Cambridge, Mass.: Cultural Survival.

Clifford, James. 1997. *Routes: Travel and Translation in the Late Twentieth Century*. Cambridge: Harvard University Press.

Colson, Elizabeth. 1971. *The Social Consequences of Resettlement: The Impact of the Kariba Resettlement upon the Gwembe Tonga*. Manchester: Manchester University Press.

Constitution of the Federal Democratic Republic of Ethiopia. 1995. Addis Ababa.

Cuny, Frederick C. 1994. *Disasters and Development*. Dallas: Intertect Press.

Daley, Patricia. 1991. "Gender, Displacement, and Social Reproduction: Settling Burundi Refugees in Western Tanzania." *Journal of Refugee Studies* 4, no. 3, 248–65.

Daniel, E. Valentine, and John Chr. Knudsen, eds. 1995. *Mistrusting Refugees*. Berkeley: University of California Press.

Davis, J. 1992. "The Anthropology of Suffering." *Journal of Refugee Studies* 5, no. 2, 149–61.

Defo Kuate, and Alberto Palloni. 1995. "Determinants of Mortality among Cameroonian Children: Are the Effects of Breastfeeding and Pace of Childbearing Artifacts?" *Genus* 51, no. 3–4, 61–96.

de Waal, Alex. 1991. *Evil Days: Thirty Years of War and Famine in Ethiopia*. London: Africa Watch Report/Human Rights Watch.

———. 1989. *Famine That Kills: Darfur, Sudan, 1984–85*. Oxford: Clarendon.

Deng, Francis M., and Larry Minear. 1992. *The Challenges of Famine Relief: Emergency Operations in the Sudan*. Washington: Brookings Institution.

Dolan, Chris. 1999. "Repatriation from South Africa to Mozambique—Undermining Durable Solutions?" In *The End of the Refugee Cycle: Refugee Repatriation and Reconstruction*, edited by Richard Black and Khalid Koser, 85–109. Oxford: Berghahn Books.

Douglas, Mary. 1966. *Purity and Danger: An Analysis of the Concepts of Pollution and Taboo*. London: Routledge.

Drucker, D. 1988. "South Kassala Agricultural Project Human Resources Survey, 28 March–13 May 1988." UNHCR/TSS (with the World Bank) MR 21/88: Sudan.

Duffield, Mark, and John Prendergast. 1994. *Without Troops and Tanks: Humanitarian Intervention in Ethiopia and Eritrea*. Trenton, N.J.: Red Sea Press.

Eastmond, Marita, and Joakim Öjendal. "Revisiting a 'Repatriation Success': The Case of Cambodia." In *The End of the Refugee Cycle: Refugee Repatriation and Reconstruction*, edited by Richard Black and Khalid Koser, 38–55. Oxford: Berghahn Books.

Engels, F. 1972 [1884]. *The Origin of the Family, Private Property, and the State, in the Light of the Researches of Lewis H. Morgan*. New York: International Publishers.

Escobar, Arturo. 1995. *Encountering Development: The Making and Unmaking of the Third World*. Princeton: Princeton University Press.

Feld, Steven, and Keith H. Basso, eds. 1996. *Senses of Place*. Santa Fe: School of American Research Press.

Foster, George. 1965. "Peasant Society and the Image of the Limited Good." *American Anthropologist* 67, no. 2, 293–315.

Foucault, Michel. 1972. *Archaeology of Knowledge and the Discourse on Language*. New York: Pantheon.

——. 1973. *The Order of Things: An Archaeology of the Human Sciences*. New York: Vintage.

Geneva Conventions Relating to the Protection of Victims of Non-International Armed Conflicts (Protocol II), 12 Aug. 1949.

Gmelch, George. 1980. "Return Migration." In *Annual Review of Anthropology* 9, 135–59.

Gordon, Milton. 1964. *Assimilation in American Life: The Role of Race, Religion, and National Origins*. New York: Oxford University Press.

Gow, Peter. 1995. "Land, People, and Paper in Western Amazonia," In *The Anthropology of Landscape*, edited by Eric Hirsch and Michael O'Hanlon, 43–62. Oxford Studies in Social and Cultural Anthropology. Oxford: Clarendon Press.

Greenhouse, Carol J., Elizabeth Mertz, and Kay B. Warren. 2002. *Ethnography in Unstable Places: Everyday Lives in Contexts of Dramatic Political Change*. Durham, N.C.: Duke University Press.

Habte-Selassie, Elias. 1992. "Eritrean Refugees in the Sudan: A Preliminary Analysis of Voluntary Repatriation." In *Beyond Conflict in the Horn: Prospects for Peace, Recovery, and Development in Ethiopia, Somalia, Eritrea, and Sudan*, edited by Martin Doornbos, Lionel Cliffe, Abdel Ghaffar M. Ahmed, and John Markakis. Trenton, N.J.: Red Sea Press.

Hailu, Asrat, and Dominique Frommel. 1993. "Leishmaniasis." In *The Ecology of Health and Disease in Ethiopia*, edited by Helmut Kloos and Zein Ahmed Zein, 375–88. Boulder, Colo.: Westview Press.

Hammond, Laura. 2003. "How Will the Children Come Home? Emplacement and the Creation of the Social Body in an Ethiopian Returnee Settlement." In *Children's Places: Cross-Cultural Perspectives*, edited by Karen Fog Olwig and Eva Gullov. London: Taylor and Francis.

——. 2000. "This Place Will Become Home: Emplacement and Community Formation in a Tigrayan Returnee Settlement, Northwest Ethiopia." Ph.D. diss. Madison: University of Wisconsin.

——. 1999. "Examining the Discourse of Repatriation: Towards a More Proactive Theory of Return Migration." In *The End of the Refugee Cycle: Refugee Repatriation and Reconstruction*, edited by Richard Black and Khalid Koser, 227–46. Oxford: Berghahn Books.

——. 1998. "'Express Lane' Repatriation: Opportunity or Obstacle to Development in Postwar Somaliland?" Paper presented to the International Association for the Study of Forced Migration's International Research and Advisory Panel, Jerusalem.

——. 1996a. "Tradition, Change, and Cultural Variation in Postwar Tigray." In *Aethiopia*, edited by Xavier van der Stappen. Paris: Cultures and Communication.

——. 1996b. "Returnees, Local Farmers, and Big Business: The Politics of Land Allocation in Humera, Ethiopia," in *After the Derg: An Assessment of Rural Land Tenure Issues in Ethiopia: Proceedings of a Workshop Held at Addis Ababa University, 5–6 May 1994*. Trondheim, Norway: Trondheim University Press.

——. 1989. "The Formation of an Ethiopian Community in New York City: Family Ties, Regional Identities, and Mutual Assistance." Undergraduate thesis. Bronxville, N.Y.: Sarah Lawrence College.

Hancock, Graham. 1992. *The Sign and the Seal: The Quest for the Lost Ark of the Covenant.* London: Heinemann.

Hareide, Dag. 1991. *Vulnerability to Famine.* Oslo: Alternative Future Project.

Harrell-Bond, Barbara. 1986. *Imposing Aid: Emergency Assistance to Refugees.* Oxford: Oxford University Press.

Harrell-Bond, Barbara E., and E. Voutira. 1992. "Anthropology and the Study of Refugees." *Anthropology Today* 8, no. 4, 6–10.

Heiden, David. 1992. *Dust to Dust: A Doctor's View of Famine in Africa.* Philadelphia: Temple University Press.

Hendrie, Barbara. 1992. "The Tigrayan Refugee Repatriation: Sudan to Ethiopia, 1985–1987." In *Repatriation during Conflict in Africa and Asia*, edited by F. Cuny, B. Stein, and P. Reed. Dallas: Intertect.

Hinton, Alexander Laban. 2002. *Annihilating Difference: The Anthropology of Genocide.* Berkeley: University of California Press.

Hirsch, Eric, and Michael O'Hanlon. 1995. *The Anthropology of Landscape.* Oxford Studies in Social and Cultural Anthropology. Oxford: Clarendon.

Holt, Julius, and Jennifer Bush. 2001. "Food Economy Training Course and Field Assessment in Central Tigray." Unpublished report submitted to Oxfam-Canada.

Holt, Julius, and Mark Lawrence. 1993. "Making Ends Meet: A survey of the Food Economy of the Ethiopian North-east Highlands." London: Save the Children.

Horst, Cindy. 2002. "Transnational Nomads, Somali Coping with Refugee Life in Dadaab, Kenya." A paper presented to the American Anthropological Association meeting, New Orleans.

Humphrey, Caroline. 1995. "Chiefly and Shamanist Landscapes in Mongolia." In *The Anthropology of Landscape*, edited by Eric Hirsch and Michael O'Hanlon, 135–62. Oxford Studies in Social and Cultural Anthropology. Oxford: Clarendon.

Hutchinson, Sharon. 1998. *Nuer Dilemmas: Coping with Money, War, and the State.* Berkeley: University of California Press.

——. 1992. "'Dangerous to Eat': Rethinking Pollution States among the Nuer of Sudan." *Africa* 62, no. 4, 490–504.

——. 1990. "Rising Divorce among the Nuer, 1936–1983." *Man* (n.s.) 25, 393–411.

Hyndman, Jennifer. 2000. *Managing Displacement: Refugees and the Politics of Humanitarianism*, Minneapolis: University of Minnesota Press.

Jackson, Jeremy. 1994. "Repatriation and Reconstruction in Zimbabwe during the 1980s." In *When Refugees Go Home: African Experiences*, edited by Tim Allen and Hubert Morsink, 126–66. Trenton, N.J.: Africa World Press.

Kalipeni, Ezekiel, and Paul T. Zeleza. 1999. *Sacred Spaces and Public Quarrels: African Cultural and Economic Landscapes*, Trenton, N.J.: Africa World Press.

Kearney, M. 1995. "The Local and the Global: The Anthropology of Globalization and Transnationalism." *Annual Review of Anthropology* 24, 547–65.

Kibreab, Gaim. 1999. "Revisiting the Debate on People, Place, Identity, and Displacement." *Journal of Refugee Studies* 12 no. 4, 384–428.

———. 1996a. *People on the Edge in the Horn.* Trenton, N.J.: Red Sea Press.

———. 1996b. "Ready and Willing . . . but Still Waiting: Factors Influencing the Decision of Eritrean Refugees in the Sudan to Return Home." Uppsala: Life and Peace Institute.

———. 1990. *From Subsistence to Wage Labour: Refugee Settlements in the Central and Eastern Regions of the Sudan.* Trenton, N.J.: Red Sea Press.

———. 1989. "Local Settlements in Africa: A Misconceived Option?" *Journal of Refugee Studies* 2, no. 4, 468–90.

Korn, David A. 1986. *Ethiopia, the United States and the Soviet Union.* London: Croon Helm.

Koser, Khalid. 1997. "Information and Repatriation: The Case of Mozambican Refugees in Malawi." *Journal of Refugee Studies* 10, no. 1: 1–18.

Kuhn, Thomas. 1970. *The Structure of Scientific Revolutions.* Chicago: University of Chicago Press.

Kundera, Milan. 2003. *Ignorance.* New York: Harper Collins Publishers.

Larkin, Mary Ann, Frederick Cuny, and Barry N. Stein. 1992. *Repatriation under Conflict in Central America.* Washington, D.C.: Hemispheric Migration Project Center for Immigration Policy and Refugee Assistance, Georgetown University and the Intertect Institute.

Lavie, Smadar, Kirin Narayan, and Renato Rosaldo, eds. 1993. *Creativity/Anthropology.* Ithaca: Cornell University Press.

Lepowsky, Maria. 1993. *Fruit of the Motherland: Gender in an Egalitarian Society.* New York: Columbia University Press.

———. 1990. "Big Men, Big Women, and Cultural Autonomy." *Ethnology* 29, no. 10, 35–50.

Leslau, Wolff. 1976. *Concise Amharic Dictionary.* Berkeley: University of California Press.

Limón, Jose. 1994. *Dancing with the Devil.* Madison: University of Wisconsin Press.

———. 1989. "Carne, Carnales, and the Carnivalesque: Bakhtinian Batos, Disorder, and Narrative Discourse." *American Ethnologist* 16, 471–86.

Loizos, Peter. 1981. *The Heart Grown Bitter: A Chronicle of Cypriot War Refugees.* Cambridge: Cambridge University Press.

MacClancy, Jeremy, ed. 2002. *Exotic No More: Anthropology on the Front Lines.* Chicago: University of Chicago Press.

Makanya, Stella Tandai. 1994. "The Desire to Return: Effects of Experiences in Exile on Refugees Repatriating to Zimbabwe in the Early 1980s." In *When Refugees Go Home: African Experiences.* edited by Tim Allen and Hubert Morsink, 126–66. Trenton, N.J.: Africa World Press.

Malkki, Liisa H. 1996. "Speechless Emissaries: Refugees, Humanitarianism, and Dehistoricization." *Cultural Anthropology* 11, no. 3, 377–404.

———. 1995a. *Purity and Exile: Violence, Memory, and National Cosmology among Hutu Refugees in Tanzania.* Chicago: University of Chicago Press.

———. 1995b. "Refugees and Exile: From 'Refugee Studies' to the National Order of Things." *Annual Review of Anthropology* 24, 495–523.

———. 1994. "Citizens of Humanity: Internationalism and the Imagined Community of Nations." *Diaspora* 3, no. 1, 41–68.

———. 1992. "National Geographic: The Rooting of Peoples and the Territorialization of National Identity among Scholars and Refugees." *Cultural Anthropology* 7, no. 1, 24–44.

———. 1990. "Context and Consciousness: Local Conditions for the Production of Historical and National Thought among Hutu Refugees in Tanzania," In *Nationalist Ide-*

ologies and Production of National Cultures, edited by Richard G. Fox. American Ethnological Society Monograph Series no. 2. Washington, DC: American Anthropological Association.

Malthus, Thomas R. 1958 [1798]. *An Essay on the Principle of Population*, New York: Dutton.

Maren, Michael. 1997. *The Road to Hell: The Ravaging Effects of Foreign Aid and International Charity*. New York: Free Press.

Max Planck Institute for Biophysical Chemistry. (Feb.) 2000. "Cure for Fatal Tropical Disease—Oral Treatment of Leishmaniasis." Press release, Göttingen.

May, Clifford D. 1985a. "Ethiopia's Other Scourge: Rebel War." *New York Times*, Jan. 5, 1985.

——. 1985b. "Ethiopia Refugees Leaving the Sudan." *New York Times*, May 25, 1985, A3.

——. 1985c. "Cholera Reported Spreading in Ethiopia Capital and Sudan." *New York Times*, Aug. 1, 1985, A2.

——. 1985d. "The Famine Workers." *New York Times Magazine*, Dec. 1, 1985, 60.

McCann, James C. 1999. *Green Land, Brown Land, Black Land: An Environmental History of Africa, 1800–1990*. Portsmouth, N.H.: Heinemann.

——. 1998. "A Tale of Two Forests: Narratives of Deforestation in Ethiopia, 1840–1996." Boston University African Studies Center Working Paper no. 209.

——. 1995. *People of the Plow: An Agricultural History of Ethiopia, 1800–1990*. Madison: University of Wisconsin Press.

——. 1990. "A Dura Revolution and Frontier Agriculture in Northwest Ethiopia, 1898–1920." *Journal of African History* 31, 121–34.

McSpadden, Lucia Ann. 1999. "Contradictions and Control in Repatriation: Negotiations for the Return of 500,000 Eritrean Refugees." In *The End of the Refugee Cycle: Refugee Repatriation and Reconstruction*, edited by Richard Black and Khalid Koser, 69–84. Oxford: Berghahn Books.

Mebtouche, Larbi. 1987. "Refugees in Eastern Sudan: Aid and Development (5–30 Oct. 1987)." Mission Report 87/50 Geneva: UNHCR/TSS.

Médecins Sans Frontières. 1985. *Mass Deportations in Ethiopia*, Paris: Médecins Sans Frontières.

Migdal, Joel. 1988. *Strong Societies and Weak States: State-Society Relations and State Capabilities in the Third World*. Princeton: Princeton University Press.

Miller, Judith. "Up to Four Million in Sudan Said to Face Starvation." *New York Times*, Jan. 12, 1985, A10.

Morphy, Howard. 1995. "Landscape and Reproduction of the Ancestral Past." In *The Anthropology of Landscape*, edited by Eric Hirsch and Michael O'Hanlon, 184–209. Oxford Studies in Social and Cultural Anthropology. Oxford: Clarendon.

Nagengast, Carole. 1994. "Violence, Terror, and the Crisis of the State." *Annual Review of Anthropology* 23, 109–36.

Negussie, Gizaw. 1976. "Organization and Financing of Agricultural Cooperatives in Ethiopia," M.S. thesis, Sartafé: New Mexico State University.

Nieburg, P., A. Berry, R. Steketee, N. Binkin, T. Dondero, and N. Aziz. 1988. "Limitations of Anthropometry during Acute Food Shortages: High Mortality Can Mask Refugees' Deteriorating Nutritional Status." *Disasters* 12, 253–58.

Nordstrom, Carolyn. 1997. *A Different Kind of War Story*. Philadelphia: University of Pennsylvania Press.

Nordstrom, Carolyn, and C. G. M. Robben, eds. 1995. *Fieldwork under Fire: Contemporary Studies of Violence and Survival*. Berkeley: University of California Press.

Ogata, Sadako (United Nations High Commissioner for Refugees). 6 May 1997. Statement to the Inter-Governmental Consultations on Asylum, Refugee, and Migration Policies in Europe, North America, and Australia (IGC). Washington, D.C.

Oliver-Smith, Anthony. 1996. "Anthropological Research on Hazards and Disasters." *Annual Review of Anthropology* 25, 303–28.

Ong, Aihwa. 1999. *Flexible Citizenship: The Cultural Logics of Transnationality*. Durham: Duke University Press.

Organization of African Unity (OAU). 1969. "Convention Governing Specific Aspects of Refugee Problems in Africa." Addis Ababa.

Palloni, Alberto, and Sara Millman. 1986. "Effects of Inter-Birth Intervals and Breast-feeding on Infant and Early Childhood Mortality." *Population Studies* 40, 215–36.

Palloni, Alberto, and Marta Tienda. 1986. "The Effects of Breastfeeding and Pace of Childbearing on Mortality at Early Ages." *Demography* 23, no. 1, 31–52.

Pankhurst, Alula. 1989. "Settling for a New World: People and the State in an Ethiopian Resettlement Village." Ph.D. diss. Manchester University (U.K.).

Pankhurst, Helen. 1992. *Gender, Development, and Identity: An Ethiopian Study*. London: Zed Books.

Pausewang, Siegfried, Fantu Cheru, Stefan Brüne, and Eshetu Chole, eds. 1990. *Ethiopia: Rural Development Options*. London: Zed Books.

Pilkington, Hilary, and Moya Flynn. 1999. "From 'Refugee' to 'Repatriate': Russian Repatriation Discourse in the Making." In *The End of the Refugee Cycle: Refugee Repatriation and Reconstruction*, edited by Richard Black and Khalid Koser, 171–97. Oxford: Berghahn Books.

Pottier, Johan. 1999. "The 'Self' in Self-Repatriation: Closing Down Mugunga Camp, Eastern Zaire." In *The End of the Refugee Cycle: Refugee Repatriation and Reconstruction*, edited by Richard Black and Khalid Koser, 142–70. Oxford: Berghahn Books.

Preston, Rosemary. 1999. "Researching Repatriation and Reconstruction: Who Is Researching What and Why?" In *The End of the Refugee Cycle: Refugee Repatriation and Reconstruction*, edited by Richard Black and Khalid Koser, 18–37. Oxford: Berghahn Books.

Quirin, James. 1992. *The Evolution of the Ethiopian Jews: A History of the Beta Israel (Falasha) to 1920*. Philadelphia: University of Pennsylvania Press.

Rahmato, Dessalegn. 1991. *Famine and Survival Strategies*. Uppsala: Scandinavian Institute of African Studies.

———. 1986. "Moral Crusaders and Incipient Capitalists: Mechanized Agriculture and Its Critics in Ethiopia." Proceedings of the third annual Seminar of the Department of History. Addis Ababa: Addis Ababa University Press.

Ranger, Terence. 1994. "Studying Repatriation as Part of African Social History." In *When Refugees Go Home: African Experiences*, edited by Tim Allen and Hubert Morsink, 279–94. Trenton, N.J.: Africa World Press.

Relief Society of Tigray (REST). 30 November 1984a. Bulletin.

———. 7 January 1994b. Bulletin.

———. Jan. 1993. Central Tigray Integrated Agricultural Development Programme, 1993–1997. Addis Ababa.

Rogge, John R. 1994. "Repatriation of Refugees." In *When Refugees Go Home: African Experiences*, edited by Tim Allen and Hubert Morsink, 14–49. Trenton, N.J.: Africa World Press.

———. 1985. *Too Many, Too Long: Sudan's Twenty-Year Refugee Dilemma*, Totowa, N.J.: Rowman and Allenheld.

Rosaldo, Michelle Z. 1974. "Theoretical Overview." In *Women, Culture, and Society*, edited by M. Z. Rosaldo and L. Lamphere. Stanford: Stanford University Press.

Rosaldo, Renato. 1989. *Culture and Truth: The Remaking of Social Analysis*. Boston: Beacon Press.

Salama, Peter, Fitsum Assefa, Seisel Talley, Paul Speigel, Albertien van der Veen, and Carol N. Gorway. 2001. "Malnutrition, Measles, Mortality, and the Humanitarian Response during a Famine in Ethiopia." *Journal of the American Medical Association* 286, no. 5: 563–71.

Scheper-Hughes, Nancy. 1993. *Death without Weeping: The Violence of Everyday Life in Brazil.* Berkeley: University of California Press.

Scott, James C. 1985. *Weapons of the Weak: Everyday Forms of Peasant Resistance*, New Haven: Yale University Press.

———. 1976. *Moral Economy of the Peasant: Rebellion and Subsistence in Southeast Asia.* New Haven: Yale University Press.

Scudder, Thayer. 1962. *Ecology of the Gwembe Tonga.* Manchester: Manchester University Press.

Sen, Amartya K. 1981. *Poverty and Famines: An Essay on Entitlement and Deprivation.* Oxford: Clarendon.

Shils, Edward. 1975. *Center and Periphery.* Chicago: University of Chicago Press.

Spear, Thomas. 1990. "Review of *The Spoils of Famine: Ethiopian Famine Policy and Peasant Agriculture* by Jason W. Clay, Sandra Steingraber, and Peter Niggli." *Northeast African Studies* vol. 12, 134–38.

Sphere Project. 2004. *Humanitarian Charter and Minimum Standards in Disaster Response.* Geneva: Sphere Project.

Steffansson, Anders. 2003. "Under My Own Sky? The Cultural Dynamics of Refugee Return and (Re)Integration in Postwar Sarajevo." Ph.D. thesis, University of Copenhagen Institute of Anthropology.

Stein, Barry. 1981. "The Refugee Experience: Defining the Parameters of a Field of Study." *International Migration Review* 15, no. 1, 320–30.

Stepputat, Finn. 1999. "Repatriation and Everyday Forms of State Formation in Guatemala." In *The End of the Refugee Cycle: Refugee Repatriation and Reconstruction*, edited by Richard Black and Khalid Koser, 210–26. Oxford: Berghahn.

Strathern, Marilyn. 1988. "Commentary: Concrete Topographies." *Cultural Anthropology* 3, no. 1, 88–96.

Tareke, Gebru. 1996. *Ethiopia: Power and Protest.* Trenton, N.J.: Red Sea Press.

"Temporary Policy on Investment for Agriculture and Natural Resource Management." Lekatit 1986 (Feb. 1993). Ministry of Agriculture, Tigray Region, Mequelle.

Tessema, Negga. 1956. "The Death Customs in the Province of Tigre." University College of Addis Ababa Ethnological Society Bulletin (5), 13–23.

Transitional Government of Ethiopia (TGE). 1992. "Proposal for the Repatriation of Ethiopian Refugees from the Sudan." Addis Ababa.

Turner, Victor. 1974. *Dramas, Fields, and Metaphors: Symbolic Action in Human Society.* Ithaca: Cornell University Press.

———. 1969. *The Ritual Process: Structure and Anti-Structure.* Chicago: Aldine.

———. 1967. *The Forest of Symbols: Aspects of Ndembu Ritual.* Ithaca: Cornell University Press.

United Nations Development Programme (UNDP). 1993. Overview of Disaster Management. New York: United Nations Development Programme's Disaster Management Training Programme.

Vaughan, Meghan. 1991. *Curing Their Ills: Colonial Power and African Illness.* Oxford: Polity.

Waldron, Sidney R. 1988. "Working in the Dark: Why Social Anthropological Research Is Essential in Refugee Administration." *Journal of Refugee Studies* 1, no. 2, 153–65.

Walsh, Martha, Richard Black, and Khalid Koser. 1999. "Repatriation from the European Union to Bosnia-Herzegovina: The Role of Information." In *The End of the Refugee Cycle: Refugee Repatriation and Reconstruction*, edited by Richard Black and Khalid Koser, 110–25. Oxford: Berghahn.

Warner, W., and Leo Srole. 1945. *The Social Systems of American Ethnic Groups.* New Haven: Yale University Press.

Watts, Michael. 1992. "Space for Everything (A Commentary)." *Cultural Anthropology* 7, no. 1, 115–29.

Webb, Patrick, and Joachim von Braun. 1994. *Famine and Food Security in Ethiopia: Lessons for Africa.* London: John Wiley and Sons.

Wolde Giorgis, Dawit. 1989. *Red Tears: War, Famine, and Revolution in Ethiopia.* Trenton, N.J.: Red Sea Press.

Wolde Mariam, Mesfin. 1984. *Rural Vulnerability to Famine in Ethiopia, 1958–1977.* New Delhi: Vikas Publishing House.

Young, Allan Louis. 1970. "Medical Beliefs and Practices of Begemder Amhara." Ph.D. diss., Philadelphia: University of Pennsylvania.

Young, John. 1997. *Peasant Revolution in Ethiopia: The Tigray People's Liberation Front, 1975–1991.* Cambridge: Cambridge University Press.

——. 1994. "Peasants and Revolution in Ethiopia: Tigray 1975–1989." Ph.D. diss. Vancouver: Simon Fraser University.

Index

DATW. *See* Democratic Association of Tigray Women

Davis, John, 24, 116, 213

Dean, R. F. A., 161

Death, 12, 26, 166–67; and burial, 21, 98–99, 155–56, 168, 170–73; in childbirth, 147–50; of children, 12, 59, 144–45, 147, 150, 164–66, 169, 232 n.14; and funerals, 136, 166–70, 171, 232 n.14; institutional indifference to, 173–75; and last rites, 167; and mourning vigil, 168–69; and mutual assistance associations, 136; and preparation of corpses, 167, 232 n.12; in refugee camps, 58–61; resignation to, 21, 165–66; supernatural interpretations of, 12, 61–63, 148–50

Debt, 126, 127–28, 130–31; and community sources of credit, 131–32; and external sources of credit, 132–35; interhousehold, 139–40; and mutual assistance associations, 135–39

Decentralization, 179–80

Deforestation, 31

Democratic Association of Tigray Women (DATW), 129, 133–34, 147

Dependency, on aid, 114, 118, 194–98, 233 n.10

Derg, the, 3, 8, 29, 33–34, 225 nn. 1, 2; agricultural policies of, 34–35, 42–46, 184; counterinsurgency campaigns of, 37–41; and famine relief, 40, 52; and Humera, 44–46

Development assistance. *See* Humanitarian assistance

de Waal, Alex, 24, 35, 37, 39, 116–17, 146, 211–12; on labor conscription, 45; on migration failure, 42, 43

Diarrhea, 59, 60

Disease, 4–5, 12, 157, 170, 229 n.10; in refugee camps, 58–59, 60

Disorder, anthropology of, 212–13

Displacement. *See* Evacuation of 1984; Migration

Distress migration. *See* Evacuation of 1984; Migration

Divorce, 73, 228 n.6

Dolan, Chris, 181

"Draft Economic Policy of the Transitional Government," 185

Drought, 31, 41

Duffield, Mark, 40

Eastmond, Marita, 135, 215

Economy: effect of civil war on, 38; and Ethiopian-Eritrean war, 223; in refugee camps, 65–68, 194–98. *See also* Agriculture; Household food economy

EDU. *See* Ethiopian Democratic Union

Elderly: and birthplace, 170–72, 215–16; respect for, 94

Elections, 26, 27, 182, 187–89, 233 n.9; and land allocation, 200–201

Emplacement, 3, 9–10; as continuation of community disintegration, 24–25; defined, 25, 83; difficulties of, 213; economic practice as, 25–26, 110–11, 118–19, 135–36, 142–43; larger political context of, 13–14, 176–77, 214; and notions of home, 10–11, 27, 106, 215–17; as ongoing process, 14–16, 107, 208; and refugees' attitudes about repatriation, 214; and repatriation policy, 219–20; and ritual, 26, 145, 156; and sedentarism, 78–80, 207, 210–12; and self-help, 196–98. *See also* Community formation; Place; Space

Employment. *See* Labor

Endadutch, 104–5

Entrepreneurship, 7–8. *See also* Businesspeople; Commercial farms; Markets

EPLF. *See* Eritrean People's Liberation Front

EPRDF. *See* Ethiopian People's Revolutionary Democratic Front

EPRP. *See* Ethiopian People's Revolutionary Party

Eritrea: Ethiopian war with, 222–24, 226 n.14, 227 n.19, 230 n.3; independence of, 226 n.9, 227 n.19

Eritrean Liberation Front (ELF), 35

Eritrean People's Liberation Front (EPLF), 35, 40

Erosion, 31

Ethiopian Catholic Church, 230 n.1

Ethiopian Democratic Union (EDU), 35–36, 45, 73

Ethiopian-Eritrean war, 222–24, 226 n.14, 227 n.19, 230 n.3

collection and analysis regarding, 121–25; and emplacement, 110–11, 118–19, 142–43; expenditure profiles, 125–26; and external sources of credit, 132–35; and highland economy, 30–31, 111–14; households selected for study of, 119–21; income levels, 127–29; informal household cooperation, 128, 139–40; and labor migration, 140–42; mutual assistance associations, 135–39; in refugee camps, 65–59; and resource hiding, 109–10, 123–24; women's management of, 92

Houses, 7, 227 n.26, 228 n.5; construction of, 84, 85–89; as women's space, 89–93

Humanitarian assistance, 205–6, 207; and definition of famine, 54–55; during famine of 1984–1985, 40–41, 52–53, 57–58, 59–60; and household food economy, 114, 118, 138–39, 230 n.7; inequalities in, 190–94; medium- and long-term need for, 215, 217, 219, 220; in refugee camps, 57–58, 59–60, 65–67, 194–98; and relief workers, 56–57, 64; returnees' disappointment with, 26, 76, 81, 205; and self-reliance, 114, 118, 194–98, 218. *See also* Aid agencies; Relief Society of Tigray; United Nations *and related headings*

Human rights abuses: anthropological study of, 212–13; by the Derg, 37–41, 226 n.15

Humera: civil war in, 44–46; during Ethiopian-Eritrean war, 222; hospital in, 17–19, 148, 149, 174, 225 n.1

Humphrey, Carolyn, 82

Hutchinson, Sharon, 228 n.6

Iddir, 136

Income levels, 127–29

Infant mortality, 147, 164–66

Infibulation, female, 154, 231 n.6

Innovation, 11–13, 78, 212; and etiquette, 110; in exile, 213–14

Insurance, 114, 115

Interest rates, 131

International organizations. *See* Aid agencies; United Nations *and related headings*

Iqub, 136

Islam. *See* Muslims

Kibreab, Gaim, 104, 196–97, 214

Kin networks, invented, 124–25

Kitchens, 91

Labor, 4, 181; under the Derg, 42–43, 45–46; for food aid, 114, 195; and household food economy, 114, 126, 128, 130, 140–42; in Sudan, 65, 67–68, 128, 140–42

Land allocation, 7, 8, 83–86, 103–6; and community service, 27, 104, 198–99; and elections, 200–201

Land ownership, public versus private, 184–85, 233 n.8

Land reform, and civil war, 34–35, 42

Landscape, 107; defined, 82–83

Language, and citizenship, 187

Lawrence, Mark, 112, 113, 114, 116, 117–18

Leslau, Wolff, 106

Livestock, 41, 229 n.9

Local government, 86, 94, 193, 198–99, 204. *See also* Politics

Lowlanders, prejudices against, 101–2

Lowlands: coping strategies in, 117–18; and highlands compared, 4–5, 8, 29–30

MacClancy, Jeremy, 212

Maheber, 136–38

Malaria, 59, 60

Malkki, Liisa, 20–21, 210–11, 214

Malnutrition, 12, 22, 164–65; and childbirth, 146; chronic, 116, 146; and nutritional requirements, 227 n.1; in older siblings, 161, 232 n.11; in refugee camps, 24, 58, 59–60. *See also* Famine

Malthus, Thomas R., 146

Marasmus, 165

Maret. *See* Relief Society of Tigray

Mariam, Saint, 150–52

Markets, 4, 7, 112, 226 n.12; during civil war, 31, 38, 39; as gathering places, 94–95; as source of nongrain foods, 125–26

Marriage, 4–5, 70–73, 228 nn.6, 7

Maternal mortality rates, 147

May, Clifford, 56

economic conditions in, 65–68, 194–98; marriage in, 70–73; mortality and morbidity rates in, 58–59, 60; politics in, 69, 73–74; social order in, 69–70

Refugee studies, 209, 233 n.1

Regional government, 132–33, 194. *See also* Politics

Relief Society of Tigray (REST), 55, 68, 113, 178, 226 n.10; and decisions to repatriate, 73, 75, 76; establishment of, 36; and evacuation of Tigray, 46–47, 52; and refugee camp political structure, 69; and repatriation assistance, 5, 179, 191–92, 205; and repatriation of 1985, 64

Relief supplies. *See* Humanitarian assistance

Relief workers, 56–57, 64. *See also* Aid agencies

Religion, 84–85, 92, 97–99, 138; Catholicism, 230 n.1; and gift giving, 128. *See also* Christianity; Ethiopian Orthodox Church; Muslims

Religious institutions, influence of, 180, 193, 202–3

Repatriation: and anthropologists as advisers to aid agencies, 219–21; and concepts of home, 10–11, 27, 106, 215–17; decisions about, 73–77; in 1985, 53, 63–65; as policy preference, 180–81, 214, 217–19; in postwar context, 27–28; and power politics, 180–81, 204–6; and refugees' adaptability to exile, 213–14; refugees' attitudes toward, 73, 75, 214; research on, 210; returnees' expectations of, 10–11, 76, 80–81; and self-reliance, 114, 118, 194–98, 218; unequal assistance for, 190–94

Representations, 9; of the homeland, 80

Resettlement program, Derg, 39

Resource maximization strategies, 111. *See also* Household food economy

Respiratory infections, 59, 60

REST. *See* Relief Society of Tigray

Risk absorption, 114

Risk minimization, 114

Rituals, 26; burial, 21, 98–99, 155–56, 168, 170–73; at childbirth, 150–52; christening, 154–56; circumcision,

152–54, 231 n.6; commemoration ceremonies, 169; funerals, 166–70, 171, 232 n.14; last rites, 167; mourning vigil, 168–69; preparation of corpses, 167, 232 n.12; scarring, 156–59, 232 n.8

Robben, C. G. M., 212

Rosaldo, Renato, 21, 50

Russian returnees, 10–11

Rwanda, 14

Safawa: household economics in, 65–68; marriage in, 70–73; political structure in, 69; social order in, 69–70

Safawa Hade, 85

Saints' days, 136–39, 202, 231 n.13

Savings associations, 136

Scarring, 156–59, 232 n.8

Scheper-Hughes, Nancy, 22, 145–46, 150, 165, 173

"Scientific socialism," 33

Scott, James C., 115, 197

Scudder, Thayer, 211

Seasonal migration, 23–24, 29, 42

Sedentarism, 78–80, 207, 210–12, 214

Self-reliance, promotion of, 114, 118, 194–98, 218

Sen, Amartya, 139, 146

Serit, 69

Sexual relations, 154–55, 161; rape, 68

Sharing, 70, 109–10, 228 n.7

Shofer, 157

Shopkeepers, and credit, 131–32, 134–35. *See also* Businesspeople

Smallpox, 170

Snakes, 101, 159, 229 n.15

Social behavior, 11–13, 109–10; and access to resources, 27, 104, 198–99, 200–201, 204

Social change: in postwar context, 27–28; and refugee studies, 209; and sedentarist orientation, 207

Social emplacement. *See* Community formation; Emplacement

Social innovation, 11–13, 78, 110, 212, 213–14

Socialism, under the Derg, 33

Social networks. *See* Community formation; Emplacement

Social order. *See* Community formation; Emplacement

Wad Kowli refugee camp, 57–61; alternative explanations of death in, 61–63; closing of, 64–65
Wage labor. *See* Labor
War crimes: anthropological study of, 212–13; by the Derg, 37–41, 226n.15
Warren, Kay, 212
Water, 22–23, 89–90, 229nn. 9, 10
Watts, Michael, 82
Waz, 157
Weaving, 122
Webb, Patrick, 114–15, 116
Wi'il, 71
Wilderness, 101–3
Wolde Giorgis, Dawit, 40–41
Wolde Mariam, Mesfin, 115

Wolkait, 99, 181. *See also* Humera
Wolkait people, 101–2, 229n.16
Women: and childbirth, 145–50; and credit, 133–34; crisis roles of, 116; and death rituals, 167–68, 170; and evil spirits, 63, 144, 145, 148–49, 170; household as space of, 89–93; in public spaces, 92–93, 95; and wilderness, 101
Women's Association, 95
Woredas, 69, 103, 193, 226n.4. *See also* Politics

Young, John, 35, 36, 43, 185, 201, 202

Zambia, 12